Creating 6-Trait Revisers and Editors for Grade 8

30 Revision and Editing Lessons

Vicki Spandel

Writer in Residence, Great Source Education Group

Boston New York San Francisco
Mexico City Montreal Toronto London Madrid Munich Paris
Hong Kong Singapore Tokyo Cape Town Sydney

Thank you to the following individuals for reviewing this book.

Tamara Doehring, Melbourne High School
Dena Harrison, Mendive Middle School
Susan Vachris, Smithtown High School West

Executive Editor: Aurora Martínez Ramos
Editorial Assistant: Kara Kikel
Executive Marketing Manager: Krista Clark
Marketing Manager: Danae April
Production Editor: Janet Domingo
Editorial-Production Service: Kathy Smith
Composition Buyer: Linda Cox
Manufacturing Buyer: Megan Cochran
Interior Design and Composition: Schneck-DePippo Graphics
Cover Administrator: Linda Knowles

For related titles and support materials, visit our online catalog at www.allynbaconmerrill.com.

Between the time website information is gathered and then published, it is not unusual for some sites to have closed. Also, the transcription of URLs can result in typographical errors. The publisher would appreciate notification where these errors occur so that they may be corrected in subsequent editions.

ISBN-13: 978-0-205-57062-1 ISBN-10: 0-205-57062-3

Printed in the United States of America
10 9 8 7 6 5 4 3 2 1 Bind-Rite 12 11 10 09 08

Allyn & Bacon
is an imprint of

www.allynbaconmerrill.com

Contents

Grade 8

Creating Revisers and Editors

Welcome!

. . . to a series of revision and editing lessons that challenge students to be daring and confident revisers.

These lessons complement and extend instructional ideas found in my book *Creating Writers Through 6-Trait Assessment and Instruction* (for teachers who work with students in grades 3 through college). In this set of lessons—as suggested in that book—students practice revision and editing skills on text that is *not their own*, and then extend what they have learned by applying those same strategies to their own writing.

Unlike other writing and revising lessons, this set shows revision *in action.* It allows students to see drafts in process, observe exactly what a thoughtful reviser does, and compare this to their own revision of the very same text. Students work individually, with partners, and in groups, and have multiple chances to experience success.

Please note that these lessons are a perfect complement to your own instruction or any materials, such as the *Write Traits Classroom Kits* (by Vicki Spandel and Jeff Hicks), that you may use to teach *ideas, organization, voice, word choice, sentence fluency,* and *conventions.*

Why do we need to teach revision differently?

Traditionally, we have not really *taught* revision, but only *assigned* it: "Revise this for Monday." Students who do not understand revision or do not know specific strategies to apply often wind up writing a longer draft, making it neater, or correcting conventional errors. This is not true revision. Revising is re-seeing, re-thinking text, and making internal changes that affect message, voice, and readability.

The six traits make it possible for us to actually *teach* revision. But to do so effectively, we have to make revision visible. This starts with providing rubrics and checklists that clarify expectations. But this is *not enough*. We must show students what revision looks like, by taking a rough draft and marking it up with arrows, carets, delete symbols, and new text. These lessons do three things:

Extend students' practice. Most students practice revision and editing only on their own work. Because very few of them write and revise every day, such an approach does not offer enough practice to ensure growth in skills and deepened understanding. By working on the text of others, students learn strategies they can apply to their own work. Through such practice, students become significantly more efficient, confident revisers.

Show students what revision looks like. Many teachers are uncomfortable writing with or in front of students, feel they do not have time to write, or are unsure what modeling looks like, and so do not attempt it. As a result, most students have never seen what other writers actually *do* when they write or revise. In addition, much of the writing students do is on computer or via text messaging. The revision is either invisible (once a change is made, the history of the change is gone) or nonexistent. In these lessons, the original text remains in place, with changes superimposed so students can track what is happening.

Make revision manageable. As students move into middle grades and beyond, their writing tends to get longer, and tackling revision on a two-, three-, or five-page document, especially when they must deal with everything at once, overwhelms many of them. With this set of lessons, they work on *smaller* text, and focus on one problem (or a small handful of problems) at a time. This gives them confidence to take on something bigger.

What if I have never worked with the traits before?

These are pick-up-and-go lessons. You will find this revision and editing practice *very* student and teacher friendly, even if you are new to the traits.

At the same time, I urge you to use these lessons in conjunction with the book *Creating Writers*, Fifth Edition (2009, Pearson Education). These lessons are an extension of ideas put forth in that text. The book offers *numerous* additional writing samples, along with instructional strategies to help you understand:

- What the six traits are
- How they influence written text
- How to use trait language in coaching your student writers

Simply put, the traits are qualities or characteristics that define good writing. Following are definitions you can share with parents, if you wish:

The 6 Traits in a Nutshell

Trait 1

Ideas

Ideas are the heart of the message: the writer's main point or storyline, together with all the details that help make it clear and vivid for the reader.

Trait 2

Organization

Organization is the overall design or structure of the writing, including the lead (or beginning), the flow of ideas, the transitions connecting those ideas, and the conclusion (ending).

Trait 3

Voice

Voice is the writer's unique way of expressing ideas—the general sound and tone of the piece, the writer's presence in the text, the link between writer and reader, the verbal fingerprints of the writer on the page.

Trait 4

Word Choice

Word choice includes all the individual words, phrases, and expressions a writer uses to convey ideas and feelings.

Trait 5

Sentence Fluency

Sentence fluency is the flow and rhythm of the language, all the variations in sentence length and structure, and the degree to which text can be read easily and with expression.

Trait 6

Conventions

Conventions involve anything a copy editor would consider in making text easier to process, including (but not limited to) spelling, punctuation, grammar and usage, capitalization, paragraphing, spacing, and layout.

How are the lessons organized?

General Overview

In this collection, you will find **30 lessons** in all, **15 revision** lessons and **15 editing** lessons. They are alternated so that students practice revision, then editing, then revision again, and so on. Revision lessons are based on the five traits of *ideas, organization, voice, word choice*, and *sentence fluency*. Editing lessons are based on the trait of *conventions*.

Each **revision lesson** is designed to be completed within roughly **50 minutes.** Each **editing lesson** is designed to be completed within about **40–45 minutes**.

Revision lessons emphasize:

- Understanding of a foundational revision strategy.
- Connection to literature.
- A chance to see the strategy modeled (by the teacher).
- Collaboration between students.
- Discussion, brainstorming, and sharing of ideas.

Editing lessons emphasize:

- Direct instruction on one editorial concern.
- Repeated practice on one editorial problem.
- An opportunity to apply editorial skills to real-world text.

For writers who need extra time or practice . . .

All lessons in this set are designed for use with eighth grade writers and revisers. If you find a lesson is difficult for some students, you can adjust the amount of revising they do (e.g., making *a few small revisions* rather than dealing with the whole text). You can also break a revision lesson into two or three parts. Also remind students to read everything aloud as they go, and encourage students to work with partners *throughout the lesson*.

Connection to personal writing . . .

In all cases, the intent is that students move from the lesson to working on their own writing, applying the same revision or editing skills.

Specific Lesson Format and Timelines

For Revision Lessons

Preparing for a Revision Lesson To prepare, *read through the entire lesson.* Make any copies or overhead transparencies you need. Note that the format is the same for each revision lesson in the set. Once you are familiar with this format, the lesson flow is very easy—and of course, you should personalize each lesson *in any way you wish.*

Introducing a Revision Lesson Each revision lesson begins with (1) a short introduction describing the focus of the lesson, and offering a relevant warm-up; and (2) a brief sample from literature or professional writing to help you illustrate an important writing feature: e.g., *revising by showing.*

> **Texts for individual lessons are short**
> The text for each revision lesson is deliberately kept short in order to make the lesson manageable for you. It is *not* intended to be fully representative of longer reports or essays your students may be writing. Unless otherwise directed, you should think of each sample as an *excerpt* from a potentially longer piece.

Teaching a Revision Lesson (with timelines) Revision lessons are designed to take about **50 minutes** (times will vary, depending on how much revising students do). Once you finish the Lesson Introduction, you have three options:

1. Do the lesson **all at once**
2. Divide the lesson into **two parts**
3. Divide the lesson into **three parts**

Regardless of which option you choose, the general flow goes like this:

Part 1

- Share Samples A and B.
- Discuss strengths and problems, and ask students what they might do to revise the *weaker* sample (**6–8 minutes**).
- *Optional:* Share and discuss our *suggested revision of the weaker sample* (**3 minutes**).

> If you wish to divide the lesson into 3 parts, pause here.

Part 2

- Share Sample C (*Whole Class Revision*).
- Read Sample C aloud as students follow along OR ask a student to read it aloud (**1 minute**).
- Invite students to work with a partner in identifying problems with Sample C, and to make notes they can use to coach you as you model revision of this sample (**6 minutes**).
- Invite students (as a class) to coach you as you model revision of Sample C (**6–8 minutes**). Read your revision aloud to close this portion of the lesson.
- *Optional:* Compare your whole class revision of Sample C with the suggested revision (**3 minutes**).

> **If you wish to divide the lesson into <u>2 parts</u>, pause here.**
>
> **If you are dividing the lesson into <u>3 parts</u>, pause here for the second time.**

Part 3

- Share Sample D (*Revising with Partners*).
- Ask students to revise Sample D independently, following the same strategies they used as a group for Sample C. Then, ask them to check with partners to compare strategies and results (**10–12 minutes**).
- Ask two or three pairs of students to share their revisions. The goal is to *hear some variations*, despite use of parallel strategies (**3–4 minutes**).
- *Optional:* Compare your revisions to our suggested revision of Sample D (**3 minutes**).

> **How much revision should students do?**
>
> **The suggested revisions for *all* problematic pieces are provided to facilitate discussion and to give you models that show *possibilities*. Your revisions do not EVER need to match ours, and do not need to be as expansive as ours. Some students will revise *extensively*; beginners may do much less.**

For Editing Lessons

Each **editing lesson** contains these basic components:

- Introduction and explanation of the focus skill for that lesson.
- Illustrations you can share with students.

- Instructions to guide you step by step through the lesson.
- A sample for editing practice.
- Edited copy that you can use as a model (for comparison) once students have finished their own editing.

Teaching an editing lesson (with timelines) Allow about **40–45 minutes** for each editing lesson. Following is a brief estimate of how long each component is likely to take:

- Introduce the focus for the lesson (**5 minutes**).
- Share illustrations (**5–10 minutes**).
- Share the Editing Practice sample with students.
- Ask students to edit individually (**10–15 minutes**).
- Invite students to compare their editing with that of a partner (**3 minutes**).
- Invite students (as a class) to coach you as you model editing of the text (**5–10 minutes**). Read your edited copy aloud (**2 minutes**).
- Check your editing against the copy provided (**3 minutes**).

An editing checklist . . .
is provided with Lesson 30. You should feel free to share this checklist at any time during your use of these lessons. Simply realize that it may be challenging for students to apply the checklist until certain elements have been taught.

What if our changes do not agree with the suggested text?

In most cases, your **editing** should agree *very* closely with the copy provided. Admittedly, however, even widely used handbooks do not all agree on such issues as use of commas. My suggestion is to choose one handbook that will be *your* final authority, and in the case of any disagreement, consult that handbook. In most cases, editing lessons are non-controversial, and disagreement should be minimal. (The resource texts for this set of lessons are *The Chicago Manual of Style*, 14th edition. 1993. Chicago: University of Chicago Press; and *Write Source: New Generation*. 2006. Wilmington. MA: Great Source Education Group. If possible, make the latter text available to student editors during lessons.)

With **revision** lessons, of course, there are no "correct" answers. What matters is that you and your students identify problems in the text and revise them in a way that makes the draft clear and readable. The suggested revisions are provided *to guide you*, to make you aware of possibilities, and also to make you more comfortable discussing samples or modeling revision. They are not meant to restrict what you can or should do as writers and revisers.

Do these lessons fit well into writing workshop?

Absolutely! Usually, writing workshop offers a combination of direct instruction, coaching, writing and revising, and sharing. These lessons provide excellent opportunities for direct instruction and coaching, while allowing students the support of working in pairs or teams, as well as connecting reading and writing.

The lessons are *not* meant to take the place of students' independent writing. Rather, they serve as a stepping stone *into* that writing—giving students just the strategies they need to revise their rough drafts with skill and confidence. Because the lessons are designed to help students become independent editors and revisers, with a strong grasp of writers' vocabulary, they fit very well into any writing workshop that encourages students to take charge of their own writing process.

What can I do to make these lessons more effective?

Many things. Here are 16 suggestions—

1. **Read *Creating Writers Through 6-Trait Assessment and Revision***, Fifth Edition (2009. Boston: Pearson Education), for teachers at grades 3 through college, and keep a copy handy to refer to as you use these lessons.
2. **Make sure students have access to handbooks** (e.g., *Write Source: New Generation,* published by Great Source Education), dictionaries, and thesauruses. Provide space on which to post a traits checklist or other lists and charts used throughout the lessons. (You will need to make your own enlarged copies.)
3. At any time you feel it is appropriate during your presentation of these revision lessons, provide students with copies of the **Student 6-Point Writing Guide**. Also provide copies of the **Student Checklist** (both appear at the end of this Introduction.) Students can use the **Writing Guide** and/or **Checklist** to assess their own writing *prior to revision.*
4. Encourage students to **keep writing folders**. Any drafts they put into those folders can be assessed and revised, then edited, using skills they develop through these lessons.
5. **Do not assess *everything*** students create. It will be overwhelming for both them and you. Also, do not assess the work they do in conjunction with these lessons except in the sense that they *complete* all revision and editing activities. Think of the lessons as rehearsal for revision of any rough drafts they may have in their writing folders.
6. **Allow extended writing time**. Encourage students to occasionally choose a draft of their own work to revise, applying strategies learned from this lesson set. Recognize that both writing and revising are reflective activities that require time, some of which should be provided during class, where student writers have access to resources, and coaching from peers and from you.

7. **When students have written a draft, let them "abandon" it mentally for a time** by putting it into the writing folder, and doing nothing more with it for three or more days. During this time, present one or more revision/editing lessons. When students return to their drafts, they will see their writing with fresh eyes, and will have in their minds specific skills to apply as they revise. The difference will impress you—and encourage them.
8. **Remind students to double space rough drafts**, and to leave large side margins, providing room for revision and editorial notes. Even if they work on computers, encourage them to format drafts in this way. That way, they can make notes on printed copy to guide the revision they later do electronically.
9. **Keep revision small and focused**. Changing one sentence or inserting one or two details is a good beginning for some students. Encourage experimentation. Do not expect most of your students to do as much revision as you will see in our examples. Those are provided for discussion purposes to help you and your students see various possibilities. There is *no expectation* that any one student will make *every possible revision.*
10. **Adapt lessons for challenged writers**. Because the lessons focus on one aspect of revision, they are already fairly manageable in scope. But you can make them simpler still by (1) asking students who are having difficulty to make only *one* small change, rather than focusing on a full paragraph or page; (2) asking students to revise only a line or two, rather than a whole sample; (3) ensuring that any student who is struggling has a partner with whom to work, even during those times when other students may be working independently; (4) encouraging struggling students to talk through their ideas for revision before putting anything on paper; and (5) using the recommended literature to provide models (sentences, words, phrases, images, details) students can refer to or even copy verbatim.
11. **Challenge those writers who are ready**. Every lesson concludes with a section called "Next Steps," which includes suggestions for "an additional challenge." *Students who need a challenge should also routinely do more than one round of revision on a single draft.* Professional writers do numerous revisions of important documents and manuscripts. Many eighth graders are ready for multiple revisions, and should consider this a matter of course.
12. **Seat students in a way that makes working in pairs (or larger teams) easy and comfortable**. Every lesson in this set encourages collaboration through discussion, oral reading, conferring, brainstorming, and assessing.
13. **Write with your students**, modeling the kinds of things you would like them to do, such as double spacing copy, adding detail, changing an ending, starting sentences differently, playing with the voice, or inserting a word or phrase you like better than your original.

14. **Share additional examples from good literature** with your students. One brief example is provided in each lesson, but if you can provide more examples from that and other recommended texts, you make the use of literary mentors far more powerful.
15. **Make yourself as comfortable as possible with the modeling process**. You will have a suggested revision to review in advance, and you can use that suggestion to guide students' responses. However, your final draft *need not look like ours*. Feel free to be inventive, and to encourage creativity in your students. What matters is for them to see the revision unfold.
16. **Provide time and/or materials to support research.** It is much easier for a writer to add details and to write with confidence when he or she knows a topic inside and out. Even minimal research (five minutes on the Internet or with a relevant resource book or journal) can make an enormous difference. While students *can* complete every lesson in this set without research, those who have access to additional information are likely to be happier with their revisions—and to sharpen their research skills in the bargain.

Have fun watching your students' revision and editing skills grow!

Checklists

Creating Revisers and Editors, Grade 8

Note to the Teacher

Following is a series of checklists intended for use with this set of lessons. Use the checklists one at a time, as you are teaching the lessons for a particular trait—or pass them all out at once. It's your choice. Here are a few things to keep in mind . . .

Encourage honesty! Good writers make *numerous changes* to their text. So in filling out a checklist, the object is not to show how *perfect* your writing is, but to be such a good reader (of your own work) that you know precisely which problems within your draft most need attention. Remind students that most early drafts—even those written by professionals—would *not* meet all the criteria listed here.

Keep revision manageable. Once students have more than one checklist going, it is a good idea to think about how many things the writer wants to take on at once. Addressing one or two writer's problems thoroughly can improve a draft measurably. This may be sufficient for struggling writers. Many eighth graders are ready for a challenge, however, and may wish to try doing more than one revision of a given draft. Multiple revisions should be the norm for such students. In addition, for many eighth graders, the lessons should be cumulative, so that they address an ever-increasing number of concerns at a time when revising their own work.

A Writing Guide is different from a checklist. A writing guide includes *numbers*, and shows a writer where his or her writing falls along a continuum of performance from beginning levels up to strong and proficient. A *6-Trait Writing Guide* (which students can use to score their own or others' writing) is provided with these lessons. It corresponds to the guide found in *Creating Writers,* Fifth Edition. Keep in mind, though, that the purpose of these lessons is to create *revisers*, not *critics*. The discussion that comes out of assessing a piece of work and talking about it with others is extremely helpful in giving writers the insight they need to write better. Scores per se are less important than the discussion itself.

A checklist, by contrast, includes no scores; it is intended as a guide to revision, a series of reminders. Like a Writing Guide, it is designed to encourage stronger writing by opening students' eyes to revision possibilities.

Personal Revision Guide

Ideas

___ Everything is clear—it makes sense

___ Examples expand my main idea

___ I know this topic well—and it shows

___ I include helpful, memorable, intriguing details

___ It's more than just a list of facts

___ My writing answers reader's questions

___ I include what matters—NOT filler!

___ My writing makes readers think

Personal Revision Guide

Organization

___ A strong lead invites you in

___ A strong ending wraps things up

___ Every detail seems to fall in the right place

___ My organization guides readers like a good road map

___ It's not *too* predictable—it includes some surprises

___ I show how ideas connect

___ The pacing is just right—not too fast or too slow

Personal Revision Guide

Voice

___ It's individual—my fingerprints are on *every page*

___ The writing is expressive—you can tell I like this topic

___ The tone and language create the right mood

___ My knowledge of the topic gives the writing conviction

___ This piece speaks to readers

___ You'll enjoy reading it aloud

___ This is the right voice for the genre and purpose

Personal Revision Guide

Word Choice

___ Every word and expression is "just right" for the moment

___ The writing is original and creative—I say things *my own way*

___ Words are used accurately

___ New or technical words are defined

___ The writing makes vivid pictures, movies in the reader's mind

___ Lively verbs put things into motion

___ Adjectives and adverbs aren't *overused*

___ Every word counts—I didn't use 20 words when 10 would do

Personal Revision Guide

Sentence Fluency

___ This writing is easy and fun to read aloud—*with expression*

___ Some sentences are long, some short

___ Sentences begin in different ways

___ Many sentence beginnings link ideas with transitions like . . . *After a while, Nevertheless, Moreover, For example, On the other hand, The next day . . .*

___ I used fragments or repetition *only for emphasis*

___ Dialogue (if used) sounds authentic and natural

Please note . . .

No checklist is included for Conventions because it appears in conjunction with the editing lessons.

Student Writing Guide, Grade 8

Ideas

6

- ❑ My writing is clear and focused—it will hold your attention.
- ❑ I know this topic inside and out.
- ❑ I help readers learn—and make them think, imagine, envision.
- ❑ Out of many possibilities, I chose the *most intriguing* details.

5

- ❑ My writing is clear and focused.
- ❑ I know a lot about this topic.
- ❑ I share information that matters—to me and to my readers.
- ❑ I include many helpful details and examples.

4

- ❑ My paper is clear and focused most of the time.
- ❑ I know this topic well enough to write about it.
- ❑ My paper has some new information and some things most people know.
- ❑ I came up with a few details and examples.

3

- ❑ I ran out of things to say. Not every part is clear, either.
- ❑ I wish I knew more about this topic!
- ❑ It was hard to come up with new information.
- ❑ I scrambled for details. I think I repeated some things.

2

- ❑ I have a topic—*sort of*—but I'm not sure what to say about it.
- ❑ I did not know enough to write about this topic.
- ❑ I made my best guesses—or just repeated things.
- ❑ I listed some ideas—but I didn't have any good details or examples.

1

- ❑ I don't have a real topic. I'm not sure what to say.
- ❑ Without a topic, how could I have information?
- ❑ I just wrote whatever came into my head.
- ❑ I wrote what I could. It isn't really *about* anything in particular.

Organization

6

- ❑ My organization guides you right through the piece.
- ❑ My lead will hook you. My conclusion will leave you thinking.
- ❑ I link ideas in ways you might not think of on your own.
- ❑ The overall design gives a real sense of purpose to my writing.

5

- ❑ The organization helps you focus on what's most important.
- ❑ I have a strong lead and a conclusion that wraps things up.
- ❑ My transitions connect ideas clearly—you don't have to make your own connections.
- ❑ The organization makes everything easy to follow.

4

- ❑ The organization supports the ideas.
- ❑ I have a lead and conclusion. They seem OK.
- ❑ My transitions link ideas pretty clearly.
- ❑ You can follow it—but sometimes you know what's coming next.

3

- ❑ If you pay attention, you can follow my story or discussion.
- ❑ My lead and/or conclusion need some work.
- ❑ You'll need to make some connections as you read this. Or else, use the old formulas: *point one, point two, etc.*
- ❑ It's either hard to follow—or else REALLY predictable!

2

- ❑ I feel like reorganizing *everything*—beginning to end!
- ❑ My lead and conclusion are the same ones you've heard before.
- ❑ I wasn't sure how to connect these ideas. I need to think about it.
- ❑ This is very hard to follow even if you pay attention.

1

- ❑ This seems totally random—there's no pattern or design here.
- ❑ It just starts and stops. There's no lead or conclusion.
- ❑ These ideas don't really go together. They're just first thoughts.
- ❑ No one can follow this. I can't follow it myself.

Student Writing Guide, Grade 8

Voice

6
- ❑ This is ME—as individual as my fingerprints.
- ❑ Trust me—you *will* want to share this aloud.
- ❑ I use voice to make the message resonate in your head.
- ❑ Hear the passion? I want you to love this topic as much as I do.

5
- ❑ It's original and distinctive. It will definitely stand out from the crowd.
- ❑ I think you will want to read this aloud.
- ❑ The voice fits my topic. I reach out to the audience.
- ❑ The paper is lively and expressive. I liked this topic.

4
- ❑ My writing strikes a spark or two. You *might* recognize me.
- ❑ You might share a line or two aloud.
- ❑ Though my voice fades at times, you can tell I'm thinking of the reader.
- ❑ This paper is sincere. This was an OK topic for me.

3
- ❑ My voice comes and goes. I'm not sure you could tell it's me.
- ❑ There could be a share-aloud moment.
- ❑ I wasn't *always* thinking of the reader. I just wrote.
- ❑ My voice is quiet in this paper. I couldn't really get into this topic.

2
- ❑ This isn't really me. It's more of an "anybody" voice.
- ❑ There could be a hint of voice in there somewhere.
- ❑ My voice is faint—just a whisper, really.
- ❑ I sound bored—or like an encyclopedia. This was NOT my topic.

1
- ❑ I'm not at home in this paper. I can't hear myself at all.
- ❑ This is definitely not a piece to share aloud.
- ❑ My voice is just—well, *missing* . . . Not even a whisper . . .
- ❑ I couldn't get excited about the topic. You won't either.

Word Choice

6
- ❑ I tried for original, creative ways to use words.
- ❑ You might read this more than once—you'll remember a phrase or two.
- ❑ Every word is important. I wouldn't cut anything.
- ❑ I used strong verbs—and precise nouns and adjectives.
- ❑ My words make vivid, memorable pictures in your mind.

5
- ❑ I wrote to make meaning clear—not to impress you.
- ❑ Once you start reading, you'll want to keep reading.
- ❑ I kept it concise.
- ❑ I used strong verbs. I didn't overdo the adjectives.
- ❑ My words help you picture things clearly.

4
- ❑ My writing is clear. I used words correctly.
- ❑ You'll notice some strong words or phrases.
- ❑ I could cut a little.
- ❑ There are some strong verbs—also vague words (*nice, fun, great*).
- ❑ My writing gives you the general picture.

3
- ❑ I used the first words that came to me—but you'll get the idea.
- ❑ Here and there I've used a word or phrase I like.
- ❑ It's a little cluttery. I should shorten it.
- ❑ I need more strong verbs. I might have too many adjectives.
- ❑ You'll need to use your imagination—or fill in some blanks.

2
- ❑ Watch out for tired words, vague words, or thesaurus overload!
- ❑ You'll have to look hard to find strong moments.
- ❑ It's very sketchy—or else it's so overdone the message is lost.
- ❑ Strong verbs rode into the sunset. Many words are vague or general.
- ❑ You'll have to work hard just to get the main idea.

1
- ❑ I wrote to fill space. I don't think any message comes through.
- ❑ It was a struggle to get *anything* on paper.
- ❑ I need more words, stronger words, *different* words—help!!

Student Writing Guide, Grade 8

Sentence Fluency

6

- ❑ This is easy to read with expression and voice.
- ❑ It flows like a good song lyric or movie script.
- ❑ You won't believe the variety in my sentences.
- ❑ If I used fragments, they add punch. My dialogue is like listening in on a good conversation.

5

- ❑ You can read this with expression.
- ❑ It has a good rhythm and flow. I like the sound of it.
- ❑ My sentences begin in different ways. Some are long, some short.
- ❑ Fragments or repetition add emphasis. Dialogue sounds real.

4

- ❑ My writing sounds natural. It's easy to read aloud.
- ❑ It flows for the most part. I might smooth out a wrinkle or two.
- ❑ I have some sentence variety. I could use more.
- ❑ Fragments or repetition sound OK. My dialogue could use some work—it's pretty natural, though.

3

- ❑ If you read this aloud, it's a bumpy ride. You can do it, though.
- ❑ I need to read this aloud myself and rewrite some sentences.
- ❑ I need MUCH more sentence variety.
- ❑ My fragments (if I used them) don't work. The dialogue doesn't quite sound like real people speaking.

2

- ❑ You can read this if you're patient—and you rehearse!
- ❑ I have run-ons, choppy sentences, or other sentence problems.
- ❑ My sentences are all alike—or it's hard to tell where they start.
- ❑ If I used fragments or repetition, it was by accident.

1

- ❑ This is very *hard* to read aloud, even for me.
- ❑ You need to re-read a lot—or fill in missing words as you go.
- ❑ It's hard to tell where sentences start or stop.
- ❑ I need to read this aloud, slowly. I need to rewrite sentences, finish sentences, and combine some sentences.

Conventions

6

- ❑ I edited this thoroughly. Only the pickiest editors will spot errors.
- ❑ My conventions are creative. They bring out meaning and voice.
- ❑ This paper shows off my control over many conventions.
- ❑ *If layout was important,* I made it appealing and eye-catching.
- ❑ This is **ready to publish.**

5

- ❑ I edited this. Errors are minor and easy to overlook.
- ❑ My conventions support the meaning and voice.
- ❑ The paper shows I know many different conventions.
- ❑ *If layout was important,* I made sure the piece had a pleasing look.
- ❑ This is ready to publish with **light touchups.**

4

- ❑ I went through it quickly. There are a few noticeable errors.
- ❑ It's very readable. The errors do not get in the way of the message.
- ❑ I have good control over basics—*end punctuation, capitals,* etc.
- ❑ *If layout was important,* I made sure it was acceptable.
- ❑ This piece needs **a good once-over** before it's published.

3

- ❑ I edited too quickly. This has noticeable, distracting errors.
- ❑ The errors could slow a reader down—or get in the way of meaning.
- ❑ Even with basics (like *easy spelling*) I had some problems.
- ❑ This needs more attention to layout (*optional*).
- ❑ This piece needs **careful, thorough editing** before it's published.

2

- ❑ Frequent, distracting errors show it's not really edited yet.
- ❑ The errors will slow a reader down—or distort the meaning.
- ❑ I made many errors, even on basics.
- ❑ I did not think too much about layout (*optional*).
- ❑ This needs **line-by-line editing** before it's published.

1

- ❑ This is not edited. There are serious, frequent errors.
- ❑ Readers will need to de-code or reread to get the meaning.
- ❑ I made many errors, even on basics like *periods* and *capitals*.
- ❑ I need to re-work the layout (*optional*).
- ❑ This needs **word-by-word editing** before it's published.

Bibliography

List of Books Referenced for Grade 8 Lesson Set

Abeel, Samantha. 2003. *My Thirteenth Winter: A Memoir*. New York: Scholastic.

*Anderson, Laurie Halse. 1999. *Speak*. New York: Farrar, Straus & Giroux.

Ash, Russell. 1996. *Incredible Comparisons*. London: Dorling Kindersley.

*Bradbury, Ray. 1991 (2nd ed). *Farenheit 451*. New York: Random House.

*Brande, Robin. 2007. *Evolution, Me and Other Freaks of Nature*. New York: Alfred A. Knopf.

Burns, Loree Griffin. 2007. *Tracking Trash: Flotsam, Jetsam, and the Science of Ocean Motion.* Boston: Houghton Mifflin.

*Cahill, Thomas. 1995. *How the Irish Saved Civilization*. New York: Doubleday.

*Cisneros, Sandra. 1991. *The House on Mango Street*. New York: Vintage.

Cox, Loretta Outwater. 2003. *The Winter Walk*. Anchorage, AK: Alaska Northwest Books.

*Davis, James C. 2004. *The Human Story: Our History from the Stone Age to Today*. New York: HarperCollins.

Dutcher, Jim and Jamie Dutcher. 2006. *Living With Wolves*. New York: Mountaineers Books.

Fleischman, Paul. 1995. *Bull Run*. New York: HarperTrophy.

*Fleischman, Paul. 2004. *Seedfolks*. New York: HarperTeen.

*Fleischman, Paul. 2004. *Whirligig*. New York: Laurel Leaf.

Fleischman, Sid. 2006. *Escape! The Story of the Great Houdini*. New York: HarperCollins.

Freedman, Russell. 2006. *The Adventures of Marco Polo*. New York: Arthur A. Levine Books.

Freedman, Russell. 2007. *Who Was First? Discovering the Americas*. Boston: Houghton Mifflin.

Gordon, David George. 1996. *The Compleat Cockroach*. Berkeley, CA: Ten Speed Press.

*Hemingway, Ernest. 1952 (renewed 1980). *The Old Man and the Sea*. New York: Scribner.

Hesse, Karen. 2003. *Aleutian Sparrow*. New York: Aladdin.

*Hesse, Karen. 2001. *Witness*. New York: Scholastic.

Hillenbrand, Laura. 2001. *Seabiscuit*. New York: Random House.

Jannot, Mark, ed. *Science Illustrated*. April/May 2008. Copenhagan, Denmark: Bonnier Publications.

Korman, Gordon. 2002. *Everest*. New York: Scholastic.

Korman, Gordon. 2000. *No More Dead Dogs*. New York: Hyperion Books.
Korman, Gordon. 2004. *Son of the Mob*. New York: Hyperion Books.
Kramer, Stephen. 2001. *Hidden Worlds: Looking Through a Scientist's Microscope.* Boston: Houghton Mifflin.
*Kurlansky, Mark. *The Big Oyster: History on the Half Shell.* 2006. New York: Random House.
*Lee, Harper. 1960. Harper Perennial Classics edition published 2006. *To Kill a Mockingbird*. New York: Harper Perennial Classics.
*Lekuton, Joseph Lemasolai. 2003. *Facing the Lions: Growing Up Maasai on the African Savanna*. Washington, DC: National Geographic.
Mack, Tracy. 2003. *Birdland*. New York: Scholastic.
Montgomery, Sy. 2006. *Tree Kangaroo: An Expedition to the Cloud Forest of New Guinea*. Boston: Houghton Mifflin.
Morell, Virginia. "Minds of Their Own: Animals Are Smarter Than You Think." March 2008. *National Geographic*. Vol. 213, No. 3.
Murphy, Jim. 1990. *The Boys' War: Confederate and Union Soldiers Talk About the Civil War*. New York: Houghton Mifflin.
*Myers, Walter Dean. 2001. *Bad Boy*. New York: HarperCollins.
MySpace Community with Jeca Taudte. 2008. *MySpace/Our Planet: Change Is Possible*. New York: HarperCollins.
Nack, William. 2002. *Secretariat: The Making of a Champion*. New York: Da Capo Press.
*Opdyke, Irene Gut with Jennifer Armstrong. 1999. *In My Hands: Memories of a Holocaust Rescuer*. New York: Random House.
Orwell, George. 2004 (50th Anniversary edition). *Animal Farm.* New York: Signet.
*Osa, Nancy. 2003. *Cuba 15*. New York: Delacorte Press.
*Paulsen, Gary. 1996. *Puppies, Dogs, and Blue Northers*. New York: Harcourt Brace.
*Paulsen, Gary. 1994. *Winterdance: The Fine Madness of Running the Iditarod.* New York: Harcourt.
Riordan, Rick. 2005. *The Lightning Thief.* New York: Hyperion Books.
Schmidt, Gary D. 2007. *The Wednesday Wars*. New York: Clarion Books.
Schmidt, Gary D. 2008. *Trouble*. New York: Clarion Books.
Sis, Peter. 2007. *The Wall*. New York: Farrar, Straus and Giroux.
*Soto, Gary. 1985. *Living Up the Street*. New York: Bantam Doubleday.
Spinelli, Jerry. 2000. *Stargirl*. New York: Alfred A. Knopf.
Swinburne, Stephen R. 1999. *Once a Wolf.* Boston: Houghton Mifflin.
Thimmesh, Catherine. 2006. *Team Moon: How 400,000 People Landed Apollo 11 on the Moon*. Boston: Houghton Mifflin.
Thomas, Dylan. 1993. *A Child's Christmas in Wales*. London: Orion House.
Van Draanen, Wendelin. 2003. *Flipped*. New York: Alfred A. Knopf.
*Zusak, Marcus. 2005. *The Book Thief.* New York: Alfred A. Knopf.

*Indicates a book intended for a young adult to adult audience. May contain mature language or themes.

Lessons for Grade 8

Revising to Be Specific: CDE

Lesson 1

Trait Connection: Ideas

Introduction

In a book titled *Evolution, Me, & Other Freaks of Nature**, high school biology teacher Ms. Shepherd is giving her class a lesson about being specific. She is asking them to notice their surroundings—beginning with the color of her shirt. They immediately tell her it's red. But that answer doesn't satisfy her—she wants specifics: "Not 'red,' " Ms. Shepherd said. " 'Red' is general—'red' is boring. 'Puce' is specific. These are the distinctions we scientists must make." Ms. Shepherd goes on to challenge her class to an interesting observational game, passing out potatoes and asking them to document all the *facts* they can about their potatoes over the next two days. No invented family histories or cute names—just facts, observable and measurable—and very *specific*. The team with the longest list wins the game. If you were in Ms. Shepherd's class and had to keep an eye on a potato for the next two days, how many specifics do you think *you* could come up with? In this lesson, we'll explore three key ways of being specific: clarification (telling the reader a bit more), description (providing an image), and example—C, D, and E for short. You don't need to use them *all* at any one time. Just keep all three in mind as possibilities.

*Quotation from Robin Brande, *Evolution, Me & Other Freaks of Nature*. 2007. New York: Alfred A. Knopf, page 11.

Teacher's Sidebar . . .

When Ms. Shepherd says *puce* is preferable to *red,* she is giving her students an example of *clarification.* So often, we tell students to "be specific," but many of them do not know what that means. The purpose of this lesson is to help students identify three strategies—*clarifying, describing,* or *giving an example*—they can use to be specific. Note that some revisions rely partially on research. While research is not essential for this lesson, students may find that seeking additional information on any given topic makes revision easier and more rewarding.

Focus and Intent

This lesson is intended to help students:

- Understand the concept of *being specific.*
- Distinguish between specific images or details and generalities.

- Revise a general passage using clarification, description, and/or examples to give it specificity.

Teaching the Lesson

Step 1: Using C-D-E strategy

Some of the following passages are written in generalities. In others, the writer has used clarification (C), descriptive detail (D), or examples (E) to make the writing specific. First, identify those passages that are specific. Put a check (✓) in the blank. Then, see if you can determine which strategy (or strategies) the writer used. Circle the letter of each you think is appropriate.

___ 1. Portland, Oregon has been identified as one of the "greenest" cities in the entire country. It has one of the best recycling programs in the nation, an unrivaled system of hiking and bike trails designed to encourage fuel-free transportation and reduce traffic, and plans for a solar powered energy system to promote use of non-polluting energy.

C D E

___ 2. Our current national health system needs thorough evaluation and possible revision. Many people are unhappy with the current state of affairs. They are not receiving or cannot afford the medical attention to which they feel they should be entitled. Some people say that our health care system is not competitive with comparable systems worldwide.

C D E

___ 3. Animals moved onto the endangered species list (those threatened with extinction within a generation) do not necessarily remain there indefinitely. The peregrine falcon, for example, was listed as endangered in 1972, when a ban prohibiting killing them was enacted. Since then, many have taken to nesting on skyscrapers (which are not unlike the cliffs on which they would normally nest), and their numbers are growing—prompting their delisting in 1999.

C D E

___ 4. We think of prescription drugs as a remedy for things that ail us. Taking drugs in combination, however, can prove dangerous. These combinations lead to adverse side effects that may have unexpected and negative consequences. It is always wise to check with a pharmacist to determine potential interactions.

C D E

Now take a second look. For those passages written in generalities, what strategies could the writer use to make the passage as specific as possible?

Note to the teacher: 2 and 4 are written in generalities. Sample 1 relies primarily on examples for specificity; Sample 3 relies on clarification and an expanded example.

Step 2: Making the Reading-Writing Connection

The March 2008 edition of *National Geographic* includes an article exploring the intelligence of animals. The article asserts that animals have more reasoning power than they have been given credit for in the past, and a greater ability to communicate, whether with one another or with humans. Researcher Irene Pepperberg spent years working with a parrot named Alex, who could count, identify shapes, colors, and sizes—and even do simple arithmetic. But for author Virginia Morell, who observed the parrot firsthand, a defining moment came in the form of a simple request from Alex—one that came entirely unprompted:

Sample

"Wanna go tree," Alex said in a tiny voice.

Alex had lived his entire life in captivity, but he knew that beyond the lab's door, there was a hallway and a tall window framing a leafy elm tree. He liked to see the tree, so Pepperberg put her hand out for him to climb aboard. She walked him down the hall into the tree's green light.

"Good boy! Good birdie," Alex said, bobbing on her hand.

(From "Minds of Their Own: Animals Are Smarter Than You Think" by Virginia Morell. March 2008. *National Geographic.* Vol. 213, No. 3, page 45.)

Based on this short passage, what do we learn about Alex—and his relationship to trainer/researcher Irene Pepperberg? Does the passage provide reinforcement for Pepperberg's assertion that in his own way, Alex can think? Would you call this clarification? Description? An example? Or a combination? Imagine if Morell had simply said, "Alex is capable of making requests." What would you picture in your mind? How much would that generality diminish the power of her assertions about Alex—or animals in general? When Alex says, "Good birdie," what do you think he means to convey?

Step 3: Involving Students as Evaluators

Ask students to review Samples A and B, looking for specifics versus generalities. Which author does a better job of incorporating specifics—through clarification, description, or examples? Which resorts to generalities? Have students work with a partner, highlighting specifics from each passage and making marginal notes about ways to turn generalities into specifics.

Discussing Results

Most students should find Sample B stronger. Discuss differences between the two pieces, asking students to identify specifics from Sample B and generalities from A. Talk about opportunities the writer has missed to strengthen Sample A. One possible revision of this passage is provided.

Step 4: Modeling Revision

- Share Sample C (*Whole Class Revision*) with students. Read the original aloud.
- Talk about specifics versus generalities—and underline all the generalities you identify.
- Brainstorm ways (clarification, description, example) in which you could transform the generalities into specifics. Remember that it is not necessary to use *every* strategy within one passage—though you can, if you wish.
- If time permits, allow students to do some research on the Internet about sleep deprivation.
- Revise the passage by making it as specific as possible. Be as creative with details as you need to be. It is fine to "invent" facts for purposes of this practice (though not in students' own work!).
- Compare your revision to ours, keeping in mind that we have done more revision (for purposes of modeling) than you are likely to do.

Step 5: Revising with Partners

Pass out copies of Sample D (*Revising with Partners*). Ask students to follow the basic steps you modeled with Sample C. *Working with partners,* they should:

- Read the passage aloud.
- Look for specifics versus generalities.
- Revise by first underlining generalities—then brainstorming ways to transform them into specifics. Encourage students to use more than one strategy, though they need not use all three.
- If time permits, allow students to do some research on the topic of expanding brain power through new experience and activities such as problem solving.
- Read the revised version aloud to see how much difference specifics make.

Step 6: Sharing and Discussing Results

When students have finished, ask several pairs of students to share their revisions aloud. Did teams find different ways to transform generalities? What do their revisions tell you about what it means to "be specific"? Compare your revisions with ours (keeping in mind that ours may be more extensive).

Next Steps

- Invite students to look for generalities in their own writing, and to think about ways of transforming them. Remind them that exchanging even *two* generalities for specific information can dramatically transform the power of any piece of writing.
- When students share their writing in response groups, ask listeners to listen for generalities—and to write them on 3×5 cards to be turned in to the writers. This can be helpful feedback for revising. If only one listener identifies a "generality," inattentive listening may be the culprit. But if *three* listeners identify it, chances are good that the writing needs to be more specific.
- Watch and listen for passages showing details in the literature you share. Recommended:
    - Any edition of *National Geographic* magazine.
    - *Quest for the Tree Kangaroo: An Expedition to the Cloud Forest of New Guinea* by Sy Montgomery. 2006. Boston: Houghton Mifflin.
    - *Team Moon: How 400,000 People Landed Apollo 11 on the Moon* by Catherine Thimmesh. 2006. Boston: Houghton Mifflin.
- *For an additional challenge:* Try Ms. Shepherd's experiment, described in the introduction to this lesson. Provide students with a potato—or any small, portable object of your choice (e.g., pine cone, orange, rock). Ask students to list as many documentable observations (e.g., weighs four ounces, versus "it's pretty") as they can over the next two to three days. Compare lists. Who came up with the most facts? Who thought of details others might not think of? Who came up with the most specific details about color, shape, size, texture, or smell? Compare lists and talk about what this experiment teaches you about specifics.

Sample A

Generalities? or Specifics?

Killer Bugs

People who were around in the late 1960s recall very clearly the excitement of going to the moon. It was an amazing time! For the first time in our history, people would actually set foot on the moon, some 240,000 miles from home!

Of course, there could be dangers. Some contamination from the moon could make its way back to Earth. Scientists were particularly worried about germs. This possibility posed a grave threat, to say the least.

Fortunately, NASA was prepared. They took careful precautions to make sure no bacterial infection would spread from the moon to Earth.

Sample B

Generalities?
or Specifics?

A Toddler in Dog's Clothing?

Betsy, a six-year-old border collie, shows signs of intelligence that have her owners—along with scientists and dog trainers—abuzz. She can identify objects by name faster than a great ape. Her vocabulary is currently estimated at roughly 340 words, and it continues to grow. The average toddler learns from one to ten new words per day; though no one can be sure Betsy is learning that many, her expanding vocabulary is impressive. Even at the age of just ten weeks, Betsy knew the words for simple objects like *ball, rope, paper*, and *keys*—and would retrieve such objects on command. Most amazing of all is Betsy's apparent ability to link not only *objects* with words, but photographs of those objects.

Scientists theorize that dogs like Betsy, who come from a herding species, may have a special bond with humans that makes them sensitive to human forms of communication. They also believe that this ability to "read" humans through gestures, facial expressions, *and* language patterns has evolved over time.

Information in this passage is based on Virginia Morell. "Minds of Their Own: Animals Are Smarter Than You Think." *National Geographic*. March 2008. Vol. 213, No. 3. Pages 49–51.

Revision of Sample A

Stopping

Killer Bugs

on July 20 (or 21, depending on where you live), 1969

People who were around ~~in the late 1960s~~ recall very clearly the excitement of going to the moon. ~~It was an amazing time!~~ For the first time in our history, people would actually set foot on the moon, some 240,000 miles from home!

They anticipated numerous dangers, including fuel problems, and dealing with extremes of hot and cold. In addition, though there was no evidence of life on the moon, scientists feared that unseen, deadly microorganisms

~~Of course, there could be dangers. Some contamination~~ from the moon could make their ~~its~~ way back to Earth. ~~Scientists were particularly worried about germs. This possibility posed a grave threat, to say the least.~~

The fear was that if this happened, contamination could spread worldwide, perhaps destroying some or all of life on Earth.

Fortunately, NASA was prepared. ~~They took careful precautions to make sure no bacterial infection would spread from the moon to Earth.~~

Upon their return, astronauts Neil Armstrong and Buzz Aldrin were sealed in biological isolation garments—then put into quarantine for nearly a month. They were accompanied by special germ-free mice. When the mice survived, NASA declared the mission germ-free, and the astronauts were released. Who knows what might have happened had the mice died!?

Information for this revision is taken from Catherine Thimmesh, *Team Moon: How 400,000 People Landed Apollo 11 on the Moon.* 2006. Boston: Houghton Mifflin, pages 4, 8, and 50.

Sample C: Whole Class Revision

Generalities? or Specifics?

Research indicates that few Americans get enough sleep. Perhaps you are one of the millions of people who try to get by on very little sleep per night. There are many reasons people do this. Sometimes they deprive themselves of sleep deliberately—for a number of different reasons. But just as often, factors outside their control interrupt sleep. Either way, sleep deprivation has a wide range of consequences.

Luckily, people can do a number of things to improve their sleeping experience. Those who do report almost immediately feeling benefits from the increased sleep.

Sample D: Revising with Partners

Generalities? or Specifics?

As people grow older, their brains tend to shrink. This is particularly true at a certain age. It is possible for our minds to lose some of their thinking power—but it is not necessary.

Nerve cells send out spindly limbs, like tree branches, that reach toward other nerve cells. When they meet, they form synapses. Brain signals follow along these paths.

Familiar activities allow nerve signals to follow paths they already know well. New activities prompt cells to make new connections. This in turn can increase brain power.

Suggested Revisions of C and D

Sample C: Whole Class Revision

Getting Some Sleep (title added)

Research indicates that few Americans get enough sleep. Perhaps you

five or six hours of

are one of the millions of people who try to get by on ~~very little~~ sleep

or even less. **People go without sleep for many reasons.**

per night. ~~There are many reasons people do this.~~ Sometimes they

to study, squeeze in some extra work, or just have fun.

deprive themselves of sleep deliberately—~~for a number of different~~

~~reasons.~~ But just as often, factors outside their control interrupt sleep.

Noise, stress, too much light, overeating, or consumption of caffeine or alcohol can all disrupt sleep. No matter what the cause,

~~Either way,~~ sleep deprivation has a wide range of consequences. **Sleep deprived people may fall asleep at work or while driving, may tend to forget even simple things (their own phone number), and may have trouble problem solving.**

Luckily, people can do a number of things to improve their sleeping experience. **They can change eating habits, make sure a bedroom is as dark and quiet as possible, or develop a pre-sleep routine that involves something soothing, such as music or reading.**

strive for a minimum of seven to eight hours of sleep per night

Those who ~~do~~ report almost immediatel~~y~~ ~~feeling~~ benefits. ~~from the increased sleep.~~

Sample D: Revising with Partners

Give Your Brain a Workout (title added)

Once people grow older than 30,

~~As people grow older,~~ their brains tend to shrink. ~~This is particularly true at a certain age.~~ It is possible for our minds to lose some of their thinking power—but it is not necessary. Many activities maintain—or even dramatically expand—brain power.

Nerve cells send out spindly limbs, like tree branches, that reach toward other nerve cells. When they meet, they form synapses. Brain signals follow along these paths.

such as eating the same foods, talking to the same people, or visiting the same familiar places,

Familiar activities allow nerve signals to follow paths they

even something as simple as solving a puzzle or driving to work a different way,

already know well. New activities prompt cells to make new connections. This in turn can increase brain power. People who constantly expose themselves to new situations are literally giving their brains a workout.

Some information for this revision is taken from Eric Haseltine, "Train Your Brain" in *Discover Mind Games,* an imprint of *Discover Magazine*. April 2008. New York: William C. Hostetter. Page 18.

Inserting Needed Commas

Trait Connection: **Conventions**

Introduction (Share with students in your own words—or as a handout.)

To some writers and editors, commas seem mysterious. When should we use them? *Why* do we use them? Commas shouldn't just pop up arbitrarily like dandelions in the garden. They should guide the reader, making reading of the text simpler—and making meaning clear. Following are four important uses for the comma:

1. To separate items in a series:

   Roger grabbed his backpack, bolted out the door, and headed for adventure.

2. To set off a sentence *introduction*:

   Unfortunately, the rain is not supposed to stop.

   Keeping well to the right, we headed down the bumpy road.

3. To set off a sentence *interruption*:

   The rain, sorry to say, will persist right through the week.

   The weary travelers, keeping well to the right, headed down the bumpy road.

4. To set off an *appositive* (words that rename or describe a noun):

   Mr. Brown, the best teacher on the whole staff, was fired for keeping a poisonous snake in the classroom.

   Helen, a book lover, often stayed up well past 2 a.m. reading mysteries.

While there are many other uses for commas, these four basics give any comma user a solid beginning. Remember, when you use commas carefully, you tell the reader where to pause in order to read your text properly. How important are those little pauses? Well, consider the difference between these two statements spoken by a football coach:

Let's kick, John!
Let's kick John!

See? That little comma makes quite a difference, especially to John!

In the text that follows, you'll find opportunities to insert several missing commas, which will make a difference in how the text is read. Read the text once silently, then again aloud (softly, of course). Think about where and why you want the reader to pause. Use the examples from the preceding page as guidelines to help you spot places where needed commas have been omitted, and insert them by tucking them inside a caret, like this: ^,

Marcus a careful proofreader edited the copy reread it to check his corrections and then popped his manuscript in the mail. Unfortunately it was Sunday a day with no mail delivery.

Teaching the Lesson (General Guidelines for Teachers)

1. Share the examples above, or make up your own examples to practice inserting needed commas.
2. Remind students that reading text aloud, with inflection, is a good way to both look and listen for those pauses that signify a comma is needed.
3. Share the editing lesson on the following page. Students should read the passage both silently and aloud, looking and listening for spaces where they could insert a comma.
4. Ask students to edit individually first, then check with a partner. Students should feel free to use a handbook, such as *Write Source: New Generation* (Wilmington, MA: Great Source Education Group, 2006).
5. When everyone is done, ask them to coach you as you edit the same copy.
6. When you finish, read your edited copy aloud, explaining the reason behind each comma you insert. Then compare your edited copy with our suggested text on page 35.
7. If students have difficulty with this activity, review the rules for using commas. Then, repeat the practice, this time reading the passage aloud, sentence by sentence, as students work—and exaggerating pauses.

Editing Goal: Fill in 23 commas.
Follow-Up: Look for opportunities to use commas in your own work.

Revision of sample sentence:

Marcus^, a careful proofreader^, edited the copy^, reread it to check his corrections^, and then popped his manuscript in the mail. Unfortunately^, it was Sunday^, a day with no mail delivery.

Editing Practice

Insert missing commas to—

- **Separate items in a series.**
- **Set off a sentence introduction.**
- **Set off a sentence interruption.**
- **Set off an appositive *(words that rename or describe a noun).***

In Shakespeare's time theater was much different from theater today. For one thing all of the parts were played by men. Cleopatra Juliet Lady Macbeth and many other female Shakespearean characters were all played by men. That must have been a challenge to say the least for both the actors and those in the audience. In addition actors did not wear costumes. They simply dressed in their everyday clothes. If we were able to somehow go back in time however they would probably appear "in costume" to us. After all people dressed quite differently in the 1600s. William McCready a leading actor of the 1800s is thought to have been among the first to actually "dress the part." Later such enhancements as lighting set design and revolving stages all added to the excitement of theater productions. These days people actually receive awards including the coveted Tony Award for costumes set design or other features that were not even on the drawing board during Shakespeare's day. Shakespeare himself if he were still alive today would likely find that both amusing and satisfying.

Edited Copy

23 commas inserted

In Shakespeare's time, theater was much different from theater today. For one thing, all of the parts were played by men. Cleopatra, Juliet, Lady Macbeth, and many other female Shakespearean characters were all played by men. That must have been a challenge, to say the least, for both the actors and those in the audience. In addition, actors did not wear costumes. They simply dressed in their everyday clothes. If we were able to somehow go back in time, however, they would probably appear "in costume" to us. After all, people dressed quite differently in the 1600s. William McCready, a leading actor of the 1800s, is thought to have been among the first to actually "dress the part." Later, such enhancements as lighting, set design, and revolving stages all added to the excitement of theater productions. These days, people actually receive awards, including the coveted Tony Award, for costumes, set design, or other features that were not even on the drawing board during Shakespeare's day. Shakespeare himself, if he were still alive today, would likely find that both amusing and satisfying.

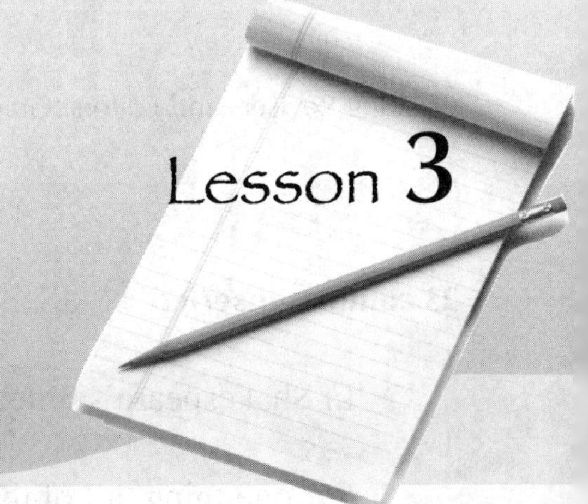

Lesson 3

Revising a Thesis

Trait Connection: **Ideas**

Introduction

A thesis and a good lead often work hand in hand, but they are not necessarily the same (though they *can* be). A lead, as you likely know, is designed to hook readers, to "lead" them into a story or conversation. A thesis, on the other hand, sets the direction for a conversation. *This*, the thesis tells us, *is the primary focus of this discussion*. No wonder a good thesis is so important. It tells the reader what to look and listen for. But it's important to the writer as well. Many writers begin an informational piece with no clear thesis in mind at all—and wind up deluging the reader with chunks of information that are related *only* because they share a common topic. You can certainly *revise* your thesis as you go—but don't head off without one, or you run the risk of confusing both your reader and yourself about what your main point really is. In this lesson, you'll look at some pieces in which the thesis is either weak or missing. Your job as a reviser will be to determine the writer's main point, and revise (or create) a thesis accordingly.

Teacher's Sidebar . . .

Contrary to the common myth, a thesis is not always the first statement of a piece. It may not appear until several sentences into a document—or even further down the road. Remember, too, that the thesis and lead can be different (though they are not always). For example, an informational piece on how chimpanzees' behavior resembles that of humans might begin with a description of a chimp family socializing, or with a story about chimpanzees escaping an attack by a leopard. In that case, the thesis *(The behavior of chimpanzees in the wild is remarkably like that of humans)* may be delayed. (A thesis can even be implied, of course—and never stated outright at all—but we won't deal with that in this lesson.) Here's the key: *Look for the statement that captures the main point of the discussion.*

Focus and Intent

This lesson is intended to help students:

- Understand the purpose of a thesis.
- Distinguish between a thesis and a lead.
- Revise a piece in which the thesis is weak or missing.

Teaching the Lesson

Step 1: Spotting a Thesis

Which of the following would you say is likely to be a *lead*—and which is more likely to be a *thesis?* Notice in making your distinctions that whereas a strong thesis can also be a lead, a lead (no matter how good) cannot *always* be a thesis.

1. New Guinea, the second largest island on Earth, has extremely diverse natural habitats, ranging from tropical rainforests to glaciers.

   ___ Lead ___Thesis ___ Both

2. Rufus the elephant stood staring at himself in the mirror. By the way he kept touching a painted patch on the top of his head, we were convinced he *knew* he was seeing his own reflection.

   ___ Lead ___Thesis ___ Both

3. The cassowary, a bird as large as a human, has such small wings that it cannot fly. But perhaps it doesn't need to. The aggressive cassowary can leap into the air, and attack an enemy with deadly, sharp claws. This bird is a living reminder that birds are descended from dinosaurs.

   ___ Lead ___Thesis ___ Both

4. As a graduate student, Anthony studied sea lions in California. That was when he knew what his life's work would be.

   ___ Lead ___Thesis ___ Both

Note to the teacher: Passage 1 reads like a thesis. It sets up a discussion. It may or may not also be the lead for this piece. Passage 2 is definitely a lead; it intrigues us, but though we can guess what the following discussion might be about, we do not yet know for sure. Passage 3 again sets the stage for a discussion—about birds descending from dinosaurs. Notice, however, that it also doubles as a strong lead. Passage 4 makes a good lead, but again, it is not a thesis because it introduces a story, not a discussion.

Step 2: Making the Reading-Writing Connection

Russell Freedman's book *Who Was First? Discovering the Americas* opens with an introductory chapter titled "Before Columbus." Like many a good title, this one hints at the thesis to come, but the opening line simply teases us to question traditional beliefs: "For a long time, most people believed that Christopher Columbus was the first explorer to 'discover' America—the first to make a successful round-trip voyage across the Atlantic." It is only at the end of this introductory chapter that we get the true thesis for Freedman's five-chapter book:

Sample

As we dig deeper and deeper into the past, we find that the Americas have always been lands of immigrants, lands that have been "discovered" time and again by different peoples coming from different parts of the world over the course of countless generations—going far back to the prehistoric past, when a band of Stone Age hunters first set foot in what truly was an unexplored New World.

(From *Who Was First? Discovering the Americas* by Russell Freedman. 2007. Boston: Houghton Mifflin, page vii.)

With this one-sentence, full-paragraph thesis, Freedman lays out the topic of the discussion to come. Now we know exactly where we are going—even though we don't know all the answers yet. A good thesis should provoke some questions. Does Freedman's thesis do that in your mind? What questions do you have?

Step 3: Involving Students as Evaluators

Ask students to review Samples A and B, looking for a strong thesis. Which author includes a thesis that thoughtfully sets up the discussion to come? Does that thesis also serve as a lead—or does the writer need to expand the piece to include a lead? Have students work with a partner, highlighting the thesis or attempted thesis from each piece and talking about what works or what could make the piece stronger.

Discussing Results

Most students should find Sample B stronger. It has a thesis that can also double as the lead. Discuss differences between the two pieces, asking students to consider what the thesis for Sample A might be. What is this writer's main point? One possible revision of this passage is provided. Note that the thesis is reinforced by the closing statement that is supportive—even expansive—without being redundant.

Step 4: Modeling Revision

- Share Sample C (*Whole Class Revision*) with students. Read the original aloud.
- Talk about the thesis. Is there one? Does the piece have a lead?
- Brainstorm ways of making the thesis stronger. Discuss the writer's topic, and see if you can identify the main point of the discussion.
- Revise the passage by strengthening the thesis or creating a new one. If your thesis does not also serve as an effective lead, feel free to expand the piece to include a lead as well.
- Give the piece a title. (We have not done this because, as you likely have noticed, a good title often gives away the thesis!)
- Compare your revision to ours, keeping in mind that we have included both a lead and a thesis; your revision may or may not include both.

Step 5: Revising with Partners

Pass out copies of Sample D (*Revising with Partners*). Ask students to follow the basic steps you modeled with Sample C. *Working with partners,* they should:

- Read the passage aloud.
- Look and listen for a strong thesis.
- Revise by first discussing the writer's main point: *What is the central assertion in this discussion?*
- Revise the thesis or create a new one so that the central point of the discussion is crystal clear. If the revised thesis does not double as a lead, they should expand the writing to include a lead as well.
- Give the piece a title.
- Read the revised version aloud to hear how it sounds with a strong, clear thesis.

Step 6: Sharing and Discussing Results

When students have finished, ask several pairs of students to share their revisions aloud. Are their thesis statements similar—or very different? Did anyone add a lead as well as a thesis? Compare your revisions with ours (keeping in mind that ours may be more extensive).

Next Steps

- Invite students to look and listen for a strong thesis in their own writing. Remind them to distinguish between a lead and a thesis, remembering that while they are sometimes the same, a lead (even a very good one) does not *always* serve double duty as a thesis, particularly when a piece opens with an image or anecdote.
- Talk about the impact of a good thesis on organization.
- Look at the first paragraphs of textbooks your students may currently be using in any subject: math, social studies, science, art. How many include a thesis statement? How many include a lead? How often are they the same?
- When students share informational or persuasive writing in response groups, ask listeners to see if they can identify the thesis. Have them write it (in their own words) on 3 × 5 cards to be turned in to the writers after sharing. In any strong informational or persuasive piece, the thesis should be very clear to listeners/readers.
- Show the class a videotaped lecture or speech. See if your students can identify the thesis. Is there one? Does the speaker state it outright? At what point?
- Watch and listen for good thesis statements in the informational literature you share. Recommended:

- *Who Was First? Discovering the Americas* by Russell Freedman. 2007. Boston: Houghton Mifflin.
- Any edition of *Discover* magazine.
- **The Big Oyster: History on the Half Shell* by Mark Kurlansky. 2006. New York: Random House. (Look for a new thesis in each chapter.)
- *The Compleat Cockroach* by David James Gordon. 1996. Berkeley: Ten Speed Press. (Look for a new thesis in each chapter.)

- *For an additional challenge:* Many longer works—such as books—have more than one thesis statement. Sometimes, there is an overriding, controlling thesis, plus a sub-thesis to define the content of each chapter. Ask students who need a challenge to do an analysis of any longer nonfiction piece (any of the books from the recommended list will work). See if they can identify the *primary* lead and primary thesis (those that define the purpose of the book itself)—plus the lead and thesis for each chapter. What does this analysis teach them about the organizational structure of a longer piece? What can they use from this analysis in designing a longer piece—even a longer research piece—of their own?

*Indicates a book written for a young adult through adult audience. These books may contain mature language or themes.

Sample A

Strong Thesis?
Good lead?
Both?

Have a Cup of Coffee

In many cultures, coffee has been used for trading purposes, much like tea or salt. For some people, it is traditional to enjoy coffee with bread or other baked treats, such as scones or cakes. In other cultures, coffee is almost a meal in itself, especially when enhanced with cream, milk, sugar, or flavorings like cinnamon. For people who may be sensitive to caffeine, other drinks, such as hot chocolate, tea or even plain steamed milk, may be substituted for coffee so that they can take part in the social custom of "having a cup of coffee." This custom continues to grow in popularity, as companies like Starbucks spread across many parts of the globe. It is not necessary to be a coffee lover or even a coffee drinker to enjoy the coffee house experience. The music and opportunity for conversation are enough to draw many people into the coffee house culture.

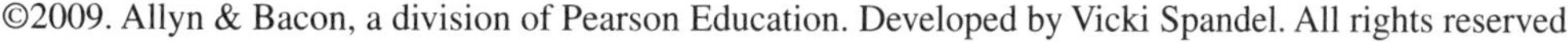

Sample B

Strong Thesis?
Good lead?
Both?

Supreme Recycling

Some people don't dispose of their old tires. They save them. What's more, they collect tires from anyone else willing to donate their cast-offs. Why would anyone do such a crazy thing? As it turns out, it may not be so crazy at all.

Old tires, especially when filled with earth, make some of the best insulating material in the world, and in a time when the Earth is running out of wood, they are top-notch construction material. As anyone who has looked closely at a car will tell you, a tire has a sizeable diameter—often exceeding two feet. When tires are filled with earth (or any non-degradable insulating material) and stacked one upon the other, they form a wall that is sturdy, long-lasting, impervious to damage by burrowing insects, and remarkably good at holding in either heat or cold. Thinking that a house made of tires might not be attractive? Think again. A little coating of plaster and paint makes the wall look as traditional as that of any contemporary home.

The tires may be hidden away behind a chic décor. But they continue to do their work as insulators. What's more, they're likely to remain in place long after more traditional walls have crumbled. So—think twice before disposing of those old tires.

Revision of Sample A

Coffee—The Social Beverage

~~Have a Cup of Coffee~~

The expression "Have a cup of coffee" resonates in many cultures, but as it turns out, it's often less about the coffee itself than about the social experience.

(is so highly valued that it)

In many cultures, coffee ^ has been used for trading purposes, much like tea or salt. For some people, it is traditional to enjoy coffee with bread or other baked treats, such as scones or cakes. In other cultures, coffee is almost a meal in itself, especially when enhanced with cream, milk, sugar, or flavorings like cinnamon. For people who may be sensitive to caffeine, other drinks, such as hot chocolate, tea or even plain steamed milk, may be substituted for coffee so that they can take part in the social custom of "having a cup of coffee." This custom continues to grow in popularity, as companies like Starbucks spread across many parts of the globe. It is not necessary to be a coffee lover or even a coffee drinker to enjoy the coffee house experience. The music and opportunity for conversation are enough to draw many people into the coffee house culture. **"Let's have a cup of coffee" really means, "Let's spend time together." The coffee house is not just for coffee; it's a gathering place.**

Sample C: Whole Class Revision

Strong Thesis?
Good lead?
Both?

As they explore Old West ghost towns, visitors uncover a wide range of relics, including dust-covered furniture, old dishes and cooking utensils (not all of which look familiar), and old kerosene lamps. It is not unusual to find a general store still stocked with some of its original goods. Visitors are often enchanted to find that beneath all the desert dust and sagebrush lies a world not unlike what they have come to expect by viewing western films. What really hits home, however, is the apparent difficulty of life in the nineteenth century, well beyond the range of conveniences. People often had no sidewalks, and there might be a single well for the entire town—one with a relatively small output at that. Shade trees were likely nonexistent, and furniture was anything but luxurious. Canned food, trekked sometimes for hundreds of miles, was scarce and expensive. Window panes were costly, too—so windows were small. With little natural light and only kerosene lamps, homes—and schools—were dark.

Sample D: Revising with Partners

Strong Thesis?
Good lead?
Both?

Plants take in carbon dioxide and release oxygen into the atmosphere. They *can* become full of CO_2. When this happens, their stomata (the tiny holes that collect the CO_2) close. At that point, the plants draw in less water. Why does this matter? Because with no plants to draw it in, the water has nowhere to go—and simply joins the run-off. According to the Hadley Center for Climate Prediction and Research, the amount of runoff over the next century could increase by 24 percent over pre-industrial levels. What would that mean for humans? Drought relief in some very dry regions. But for those areas already troubled by flooding, things could grow worse.

Information for this sample is taken, in part, from Jocelyn Rice, "Sliced Leaves at Work," *Discover Magazine*. April 2008. P. 17.

Suggested Revisions of C and D

Sample C: Whole Class Revision

Harder Than It Looks—and Then Some (title added)

Perhaps you've heard the expression, "It's harder than it looks." That definitely applies to life in the Old West—as hundreds of tourists flocking to U.S. ghost towns are discovering.

As they explore ~~Old West ghost towns~~ **the ruins of those towns,** visitors uncover a wide range of relics, including dust-covered furniture, old dishes and cooking utensils (not all of which look familiar), and old kerosene lamps. It is not unusual to find a general store still stocked with some of its original goods. Visitors are often enchanted to find that beneath all the desert dust and sagebrush lies a world not unlike what they have come to expect by viewing western films. What really hits home, however, is the apparent difficulty of life in the nineteenth century, well beyond the range of conveniences. People often had no sidewalks, and there might be a single well for the entire town—one with a relatively small output at that. Shade trees were likely nonexistent, and furniture was anything but luxurious. Canned food, trekked sometimes for hundreds of miles, was scarce and expensive. Window panes were costly, too—so windows were small. With little natural light and only kerosene lamps, homes—and schools—were dark. **Many tourists leave with a renewed respect for the "pioneer spirit" that helped people survive under such stark circumstances.**

Sample D: Revising with Partners

Drought Relief or Flooding? (title added)

Most people know that
^plants take in carbon dioxide and release oxygen into the atmosphere.

What many of us may not have known is that plants
^~~They~~ *can* become full of CO_2. When this happens, their stomata (the tiny holes that collect the CO_2) close. At that point, the plants draw in less water. Why does this matter? Because with no plants to draw it in, the water has nowhere to go—and simply joins the run-off. According to the Hadley Center for Climate Prediction and Research, the amount of runoff over the next century could increase by 24 percent over pre-industrial levels. What would that mean for humans? Drought relief in some very dry regions. But for those areas already troubled by flooding, things could grow worse. **In short, too few plants and too much CO_2 could make for a very soggy future.**

Information for this sample is taken, in part, from Jocelyn Rice, "Sliced Leaves at Work," *Discover Magazine*. April 2008. P. 17.

Deleting Unneeded Commas

Lesson 4

Trait Connection: **Conventions**

Introduction (Share with students in your own words—or as a handout.)

In the previous lesson, we looked at four common uses for the comma:

1. To separate items in a series:

   Denise loved roller skating, skiing, sky diving, and sleeping in.

2. To set off a sentence *introduction*:

   As soon as you hear the signal, begin the race.

3. To set off a sentence *interruption*:

   A six-course meal, while delightful, can take hours to serve.

4. To set off an *appositive* (*words that rename or describe a noun*):

   Bailey, an animal rights advocate, is a strict vegetarian.

Commas are also used to separate two independent clauses (clauses that could be sentences on their own) when the second one begins with a conjunction: *and, but, for, nor, or, so*, or *yet*. The comma comes before the conjunction, like this:

> I could not persuade anyone to attend the theater with me, so I gave my tickets away.
>
> Jack loves motorcycles, but I prefer 10-speed bikes.
>
> Humpback whales migrate to warm waters to give birth, and later return to northern waters later to feed.

Commas cannot just pop up *anywhere*, though. Then they become pesky, like weeds. Here, for example, are two places NEVER to use a comma:

1. Never use a comma to separate two independent clauses when the second does NOT begin with *and, but, for, nor, or, so,* or *yet:*

   I could not persuade anyone to attend the theater with me, I gave my tickets away.

That little infraction is known as a "comma splice." It gets that name because the writer has tried to "splice" two sentences together with a comma, and that does not work. The comma isn't powerful enough. The writer can write two sentences, insert a conjunction (*and, but, so, for,* etc.), or separate the clauses with a semicolon, like this:

> I could not persuade anyone to attend the theater with me. I gave my tickets away.
>
> I could not persuade anyone to attend the theater with me, <u>so</u> I gave my tickets away.
>
> I could not persuade anyone to attend the theater with me; I gave my tickets away.

2. Never insert a comma between a *subject* and *verb*:

> The brightest star in the sky, actually gives out more light than the sun.

The subject of this sentence is *The brightest star in the sky*. The verb is *gives out*. That comma has no place in this sentence because there is absolutely no reason on earth for the reader to pause after *sky*. When you make a reader pause for no reason it's like tripping him (or her). Don't make your reader stumble. Get rid of commas that do not belong, using as delete mark—like this:

> The brightest star in the sky, actually gives out more light than the sun.

In the lesson that follows, delete the commas that don't belong and only trip the reader. Also correct any comma splices you find.

Teaching the Lesson (General Guidelines for Teachers)

1. Share the examples above, or make up your own examples to practice correcting comma splices and deleting commas that "trip the reader" and interrupt the flow.
2. Share the editing lesson on the following page. Students should read the passage silently and aloud, looking and listening for unneeded commas that come between subjects and verbs, and deleting them. They should also correct any comma splices by (1) adding a conjunction (*and, but, for, nor, or, so, yet*) after the comma, (2) replacing the comma with a semicolon, or (3) inserting a period to end the first sentence and a capital to begin the next.
3. Ask students to edit individually first, then check with a partner. Be sure students have access to a handbook if they wish to use one (Recommended: *Write Source: New Generation*).
4. When everyone is done, ask them to coach you as you edit the same copy.

5. When you finish, read your edited copy aloud, pausing as necessary to explain and discuss the reason behind each change. Then compare your edited copy with our suggested text on page 52.

6. If students have difficulty with this activity, review the two incorrect uses of commas covered in this lesson. Then, repeat the practice, this time reading aloud, sentence by sentence, as students work

Editing Goal: Delete 3 unneeded commas that come between the subject and verb. Correct 4 comma splices.
Follow-Up: Watch out for unneeded commas in your own work.

Editing Practice

Delete commas that—
- **Separate subject and verb.**
- **Incorrectly "link" two sentences (also known as a *comma splice*).**

Correct "comma splices" by—
- **Replacing the comma with a semicolon, OR**
- **Forming two sentences, OR**
- **Inserting a conjunction (*and, but, so, for,* etc.) after the comma.**

People often say nothing beats home cooking, home cooking is a little different for everyone, however! In some parts of the world, it might mean fire-roasted pig with yams. In others, it means homemade pasta and cooked tomatoes. In many cultures, rice, bread, or vegetables (cooked or raw), serve as the main dish. Favorite foods, are not always "cooked" at all. For example, consider sushi, a dish made of raw fish, seaweed, and rice. Sushi is popular worldwide, it certainly reminds many people of home. Consider your own favorite dish, chances are, that food represents "home" to you. Next time you have company from another country or region, think about preparing a dish that is a favorite for them. Cooking foods from another culture, is a real adventure. Your guests will have a good time, so will you!

Edited Copy

3 interruptive, "trip the reader" commas deleted
4 comma splices corrected

People often say nothing beats home cooking, home cooking is a little different for everyone, however! In some parts of the world, it might mean fire-roasted pig with yams. In others, it means homemade pasta and cooked tomatoes. In many cultures, rice, bread, or vegetables (cooked or raw), serve as the main dish. Favorite foods, are not always "cooked" at all. For example, consider sushi, a dish made of raw fish, seaweed, and rice. Sushi is popular worldwide, and it certainly reminds many people of home. Consider your own favorite dish; chances are, that food represents "home" to you. Next time you have company from another country or region, think about preparing a dish that is a favorite for them. Cooking foods from another culture, is a real adventure. Your guests will have a good time, and so will you!

Revising to Support a Point

Lesson 5

Trait Connection: **Ideas**

Introduction

A writer who does not know a topic well—or who is writing an analysis based on a book he or she has not *actually read*—is likely to resort to generalities of this sort: *The Roman Empire was vast and powerful* . . . or, *Atticus Finch was a courageous, moral person*. Some critics call writing like this "fluff." First, it's too broad and sweeping to be meaningful; it simply doesn't cut beneath the surface to uncover anything new that would enlighten or intrigue a reader. Second, it's unsubstantiated. *How do we know* Rome was powerful? *How do we know* Atticus Finch was a moral, upstanding person? Where's the evidence? In this lesson, you'll have a chance to revise in two ways: first, by saying something specific that makes a point, and second, by supporting that point through your own knowledge or a quotation taken from reading or research.

Teacher's Sidebar . . .

Though *extensive* research is not necessary for this lesson, a major part of students' revision will be based on brief analyses of *The Old Man and the Sea* by Ernest Hemingway. You may wish to build in time for students to become at least somewhat familiar with that text; also, it is vital for them to have copies of the book from which to work. These lessons are based on the 2003 Scribner paperback edition of *The Old Man and the Sea*. Other editions may certainly be used, with the understanding that page numbers may vary slightly.

Focus and Intent

This lesson is intended to help students:

- Understand the importance of specific, documented detail.
- Distinguish between generalities and substantiated assertions.
- Revise an analysis based on generalities to give it (1) specific assertions, and (2) documentation to support those assertions.

Teaching the Lesson

Step 1: Reaching for Support

Not everything you say in a research report or literary analysis needs to be documented. Some things are generally accepted by most readers as part of what is called "common knowledge," information that can be gathered through the average person's experience without need for verification. For example, let's say you are writing an analysis based on Harper Lee's book *To Kill a Mockingbird*. You might say, as part of your analysis, that the story takes place in the South, or that it involves a trial, or that it reflects the racial tension predominant at the time. Such things are generally accepted as true and do not require documentation. On the other hand, if you say that the mockingbird (from the book's title) symbolizes the innocence of Boo Radley, or that Bob Ewell is an evil person, you must be prepared to document those assertions through quotations or summaries of the characters' actions and motives. Consider the following assertions taken from research reports or literary analyses. Identify those that require further documentation by putting a check (✓) in the blank. In deciding whether an assertion needs support, a good question to ask is, "Would a typical reader question this or want evidence to verify that it is true?"

___ 1. Some elephants can be trained to paint—even to paint self-portraits.

___ 2. Harry Houdini was a master escape artist.

___ 3. Escape artist Harry Houdini was a vain person who did not appreciate competition.

___ 4. Genghis Khan, a cruel warrior capable of supreme violence, once ruled over an empire larger than that of Rome at its peak.

___ 5. *To Kill a Mockingbird* by Harper Lee is a Pulitzer Prize-winning novel about an attorney's struggle to defend a man unjustly accused of rape.

Note to the teacher: Sample 1 is certainly not common knowledge—yet, anyway. It is based on a video clip, "Elephant Show in Thailand," that appeared on *Good Morning America* on April 2, 2008, and was narrated by the program anchor Chris Cuomo. This video clip subsequently appeared for a time on *YouTube*. Sample 2 is common knowledge and needs no documentation. Sample 3 is based on *Escape! The Story of the Great Houdini* by Sid Fleischman (2006, New York: HarperCollins), pages 126–129. Sample 4 is based on *The Human Story: Our History from the Stone Age to Today* by James C. Davis (2004, New York: Harper), pages 104–106. Sample 5 is common knowledge since it can be obtained through discussion, familiarity with the film based on the book, or a cursory look at the book jacket.

Step 2: Making the Reading-Writing Connection

In Chapter 6 of his sweeping book *The Human Story: Our History from the Stone Age to Today*, author James C. Davis describes the toughness of the Mongol soldiers, documenting how this relatively small group managed to overwhelm all of Northern China in the late twelfth and early thirteenth centuries. Davis gives ample evidence of the Mongols' legendary thick-skinned robustness, citing their ability to ride for hundreds of miles without stopping, living on curdled milk and the blood from their horses (pages 103, 106). He also notes that opposing warriors were overcome in battle not only by the skill and resoluteness of the Mongols—but by their smell as well: "Because they held that water was divine and must not be polluted, they never washed. Their filthy leather jackets shone with grease, and their southern neighbors, the Chinese, said the Mongols smelled so awful that no one could come near them" (p. 102). Davis saves the "closer" comment, his most telling tidbit, for last—quoting Genghis Khan himself:

Sample

Another point: the men who led these conquering peoples had iron wills. They astound us with their readiness to squash a million souls like bugs. Genghis Khan is said to have said, "I have committed many acts of cruelty and had an incalculable number of men killed, never knowing what I did was right. But I am indifferent to what people may think of me."

(From *The Human Story: Our History from the Stone Age to Today* by James C. Davis. 2004. New York: HarperCollins, page 106.)

Do you feel that this quotation helps define twelfth-century Mongol warriors—as well as Genghis Khan himself? As a follow-up, you may wish to read Chapter 6 of Davis's well-researched history of humanity for yourself. See if the information Davis chooses to share leaves you convinced that the Mongols were formidable, sometimes cruel warriors—and unpleasant to approach!

Step 3: Involving Students as Evaluators

Ask students to review Samples A and B, looking for strong, clear assertions that are well documented. Which author relies on sweeping statements and generalities? Which takes care to express ideas in specific terms—and then to back those up with an explanation and/or quotation? Which one makes assertions that should be supported, but are not? Have students work with a partner, highlighting the assertions each writer makes and making marginal notes about the need for specifics—or for authentication.

Discussing Results

Most students should find Sample A stronger. Writer A makes very specific assertions, and backs each one with information from the text. By contrast, Writer B either deals in generalities, or makes assertions that a reader might question—but for which there is no documentation. Please note that the examples used in this lesson are *not* intended as complete literary analyses, but as excerpts used for illustrative purposes.

Step 4: Modeling Revision

- If students are not familiar with the text *The Old Man and the Sea* by Ernest Hemingway, you may wish to give them time to read or at least skim the book. Also make sure copies are available for their reference.

- Share Sample C (*Whole Class Revision*) with students. Read the original aloud.
- Talk about the assertions this writer makes. How many are generalities? For those that are specific, does the writer provide evidence from the book? (Most students should say that this writing is a mix of *generalities and unsupported assertions.*)
- Discuss ways of making the assertions stronger through reference to Hemingway's text. Give students time to review the text for events or quotations that will support the writers' key points.
- Revise the passage by offering appropriate support in the form of brief summaries or quotations from the book. Note that it is fine to modify the wording of the writer's original assertions if you feel this is appropriate.
- Give the piece a new title to reflect the writer's thesis.
- Compare your revision to ours, keeping in mind that you may have selected different summaries and/or quotations to support key points. What matters is that all assertions are *specific and supported.* Please note that we are likely to have included *many* more quotations (for purposes of illustrating possibilities).

Step 5: Revising with Partners

Make sure students have access to the book *The Old Man and the Sea* by Ernest Hemingway. It is not necessary for them to read the *entire* text (though many will find that helpful). Then, pass out copies of Sample D (*Revising with Partners*). Ask students to follow the basic steps you modeled with Sample C. *Working with partners,* they should:

- Read the passage aloud.
- Look and listen for generalities or unsupported assertions.
- Discuss with their partners what is needed: more specific assertions and/or support from the text.
- Revise the writing so that it makes specific, supportable points; then find and document support from the book *The Old Man and the Sea.*
- Give the piece a new title to reflect the key points.
- Read the revised version aloud to hear how it sounds with specific, well-documented assertions. *Please note that adding even one or two relevant quotations will substantively improve the text.*

Step 6: Sharing and Discussing Results

When students have finished, ask several pairs of students to share their revisions aloud. Are the generalities gone? Are all questionable assertions documented with evidence from the text itself? Compare your revisions with ours, keeping in mind that we have likely made different changes, and are likely to have used *many* more quotations (for purposes of illustrating possibilities).

Next Steps

- Invite students to review their own research writing and/or literary analysis, turning generalities into specifics and providing evidence for any questionable assertions. Remind them that it is not necessary to document *everything*, but they should document what a thoughtful reader might question or disagree with.
- Look carefully through any textbooks your students may currently be using in any subject: math, social studies, science, art. How many include assertions for which the writer should provide evidence? Is it provided within the text? Is there a bibliography or list of recommended readings to suggest the sources from which information is taken? Recommended books with strong bibliographies or recommended reading lists:
  - **The Human Story: Our History, from the Stone Age to Today* by James C. Davis. 2004. New York: HarperCollins.
  - *The Boys' War: Confederate and Union Soldiers Talk About the Civil War* by Jim Murphy. 1990. New York: Houghton Mifflin.
  - *Escape! The Story of the Great Houdini* by Sid Fleischman. 2006. New York: HarperCollins.
  - *Team Moon: How 400,000 People Landed Apollo 11 on the Moon by Catherine Thimmesh.* 2006. Boston: Houghton Mifflin.
- Sometimes an author's extensive experience and personal knowledge base qualifies him or her to make *some* assertions an average reader (or writer) might not get by with. For example, James C. Davis, author of *The Human Story: Our History from the Stone Age to Today*, has taught history at the University of Pennsylvania for thirty-seven years. Talk about what effect this background might have on his credibility. How important is it, in general, to check the believability or authenticity of a source before quoting it?
- *For an additional challenge:* Students often write a research piece or literary analysis—and then go back to dig for just the right quotation to support what they want to say. This sometimes works, but often proves frustrating, and may even lead an impatient writer to delete an unsupported assertion or change a thesis. Writers seeking a challenge may find it helpful to highlight passages and make marginal notes as they go; if possible, suggest that they also keep an electronic file, by category (theme, character) of quotations likely to prove useful. This takes motivation and attention to task! But—writers who record such quotations after reading each chapter will find the later task of putting the paper together *significantly* easier—and will also be able to put their "fingers" on just the passage they need.

*Indicates a book written for a young adult through adult audience. These books may contain mature language or themes.

Sample A

Generalities?
Specific assertions?
Documentation?

The Consequences of Pity

During Tom Robinson's trial, both Tom and defense attorney Atticus Finch express pity for Mayella Ewell, the alleged victim. This emotional response has very different consequences for the two men.

In questioning Mayella Ewell, Atticus must try to break down her story and show that his client, Tom Robinson, is innocent of any wrong doing. He could go about this in a very aggressive fashion, but early on, he begins to pity Mayella despite the threat she poses to Tom. He suspects her father of beating her—and knows she is friendless. So in questioning the one witness whose testimony could exonerate his client, Atticus is gentle, not harsh. He shows her to be a victim of abject poverty and—potentially—her father's abuse. The jury learns that the Ewells do not have enough money for food, that their water comes from a spring, and that when the weather is cold enough to require shoes, "you could make dandy ones from strips of old tires" (page 208). Even as Atticus accuses Mayella of compromising Tom's safety and reputation, he remains sensitive to her feelings, treating her with dignity and respect.

Tom Robinson, as it turns out, pities Mayella too—and this pity will cost him dearly. Under testimony, Tom explains that he has helped Mayella countless times because "Mr. Ewell didn't seem to help her none," and besides "she didn't have no nickels to spare" (page 218). Scout (the story's narrator and Atticus Finch's daughter) tells us that "As Tom Robinson gave his testimony, it came to me that Mayella Ewell must have been the loneliest person in the world" (page 218). Under cross-examination by prosecuting attorney Mr. Gilmore, Tom admits to thinking this very thing himself: "I felt right sorry for her . . ." he tells the jury, and this expression of pity is enough to turn the trial (page 224). The jury will not forgive Tom for the crime of presumption. He has had the audacity to feel sorry for a white woman—and whether he has actually assaulted her physically suddenly becomes secondary.

Later, Scout closes her eyes as the jury is polled. She cannot bear to look. But she hears the repeated recitations of "Guilty . . . guilty . . . guilty . . . guilty . . ." And when she peeks at her brother Jem, his shoulders are jerking "as if each 'guilty' was a separate stab between them" (page 240). Atticus has lost the case, but Tom Robinson has lost his freedom—and will later lose his life.

Information to support this passage is taken from *To Kill a Mockingbird* by Harper Lee. 1960, renewed 1988, paperback edition 2006. New York: Harper Perennial Classics. Chapters 17–21, pages 189–241.

Sample B

Generalities?
Specific assertions?
Documentation?

Houdini

Harry Houdini was an extremely popular magician, illusionist, and escape artist. He was born in the late 1800s. Tradition says he was born in Appleton, Wisconsin.

Houdini performed numerous dangerous stunts, such as jumping from bridges. He is also said to have swung from a trapeze and to have picked up needles with his eyelashes!

Throughout his career, Houdini was challenged by many people who sought to undermine his claims that he could escape from anything. He came close to being stumped several times. At one point, he offered the sum of twenty-five British pounds to anyone who could restrain him in a way so that he could not free himself. A challenger from America took him up on the offer, and almost won the bet when Harry had a very difficult time escaping. After a long struggle, however, he managed to free himself, and the challenger lost.

Houdini was known the world over, and he worked hard to maintain his reputation as the greatest escape artist ever. He took chances he probably should not have taken. He also showed some vanity in promoting himself. But despite these things, he continues to be admired and imitated to this day.

Revision of Sample B

Houdini—Escape Artist or Narcissist? ~~Houdini~~

Harry Houdini was an extremely popular magician, illusionist, and escape artist. He was born in ~~the late 1800s~~ 1874 in Budapest, Hungary. His birth name was Erich Weiss, and his father was Rabbi Weiss. Tradition says he was born in Appleton, Wisconsin—but that is simply a myth Houdini liked to perpetuate (page 15).

Houdini performed numerous dangerous stunts, such as jumping from bridges, escaping from barrels of water, trunks, safes or straightjackets (pages 65–66). He is also said to have swung from a trapeze and to have picked up needles with his eyelashes! He actually picked up the needles with his teeth, a trick many other trapeze artists also performed (page 17).

Throughout his career, Houdini was challenged by many people who sought to undermine his claims that he could escape from anything. ~~He came close to being stumped several times.~~ At one point, he offered the sum of twenty-five British pounds to anyone who could restrain him in a way so that he could not free himself. A challenger from America named Hodgson took him up on the offer, ~~and almost won the bet when~~ handcuffing Harry and trussing him in heavy chains. ~~Harry had a very difficult time escaping.~~ After a long struggle, ~~however, he managed to free himself, and the challenger lost.~~ Houdini begged to be released, for as he said, "My back was aching, my circulation was stopped in my wrists, and my arms became paralyzed" (page 88). Hodgson refused—and was booed by the crowd for doing so. Two hours later, a bleeding Houdini emerged from seclusion—free. The remaining people in the crowd gave him a standing ovation (pages 88–90).

Houdini was known the world over, and he worked hard to maintain his reputation as the greatest escape artist ever. ~~He took chances he probably should not have taken. He also showed some vanity in promoting himself. But despite these things, he continues to be admired and imitated to this day.~~ He is widely admired for his skill and daring, but according to author Sid Fleischman, few people know the "real" Houdini. Fleischman, a magician himself, calls Houdini "arrogant, self-worshipful, and demanding." Fleischman admits, however, that Houdini's cockiness inspired a "cottage industry devoted to shooting down the master," and adds that "The trashing continues to this day" (page 76).

Information for Sample B is taken from *Escape! The Story of the Great Houdini* by Sid Fleischman. 2006. New York: HarperCollins.

Sample C: Whole Class Revision

Generalities?
Specific assertions?
Documentation?

The Theme of Competition

One of the main themes in *The Old Man and the Sea* is competition. This theme shows up in many parts of the book. For example, the old man competes with other fishermen. When he is out at sea, he recalls competing as a wrestler when he was a young man.

Santiago also competes with the fish he wants to capture. He even admires the fish for fighting back.

The old man's competitive spirit shows itself when he talks with the boy about baseball. He identifies with baseball heroes and admires them because they are strong.

In the end, the old man cannot beat the sharks and he knows it, but even then, competition remains one of the most important themes of the book.

Information for Samples C and D is based on *The Old Man and the Sea* by Ernest Hemingway. 1952, renewed 1980, new edition 2003. New York: Scribner.

Sample D: Revising with Partners

Generalities?
Specific assertions?
Documentation?

The Sharks

Toward the end of *The Old Man and the Sea*, Santiago has successfully caught the great fish, and is making his way home. But he has gone out very far, making the journey home dangerous.

With the appearance of the first shark, the tone of the book grows dark, and the reader knows things are only going to get worse. The shark is powerful, and eats some of the fish the old man has fought so hard to capture. The old man feels a growing sense of despair.

In a fierce battle, the old man successfully kills the first shark. But he seems to sense things will get worse. As readers, we sense this, too.

The next sharks are even more fearsome. He fights them, but he is growing tired. He thinks of the baseball player, Joe DiMaggio, and wonders what he would do in these circumstances.

One shark is particularly vicious. He manages to kill it, but in the course of the battle, he loses his knife. When the last sharks come, he is almost out of energy. In a moment of irony, he wishes the great fish were still alive.

When a battle weary Santiago finally returns to the town safely, all that remains of the fish is a skeleton.

Suggested Revisions of C and D

Sample C: Whole Class Revision

The Champion ~~The Theme of Competition~~

The theme of competition is woven throughout Ernest Hemingway's book ~~One of the main themes in~~ *The Old Man and the Sea*. ~~is competition.~~ ~~This theme shows up in many parts of the book.~~ For example, the old man competes with other fishermen. Some remember the great fisherman he used to be, while others only look at him and laugh (p. 111). When he is out at sea, he recalls competing in a 24-hour wrestling match ~~as a wrestler~~ when he was a young man—and winning! After that match, "He decided that he could beat anyone if he wanted to badly enough" (p. 70), and the memory of having been "The Champion" keeps him going.

Santiago also competes with the fish he wants to capture. He even admires the fish for fighting back. He calls him "the great fish," and says there is no one "worthy of eating him" (p. 75).

The old man's competitive spirit shows itself when he talks with the boy about baseball. He identifies with ~~baseball heroes and admires them because they are strong.~~ Joe DiMaggio because like Santiago, DiMaggio plays through pain, and refuses to give up (p. 114).

In the end, the old man cannot beat the sharks and he knows it, but even then, ~~competition remains one of the most important themes of the book.~~ his competitive spirit keeps him a champion to the end. Santiago coaches himself like the great fighter he is: "Fight them," he said. "I'll fight them until I die" (p. 113).

Sample D: Revising with Partners

Final Battle
~~The Sharks~~

Toward the end of *The Old Man and the Sea*, Santiago has successfully caught the great fish, and is making his way home. But he has gone too far out to see land (p. 46), ~~out very far,~~ making the journey home dangerous.

Hemingway foreshadows the hard times to come with this chilling line: "It was an hour before the first shark hit him" (p. 100). With this line, ~~With the appearance of the first shark,~~ the tone of the book grows dark, and the reader knows things are only going to get worse. The shark is deadly, "a fish built to feed on all the fishes in the sea . . . . a shark that had no fear at all and would do exactly what he wished" (p. 101). When it ~~powerful, and~~ eats some of the fish the old man has fought so hard to capture, Santiago ~~The old man~~ feels a growing sense of despair: "When the fish had been hit, it was as though he himself were hit" (p. 103).

In a fierce battle, the old man successfully kills the first shark. But he seems to sense things will get worse. As readers, we sense this, too. Like Santiago, we know the sharks are "closing all the time" (p. 107).

The next sharks are even more fearsome. The old man describes them as "bad smelling, scavengers as well as killers" (p. 108). He fights them, but he is growing tired. He thinks of the baseball player, Joe DiMaggio, and wonders ~~what he would do in these circumstances~~ if DiMaggio would approve of the way he has struck the sharks, with power and accuracy (p. 104).

It comes "like a pig to the trough if a pig had a mouth so wide you could put your head in it" (p. 111). Santiago

One shark is particularly vicious. He manages to kill it, but in the course of the

"in a pack" (p. 118),

battle, he loses his knife. When the last sharks come, he is almost out of energy. In a moment of irony, he wishes the great fish were still alive: **"He liked to think of the fish and what he could do to a shark if he were swimming free" (p. 115).**

When a battle weary Santiago finally returns to the town safely, all that remains of the fish is a skeleton. **Like the old man himself, it is a grim reminder of battles won and lost.**

Lesson **6**

Going on Comma Patrol

Trait Connection: **Conventions**

Introduction (Share with students in your own words—or as a handout.)

In the previous two lessons, we considered several ways to use commas—and places to avoid them. You should keep those lessons handy as you work through this one so that you can refer to them whenever you need to. Keep a handbook (such as *Write Source: New Generation*) close by also, for easy reference.

This time around, you'll need to read the copy *especially carefully*. Some commas are used correctly, but others are inserted at random and serve no purpose whatsoever. Still others are missing.

Begin by deleting those you feel don't belong. Then, read the text again, looking and listening for pauses that *should* be marked with a comma. We have NOT tried to make you crazy by asking you to make a thousand corrections. There are only a few mistakes. But you will need to read and listen carefully to find them. Think of yourself as "patrolling" the text, looking for misuse of commas. Remember: Read both silently and aloud. You will find *at least one error* relating to each of the following:

1. Use of commas in a series
2. Use of commas after introductions
3. Use of commas to set off a sentence interruption
4. Use of commas with *and, but, or, for*, etc. to join two clauses
5. Misuse of commas to "link" sentences, forming a comma splice
6. "Trip the reader" commas placed where there is *no need to pause*

Teaching the Lesson (General Guidelines for Teachers)

1. Briefly review Lessons 2 and 4 as needed, answering any questions students may have about comma use.
2. Ask students to keep Lessons 2 and 4 handy for easy reference, and to also have a handbook available in case they wish for more information on comma use.
3. Share the editing lesson on the following page. Students should read the passage *both silently and aloud*, looking and listening for unneeded commas as well as missed opportunities to use a comma correctly.
4. Ask students to edit individually first, then check with a partner.
5. When everyone is done, ask them to coach you as you edit the same copy.
6. When you finish, read your edited copy aloud, explaining the reason behind each change. Then compare your edited copy with our suggested text on page 70.
7. If students have any difficulty with this activity, review Lessons 2 or 4, or both. Then, repeat the practice, this time reading aloud with students, sentence by sentence, as they work—and exaggerating pauses.

Editing Goal: Delete 8 unneeded commas and insert 6 needed commas. Correct 2 comma splices.
Follow-Up: Insert needed commas, and delete those that merely interrupt the flow in your own work. Watch out for comma splices.

Editing Practice

Delete commas that *merely interrupt* the flow of the text.
Add any needed commas that are *missing* from the text.
Correct any comma splices.

Do you enjoy films? Have you, ever tried making a film, yourself? If you said yes to these questions you might be interested to know that something called "visual literacy" is becoming more popular, in schools today. Visual literacy, is the art of taking or making meaning via images or video. Some people, think for example that interpreting a painting or a film, is a form of "reading," even if no words are involved. Reading a film is very different, from reading a book. The text is partly in the script, it is also in the viewer's head. Students who are attracted to visual literacy often enjoy taking photographs creating paintings or sketches or making their own films. If you have ever read a graphic novel (one with comic-book-like sketches) then you have been a student of visual literacy. Here's an interesting observation. The best readers of traditional text, are not always the most skilled in visual literacy. They *may* "read" sketches or film with great skill, they may struggle to interpret images as quickly and easily as they make sense of words.

Edited Copy

8 unneeded commas deleted
6 helpful commas added
2 comma splices corrected

Do you enjoy films? Have you ever tried making a film yourself? If you said yes to these questions you might be interested to know that something called "visual literacy" is becoming more popular in schools today. Visual literacy is the art of taking or making meaning via images or video. Some people think for example that interpreting a painting or a film is a form of "reading," even if no words are involved. Reading a film is very different from reading a book. The text is partly in the script, it is also in the viewer's head. Students who are attracted to visual literacy often enjoy taking photographs creating paintings or sketches or making their own films. If you have ever read a graphic novel (one with comic-book-like sketches) then you have been a student of visual literacy. Here's an interesting observation. The best readers of traditional text are not always the most skilled in visual literacy. They *may* "read" sketches or film with great skill, they may struggle to interpret images as quickly and easily as they make sense of words.

Revising to Compare and Contrast

Lesson 7

Trait Connection: **Organization**

Introduction

Information can be packaged and presented any number of ways. For example, visual organization works well for describing a scene. Chronological organization works well in a story: *this happened, then this, and finally this*. A problem-solution structure (which we'll consider in the next revision lesson) is especially effective in proposals and persuasive pieces. But of all the ways to order information, few are more revealing and helpful than comparison-contrast. In comparing two subjects, we generally learn more about each of them. Good comparison demands two things, however: (1) the comparisons must be parallel, and (2) the points of comparison should reveal something important, relating to the writer's thesis. With respect to the first point, if a writer is comparing cats and dogs, and says that cats are intelligent, the reader expects some reference to the intelligence of dogs also. Point 2 simply refers to the fact that meaningless comparisons are not very useful: *Elephants can be trained to carry freight; so can camels*. "So what?" asks the reader. "Why are you telling me this?" As a writer, make sure that your comparisons are purposeful and make a point. If you do that—and if you keep your points of comparison parallel, you'll have a strong piece of writing.

Teacher's Sidebar . . .

A good comparison-contrast paper requires planning. It is helpful for writers to make a list of comparison points first, then zero in on those that are most interesting or revealing. They should also ask, "What is the one *overall* point that I wish to make?" It may be possible to draw a thousand points of comparison between dogs and cats, for instance, but only three or four may be relevant to the writer's primary discussion. In addition, it is important to make sure that everything addressed about one subject is addressed about the other as well (ensuring that the discussions are parallel).

Focus and Intent

This lesson is intended to help students:

- Explore comparison-contrast as one means of organizing information.
- Understand the specific features (focusing on what is relevant, ensuring that all comparison points are addressed for both subjects) that make comparison-contrast organization effective.

- Revise a comparison-contrast essay so that it (1) makes a central point (supporting the writer's thesis), and (2) draws parallel points of comparison for both subjects.

Teaching the Lesson

Step 1: Designing a Comparison-Contrast Essay

It is impossible, within the framework of a reasonably sized essay, to make every possible comparison between two books, films, restaurants—or whatever. Luckily, it is not necessary. Two to four key comparisons (or contrasts) are usually sufficient to make the writer's point. It is a good idea, however, to plan such an essay by brainstorming as many points of comparison as you can think of. Then you can delete those that are common knowledge, less interesting—or less relevant to the main point you wish to make. In this part of the lesson:

1. Ask students to identify two subjects for comparison. Possible topics: a book and the film made from it; two restaurants with similar menus; two sports; two places to live or vacation; two lifestyles—e.g., minimalist vs. materialistic.
2. Discuss the purpose of the comparison by raising this question: "What point should this comparison make for the reader?" The answer to this question can be used to form a *draft thesis*.
3. Brainstorm as many points of comparison as you can come up with in two to three minutes—making sure to keep the comparison parallel by documenting responses for both subjects.
4. Zero in on the two to four comparison points that seem most significant. Cross out the rest.
5. Modify the original thesis so that it better fits the final comparison points.

Following is one example, based on a comparison of downhill vs. cross country skiing:

Downhill	**Cross Country**
1. Mountainous terrain	1. Flatter terrain
2. ~~Wide skis~~	2. ~~Narrow skis~~
3. High speed	3. Slower pace
4. ~~Learning time: weeks to years~~	4. ~~Learning time: days to weeks~~
5. High expense	5. Moderate expense
6. ~~Requires stamina, balance and significant agility~~	6. ~~Requires stamina and balance~~
7. Risk of injury: very high	7. Risk of injury: moderate
8. Health benefits: high	8. Health benefits: high

Draft Thesis: Cross country skiing involves less risk of injury than downhill—and is less expensive as well—yet provides comparable health benefits.

Note to the teacher: Notice that points 2, 4, and 6 are all significant—and may still come up in the discussion. But by narrowing the focus, the writer stands a better chance of staying on track and supporting the thesis well.

Step 2: Making the Reading-Writing Connection

In a chapter titled "The End of the World: How Rome Fell and Why," historian Thomas Cahill (*How the Irish Saved Civilization*) takes us back to a dark day in 406 A.D. The Rhine River has frozen solid. It is the moment that the starving barbarians, camped outside apparently undefeatable Rome have been waiting for. The two forces huddle in the cold, sizing each other up, with only the frozen river dividing them. Cahill draws a sharp, vivid contrast between the elegant (and overly confident) Roman soldiers and the barbarian hordes, who are about to launch an unexpectedly effective attack. Following is his description of the Roman soldiers:

> *Their hair is cut with a thought to the shape of the head, they are clean-shaven to show off the resoluteness of the jawline, their dress—from their impregnable but shapely breastplates to their easy-movement skirts—is designed with the form and movement of the body in mind . . . Just now the* architriclinus*—the chef—is beginning to prepare the carrots: he slices each piece lengthwise, then lengthwise again, to achieve slender, elongated triangles.*

Here, by contrast, is his description of the barbarian hordes:

> *Their hair (both of head and face) is uncut, vilely dressed with oil, braided into abhorrent shapes. Their bodies are distorted by ornament and discolored by paint . . . They are dirty and they stink. A crone in a filthy blanket stirs a cauldron, slicing roots and bits of rancid meat into the concoction from time to time. She slices a carrot crosswise up its shaft, so that the circular pieces she cuts off float like foolish yellow eyes on the surface of her brew.*
>
> (From *How the Irish Saved Civilization* by Thomas Cahill. 1995. New York: Doubleday, pages 15–16.)

What points of comparison does Cahill focus on in this example? What do his contrasting descriptions tell us about the Romans—and about the barbarians? Consider his last point of comparison: the carrots. Why is this small detail so significant? Do you suppose the Roman army takes the barbarians seriously? Why?

Step 3: Involving Students as Evaluators

Ask students to review Samples A and B, looking for strong comparisons that (1) make a point, and (2) address parallel concerns for both subjects. Have students work together, highlighting points of comparison and identifying the thesis (if there is one) for each piece. Ask them to determine which is stronger, and to discuss what could be done to revise the other piece.

Discussing Results

Most students should find Sample A stronger. Writer B does not have a clear thesis as yet—and wanders through the comparison, not always addressing the same points for each subject. By contrast, Writer A has a clear thesis, and uses parallel points of comparison to support that thesis.

Step 4: Modeling Revision

- Share Sample C (*Whole Class Revision*) with students. Read the original aloud.
- Talk about the writer's thesis. Is it clear? (Most students should say *no.*) Ask about the key points of comparison: What are they? Are they parallel; that is, does the writer address the same points of comparison for both subjects? (Again, most students should say *no.*)
- As a class, identify the writer's thesis. What point is this writer trying to make?
- Then, based on that thesis, decide which points of comparison are most significant.
- Revise the passage by (1) making the thesis clear, (2) including two or three key points of comparison that support that thesis, and (3) deleting anything that is no longer needed. Note that it is fine to add new information if you wish.
- Give the piece a new title.
- Compare your revision to ours, keeping in mind that you may have selected different points of comparison—and that your thesis may be different from ours. What matters is that (1) the essay now makes a point, and (2) points of comparison are consistent, subject to subject, and support the thesis.

Step 5: Revising with Partners

Pass out copies of Sample D (*Revising with Partners*). Ask students to follow the basic steps you modeled with Sample C. *Working with partners,* they should:

- Read the passage aloud.
- Look and listen for points of comparison.
- Attempt to identify the thesis—or discuss a possible thesis.
- With their partners, discuss what is needed: a clear thesis; clear points of comparison; consistent, parallel comparisons (involving both subjects).
- Revise the writing so that it focuses on two or three key points of comparison, and has a clear thesis. (Note that it is fine to add new information.)
- Delete what is not needed.
- Give the piece a new title to direct a reader's attention to what is most important.
- Read the revised version aloud to hear the effect of the changes.

Step 6: Sharing and Discussing Results

When students have finished, ask several pairs of students to share their revisions aloud. Does each essay focus on the *most important* points of comparison? Have less relevant points been deleted to give the essay focus? Do points of comparison made for one subject parallel those made for the other? Is there now a clear thesis or main point? Compare your revisions with ours, keeping in mind that we may have focused on different points of comparison or come up with a different thesis.

Next Steps

- Talk about contexts in which comparison and contrast might be most useful. For example, what could this organizational design add to a persuasive piece of writing? How does it expand an informational piece? Could comparison be useful in a travel brochure? Editorial? Memoir? Poem? Advertisement? History textbook?
- Invite students to scan their own writing, looking for opportunities to use comparison effectively, and reviewing existing comparisons for effectiveness. Remind them that strong comparisons usually focus on two or three salient points, rather than trying to cover the full spectrum of possibilities.
- Look carefully through textbooks your students may currently be using in any subject: math, social studies, science, art. How many include comparisons, even if they run for just a paragraph rather than a full chapter? Recommended books that include comparisons:
  - **How the Irish Saved Civilization* by Thomas Cahill. 1995. New York: Doubleday. (Read the complete comparison of the Romans and the barbarians, pages 15–16.)
  - *Animal Farm by George Orwell.* 2004 (50th Anniversary Edition). New York: Signet. (Note the barnyard at the beginning of the book, pages 16–24, and the same scene at the close of the book, pages 118–128.)
  - *Incredible Comparisons* by Russell Ash. 1996. London: Dorling Kindersley.
  - *The Wall: Growing Up Behind the Iron Curtain* by Peter Sis. 2007. New York: Farrar, Straus, and Giroux. (Check the *Introduction* and *Afterward* to see the impact of comparison on a historical account.)
- *For an additional challenge:* Create a comparison essay based on Orwell's implied comparisons of the barnyard (and animals) at the beginning and ending of *Animal Farm*. Focus on those elements you feel Orwell especially wishes us to notice.

*Indicates a book written for a young adult *through* adult audience. These books may contain mature language or themes.

Sample A

Clear thesis?
Strong points of comparison?
Parallel comparisons?

Downloading versus Purchasing

When it comes to obtaining music easily, quickly, and cheaply, downloading has a clear advantage over purchasing music one CD at a time. Consider first the convenience. It is simply much easier to sit at one's own computer, reviewing new releases, and deciding *precisely* which ones to download than to have to get into a car, drive to a store, and spend hours scanning shelves of pre-packaged music.

In addition, downloading takes but a fraction of the time required to select music from a store. Music stores typically are crowded and noisy—and often music is arranged in a way that makes finding what a person wants anything but simple. Store merchants often have difficulty processing a specific request. By contrast, a person can search online by genre, title, or artist, and within seconds have a wide range of selections from which to choose.

Finally, consider the differences in cost. Many selections online are free—or available for a nominal fee, often less than a dollar. A typical CD costs anywhere from nine to eighteen dollars; some are more. That sounds like a bargain for twelve to fifteen tracks until users recall that some CDs contain only three or four selections the purchaser really wants—and many that he or she does not. That being the case, the purchaser is stuck with another CD to shelve, and the unsettling feeling that he or she has actually paid about $4 per song for the really good tracks.

Why buy bundled music when you can create an individualized collection song by song? Downloading beats individual CD purchasing on every count.

Sample B

Clear thesis?
Strong points of comparison?
Parallel comparisons?

Live Theater versus Movies

Live theater is exciting. Live theater has been popular for centuries, and reached a kind of golden age during the time of Shakespeare. Its popularity has never diminished since that time.

Plays feature dialogue. If you think about it, almost all of the action is driven by the performers speaking.

In a film, if lighting is not right or if a performer bungles lines, a scene can be shot repeatedly. Sometimes it requires three or four "takes" to get a scene just as the director envisioned it.

People come to a play partly to see the actors in an "up close and personal" kind of way. Those in front seats may be only a few feet from the stage. They can observe their every gesture and facial expression.

Theater tickets can be expensive. Some cost as much as two hundred dollars or more. The price of movie tickets is increasing also.

Revision of Sample B

See It Live!

~~Live Theater versus Movies~~

While films and live theater are both entertaining, it is hard to beat the excitement of the personal experience live theater provides. No wonder it ~~Live theater is exciting. Live theater~~ has been popular for centuries. ~~and reached a kind of golden age during the time of Shakespeare. Its popularity has never diminished since that time.~~

Unlike films, plays do not feature explosions and car chases. Plays feature dialogue. If you think about it, almost all of the action is driven by the performers speaking. That does not mean they are "action-free," however. In the theater, "action" comes from people reacting to each other, just as people do in real life. Most real life centers on conversation, not car chases.

Theater is also exciting for its unpredictability. In a film, if lighting is not right or if a performer bungles lines, a scene can be shot repeatedly. Sometimes it requires three or four "takes" to get a scene just as the director envisioned it. In live theater, actors get one chance to do it right, and if they bungle a line, it can take great skill to cover the blunder. At any moment, an actor may have to improvise. It takes imagination—and courage—to act on stage.

People come to a play partly to see the actors in an "up close and personal" kind of way. Those in front seats may be only a few feet from the stage. They can observe their every gesture and facial expression. Movies just don't offer that kind of immediacy.

Theater tickets can be expensive. ~~Some cost as much as two hundred dollars or more. The price of movie tickets is increasing also.~~ A play may cost five to twenty times as much as a movie ticket. But a playgoer is paying to see a favorite actor in person, betting that he or she can get those lines right on the first try—and not fall off the stage!

Sample C: Whole Class Revision

Clear thesis?
Strong points of comparison?
Parallel comparisons?

Text Messaging versus E-mail

E-mail is a quick and simple way to communicate with friends or business associates.

Text messaging is very popular, particularly with teenagers.

Text messaging requires a lot of dexterity. If you can type with your thumbs, you're ready to do it rapidly and well!

To make text messaging faster, many people use abbreviations, like SYL (see you later) or BTW (by the way). To people who don't use it, it can look like code, but for users, it's easy enough to decipher.

Through e-mails and text messages, people manage to communicate faster than they could ever do via regular mail.

Sample D: Revising with Partners

Clear thesis?
Strong points of comparison?
Parallel comparisons?

Television vs. Newspapers

Where do people get their news? Probably most people these days get it from television. It is easy to flick on the television and even listen casually while doing other things.

Newspapers certainly have a place in providing information about current events. Even with television, we should not forget about newspapers entirely. Newspaper journalists can dig deeply into one story and offer readers in-depth coverage of a single topic.

Newspapers offer a way of preserving news. Amazing numbers of people keep newspaper clippings from special days: the day they were born or the day they got married.

For the foreseeable future, most people will likely continue to get the majority of their news from television. After all, it's available virtually 24 hours a day now.

Suggested Revisions of C and D

Sample C: Whole Class Revision

TYP (Take Your Pick!)
~~Text Messaging versus E-mail~~

Just a few years ago, e-mail seemed like the fastest, easiest
~~E-mail is a quick and simple~~ way to communicate with friends or business associates.
The one drawback was, we couldn't always get an immediate response.
Then along came text messaging, offering immediate, on-the-spot communication.

has become
Text messaging ~~is~~ very popular, particularly with teenagers. It offers the speed of phoning with the quiet and privacy of e-mailing. It is perfect when a person does not want to be overheard.

and some people consider that a drawback.
Text messaging requires a lot of dexterity. If you can type with your thumbs, you're ready to do it rapidly and well! If not, it can be a little trickier to learn than e-mailing, which only takes standard keyboarding skills.

To make text messaging faster, many people use abbreviations, like SYL (see
and can be challenging to learn, but for regular text "messagers,"
you later) or BTW (by the way). To people who don't use it, it can look like code, ~~but for users,~~ it's easy enough to decipher.

Both allow
~~Through~~ e-mails and text messages, people ~~manage~~ to communicate faster than they could ever do via regular mail. In the end it's a tradeoff between WYG (what you gain)—quiet messages and immediacy—and WYS (what you spend)—time to master codes and acquire speedy thumbs.

Sample D: Whole Class Revision

Don't Throw the Paper Out—Yet

~~**Television vs. Newspapers**~~

These days, it's probably safe to say that most people get the majority of their news ~~Where do people get their news? Probably most people these days get it~~ from television. It is easy to flick on the television and even listen casually while doing other things. Newspapers, by contrast, require focused attention. It's hard to make dinner while reading the paper. Moreover, television can go right to the scene when news breaks. It takes hours to get a newspaper out, no matter how fast the writers and production people are.

All the same, newspapers certainly have a place in providing information about current events. Whereas many television stories blaze by in 30 to 60 seconds, newspaper stories offer detail—and allow for re-reading. ~~Even with television, we should not forget about newspapers entirely.~~ Newspaper journalists can dig deeply into one story and offer readers in-depth coverage ~~of a single topic~~ they are less likely to get in the typical television news.

Furthermore, unlike television broadcasts, newspapers offer a way of preserving news. Amazing numbers of people keep newspaper clippings from special days: the day they were born or the day they got married. Newspapers offer a record of our history.

For the foreseeable future, most people will likely continue to get the majority of their news from television. After all, it's available virtually 24 hours a day now. Television news is also more convenient, and more immediate. It lets us see things that happened just minutes earlier. Nevertheless, papers aren't likely to go away any time soon. People with scrapbooks and people with a quiet spot to concentrate still like the written record.

Handling Tricky Agreements (Part 1)

Lesson **8**

Trait Connection: **Conventions**

Introduction (Share with students in your own words—or as a handout.)

As an editor with some experience, you know how important it is for subjects and verbs to agree:

> The **dolphins** *were frolicking* (not *was frolicking*) in the ocean.
>
> **Ice** on the road *makes* (not *make*) driving treacherous.

Those examples were pretty straightforward. Following, however, are two situations that can prove tricky. Knowing about them and practicing just a bit can help you keep subjects and verbs in agreement, which will keep your readers happy (or at least less confused).

Tricky Situation 1: Words Come Between the Subject and Verb

Don't let this confuse you. Even when additional words are added in the middle of the sentence, the subject and verb must agree as if those additional in-between words were not there:

> **Andrew**, hoping to make a good impression on his friends, *practices* (not *practice*) football four hours a day.

Andrew (not *friends*) is the sentence subject. *Hint:* When you figure out what the subject is, identifying the right verb becomes *a lot* easier!

Tricky Situation 2: Compound Subjects with *nor, or, and*

Compound subjects joined with *and* are fairly simple to deal with. They are plural:

> **Rice and pasta** *are* among my favorite foods.

When subjects are joined by *or* or *nor*, however, the verb agrees with whichever part of the subject is *closer to that verb:*

> Either **potatoes or pasta** *is* good with chicken. (The word *pasta* is closer to the verb, so *is* is correct.)

Either **pasta or potatoes** *are* good with chicken. (The word *potatoes* is closer to the verb, so *are* is correct.)

Neither **Amos nor his friends** *are* on my team. (The word *friends* is closer to the verb, so *are* is correct.)

Neither **his friends nor Amos himself** *is* on my team. (The word *Amos* is closer to the verb, so *is* is correct.)

Warm-Up

Following is a short warm-up based on the kinds of examples we just shared with you. If you have any difficulty with this warm-up, review the opening examples again, or consult your handbook (*Write Source: New Generation* or another of your choice) under "subject-verb agreement." (Answers appear on the following page.)

1. Both Sam and Wally (*want, wants*) to be in the school musical.
2. Neither the twins nor Virginia (*feel, feels*) ready to play the lead.
3. Either Mackie or her friends (*is, are*) going to help with set design.
4. Sam, realizing he will be performing in front of many of his closest friends and his relatives, (*hope, hopes*) he can sing on key.
5. Wally, on the other hand, who has never been nervous performing in front of people, (*know, knows*) he will have the time of his life.

Teaching the Lesson (General Guidelines for Teachers)

1. Use our examples or your own to illustrate ways of handling tricky subject-verb agreements. (Note that two additional "tricky" situations will be addressed in Lesson 10.)
2. Ask students to complete the five sentences in the Warm-Up, and check to see if anyone has difficulty. If they do, you may wish to provide further examples or refer students to the appropriate section of whatever handbook you use in your classroom.
3. Ask students to keep our examples handy for easy reference, and to also have a handbook available in case they need more information on subject-verb agreement.
4. Share the editing lesson on the following page. Students should read the passage *both silently and aloud*, looking and listening for correct subject-verb agreement. Some sentences are correct as is, so they must read carefully.

5. Some students may find it helpful to underline the sentence subject as a first step. This makes identifying the correct verb much easier.
6. Ask students to edit individually first, then check with a partner.
7. When everyone is done, ask them to coach you as you edit the same copy. You may wish to discuss the reasons for each correction as you go.
8. When you finish, read your edited copy aloud, answering any additional questions students may have. Then compare your edited copy with our suggested text on page 87.
9. For students who have any difficulty with this activity, review the Warm-Up sentences, answering any questions. Then, repeat the practice, this time reading aloud with students as they work. Help them identify the sentence subject in each case; then match it with the verb. You may also wish to have students work with different partners in order to broaden their perspective on the lesson.

Editing Goal: Correct 7 mismatched verbs.
Follow-Up: Check for subject-verb agreement in your own work.

Answers to Warm-Up

1. **Both Sam and Wally** *want* to be in the school musical. (Compound subject joined by *and*—takes a plural verb.)
2. **Neither the twins nor Virginia** *feels* ready to play the lead. (Compound subject joined by *nor*—verb agrees with the word closer to it, *Virginia*.)
3. **Either Mackie or her friends** *are* going to help with set design. (Compound subject joined by *or*—verb agrees with the word closer to it, *friends*.)
4. **Sam**, realizing he will be performing in front of many of his closest friends and his relatives, *hopes* he can sing on key. (*Sam* is the subject—the underlined words in between do not affect the right verb, *hopes*.)
5. **Wally**, on the other hand, who has never been nervous performing in front of people, *knows* he will have the time of his life. (*Wally* is the subject—not *people*—and thus *knows* is the right verb. The underlined words between *Wally* and *knows* do not affect the right verb choice.)

Editing Practice

Correct any verb that does not agree with the sentence subject.
HINT: You may find it easier if you identify and underline the sentence subjects *first*.

More airlines these days, it seems, is charging additional money for their fares. It is understandable, with the rising price of fuel. Nevertheless, neither long-time travelers nor the occasional first-time traveler are happy about the situation. Additional fees for extra bags or an overweight bag boosts the cost of tickets for the consumer. From their point of view, travelers point out that they still have to put up with cramped seating and skimpy snacks. Even though passengers pay high prices, neither leg room nor lunch is likely to be available on most flights. These various discomforts, along with the occasional crying baby or lost luggage, is enough to make many travelers feel overcharged. But whether passengers are comfortable or not, the airlines, as they are quick to point out, still needs to make a profit. If we look at things from the airlines' point of view, ticket prices, though high, doesn't seem quite so outrageous. In addition, there are things travelers can do to make themselves more comfortable—such as stretching periodically or bringing their own snacks. Neither passengers nor the airline industry are to blame for higher fuel costs, so working together could make everyone happier.

Edited Copy

7 verbs corrected
Sentence subjects <u>underlined</u>

<u>More airlines</u> these days, it seems, ~~is~~ are charging additional money for their fares. It is understandable, with the rising price of fuel. Nevertheless, <u>neither long-time travelers nor the occasional first-time traveler</u> ~~are~~ is happy about the situation. <u>Additional fees</u> for extra bags or an overweight bag ~~boosts~~ boost the cost of tickets for the consumer. From their point of view, <u>travelers</u> point out that they still have to put up with cramped seating and skimpy snacks. Even though passengers pay high prices, <u>neither leg room nor lunch</u> is likely to be available on most flights. <u>These various discomforts</u>, along with the occasional crying baby or lost luggage, ~~is~~ are enough to make many travelers feel overcharged. But whether passengers are comfortable or not, <u>the airlines</u>, as they are quick to point out, still ~~needs~~ need to make a profit. If we look at things from the airlines' point of view, <u>ticket prices</u>, though high, ~~doesn't~~ don't seem quite so outrageous. In addition, there are <u>things</u> travelers can do to make themselves more comfortable—such as stretching periodically or bringing their own snacks. <u>Neither passengers nor the airline industry</u> ~~are~~ is to blame for higher fuel costs, so working together could make everyone happier.

Revising the Problem-Solution Structure

Lesson 9

Trait Connection: **Organization**

Introduction

The problem-solution structure is a very useful way to organize information. It's highly flexible, for one thing. You may recognize it as the underpinning structure of most narrative writing: the hero bumps into a problem of some sort—and struggles for a way to resolve it (sometimes successfully, sometimes not). It is also one lens through which to view history or science: a problem arises, and someone or some group finds a way of dealing with that problem—a way that may result in anything from a change in government to the discovery of microchips. The problem-solution structure is particularly valuable in proposal writing. A proposal is a formal document submitted to a public or private agency to request funding—funding to support research, or a new program. For example, let's say that students in a particular school district have trouble moving from kindergarten to first grade. Someone might propose funding a transitional K-1 classroom to suit the needs of children who are beyond kindergarten, but not quite ready for the academic challenges of grade one. Such a proposal would first document the problem, then propose a solution—for which funding would be sought. In this lesson, you will revise a variety of short pieces to ensure that both problem and the solution are presented clearly and convincingly—and that the solution effectively addresses the problem at hand.

Teacher's Sidebar . . .

Problem-solution pieces are weakened when the writer (1) does not understand the problem, (2) does not define that problem clearly for the reader, (3) defines the problem but simply complains without proposing *any* real solution, or (4) proposes a solution that does not really address the problem. Students will need to read carefully to first identify the weakness within the writing, and then revise accordingly.

Focus and Intent

This lesson is intended to help students:

- Explore problem-solution structure as one means of organizing information.
- Understand the specific features (understanding and clear definition of a problem, proposal of a relevant solution in convincing terms) that make for a strong problem-solution design.

- Revise a weak proposal to ensure that (1) the problem is well defined, (2) the solution is presented in clear, thorough, and convincing terms, and (3) the solution addresses the specific difficulties raised in the presentation of the problem.

Teaching the Lesson

Step 1: Designing a Problem-Solution Proposal

Everyone likes to complain now and then, but a good problem-solution proposal takes more than whining. It takes vision. First, the writer must clearly understand the problem, and that means getting to its underpinnings. For example, we know that some students do not do their homework—and this is a problem. It makes classes difficult to teach, and it results in lower grades on tests. But unless we look carefully at the reasons underlying the problem (*Why* don't some students do their homework?), no solution we propose is likely to be very effective. For example, without really examining the problem, we might come up with the superficial solution of lining the halls with posters reminding students to "Do your homework!" But this would only work if the real problem was that students were simply *forgetting* to do their homework. The problem is probably not that simple. An effective proposal first gets to the heart of the problem and then proposes a solution that addresses that problem head-on. Let's see if your students can do that by:

1. Brainstorming the real reasons that *some* students do not do homework.
2. Identifying the one, two, or three most significant reasons—those that seem to get at the heart of the problem.
3. Brainstorming a solution (or solutions) that would address the one, two, or three key "behind the problem" reasons identified in Step 2. (Note that the "solution" can involve outside intervention—so long as the cost is realistic—and can also require a multi-step approach.)
4. When you finish, draft a thesis that would serve as the driving force behind your proposal. A good proposal thesis doesn't summarize everything the writer is about to say, but it does indicate the direction in which the proposal is headed. Here's one example (be sure to come up with your own):

Draft Thesis: Students will be more likely to complete all homework assignments if we shorten in-class time and encourage students to do homework on campus, with access to written and technical resources, and assistance from teachers.

Step 2: Making the Reading-Writing Connection

The MySpace community has created a passionate proposal in the form of a 166-page paperback book titled *MySpace/Our Planet*. The book outlines in nine chapters (each of which reads like a proposal unto itself) the current "state of the ecology" for our world—together with very specific solutions to what they view as a critical problem: namely, lack of concern about human impact on the environment. In the first section of Chapter 5, "Social Life," titled "Gift Responsibility," the authors point out that Americans' love of partying may be damaging the planet. They note, for example, that we purchase about 7 billion greeting cards per year—and that it takes 2.5 million trees to produce them. During the fall-to-winter holiday season, we throw away almost 2 billion pounds *more* garbage per week than at any other time of the year (p. 64). Following are excerpts from their very specific solutions (p. 65):

- ***Give a gift they really want.*** *Put down the fruitcake. Unhand the garden gnome. Stop walking around aimlessly in the mall waiting for inspiration or filling your basket with random crapola that will just wind up in the garbage. Ask what your family and friends want . . .*
- ***Skip the paper card.*** *Try an e-card. If you do buy a paper card, look for cards that are 100 percent post-consumer recycled (PCR) . . .*
- ***Get some new(s) wrapping.*** *Most wrapping paper is not recyclable, and neither is ribbon. One abundant alternative wrapping paper is newsprint. Also consider cloth or brown paper bags . . .*

(From *MySpace/Our Planet: Change Is Possible* by the MySpace Community, with Jeca Taudte. 2008. New York: HarperCollins, pp. 64–65.)

So far as you can tell from this summary, do the authors make the problem they wish to address clear? Do they offer very specific solutions? Do those solutions address the heart of the problem? Explore the book further to ask how effectively the MySpace team tackles issues of driving, dating, spending, wearing makeup—and dozens of other behaviors that influence our eco-climate.

Step 3: Involving Students as Evaluators

Ask students to review Samples A and B, looking for a strong problem-solution structure that (1) clarifies the problem (including the *heart* of that problem), and (2) proposes a clear, relevant, compelling solution. Have students work together, highlighting both problem and solution, and making marginal notes about the clarity and insight with which each is presented. Ask them to identify the stronger piece, and to discuss what could be done to revise the other one.

Discussing Results

Most students should find Sample B stronger. Writer A wants to sound off more than analyze the real problem—and proposes a superficial solution that is little more than a restatement of the original problem. By contrast, Writer B explains the problem carefully, and proposes a solution that seems directly relevant.

Step 4: Modeling Revision

- Share Sample C (*Whole Class Revision*) with students. Read the original aloud.
- Talk about the writer's thesis. Is it clear? (Most students should say *no.*) Ask about the presentation of the problem and proposed solution: Are they clear and thorough? Does the solution address the problem head-on? (Again, most students should say *no.*)
- As a class, start by discussing the problem. What is it, specifically? What else does the writer need to say to make it clear?
- Then, discuss the solution. Again, what else must the writer say to make the solution both clear and relevant?
- Revise the passage by (1) stating the problem clearly, (2) making the solution both clear and relevant, and (3) revising the thesis to give direction to the piece. *It is fine to add new information from your personal knowledge or research.*
- Give the piece a new title.
- Compare your revision to ours, keeping in mind that you may have defined the problem or solution differently—and that if you did, that would influence both your thesis and title. In addition, we have researched an article on exotic pets in order to find relevant information to back our proposal. It is not necessary for your students to do this, but you may wish to point out how helpful it is to have such support.

Step 5: Revising with Partners

Pass out copies of Sample D (*Revising with Partners*). Ask students to follow the basic steps you modeled with Sample C. *Working with partners,* they should:

- Read the passage aloud.
- Look and listen for a clear, thorough definition of the problem and proposed solution.
- Take time to discuss both problem and solution, focusing on what more the writer needs to say to make each clear.
- Revise the writer's statement of the problem to make it clear.
- Revise the proposed problem so that it is clear, thorough, and relevant to the problem as it is now defined.
- Revise the thesis so that it sets a clear, purposeful direction for the writing to follow. (Please keep in mind that this sample is deliberately kept short; a final draft would likely be longer.)
- Give the piece a new title to reflect the revisions.
- Read the revised version aloud to listen for clarity and for a close connection between problem and solution.

Step 6: Sharing and Discussing Results

When students have finished, ask several pairs of students to share their revisions aloud. Did teams define the problem in similar ways? Did they come up with similar solutions? Which team discovered the most creative solution? Compare your revisions with ours, keeping in mind that we may have focused on different problems or come up with different solutions. In addition, we chose to rewrite the original second paragraph because it is so general. Students' revisions need not be this extreme, but it is important to recognize rewriting as one option for revision.

Next Steps

- Talk about how the problem-solution design influences literature. Consider, for example, *To Kill a Mockingbird* by Harper Lee, *Of Mice and Men* by John Steinbeck, *Animal Farm* by George Orwell, *Fahrenheit 451* by Ray Bradbury, or any play by William Shakespeare. Can your students identify any poetry in which they see a problem-solution pattern?
- Ask students to complete the problem-solution piece on homework that you used to introduce this lesson—or alternatively, to write a problem-solution proposal on any topic of their choice.
- Look and listen for problem-solution patterns in the literature you share aloud (including nonfiction pieces on science or history). Recommended books that include problem-solution organizational structure:
  - *MySpace/Our Planet: Change Is Possible* by the MySpace Community, with Jeca Taudte. 2008. New York: HarperCollins.
  - *Once a Wolf* by Stephen R. Swinburne. 1999. Boston: Houghton Mifflin. (Relatively easy reading that is still highly engaging.)
  - *Team Moon: How 400,000 People Landed Apollo 11 on the Moon* by Catherine Thimmesh. 2006. Boston: Houghton Mifflin.
  - *Tracking Trash: Flotsam, Jetsam, and the Science of Ocean Motion* by Loree Griffin Burns. 2007. Boston: Houghton Mifflin.
- *For an additional challenge:* Have a look at the book titled *Sensational Scientists: The Journeys and Discoveries of 24 Men and Women of Science* by Barry Shell (2005. Vancouver: Raincoast Books). Each scientist whose story appears in the book was asked to identify the question he or she would most like answered. Their responses appear in a running category termed "Mystery," and each response presents a challenge to future generations. The problems are clear—the solutions are up to the scientists of tomorrow. Invite students to write a brief proposal based on one of these "mysteries," and to propose either a solution or a means of discovering a solution.

Sample A

Clear statement of the problem? Clear proposed solution? Strong thesis?

Fix the Traffic Problem!

Have you driven on a major city freeway lately? If so, you know how out of control the traffic problem has become. The average commute time has expanded from twenty or thirty minutes to an hour—or more. Some commuters now spend two to four hours a day on the road. This is ridiculous, people! We need to stop it now.

The solution is simple. We need fewer cars on the highway. We are using up too much fuel and polluting the air. We are keeping people from their families and creating more stress. We must reduce the number of cars on our freeway systems, and we must do it now. The problem is exacerbated by our continuing indifference. If we work together, we can solve it. Cooperation is the answer.

Sample B

Clear statement of the problem?
Clear proposed solution?
Strong thesis?

Pushing Down the Dropout Rate

Recent news stories report an increasingly high dropout rate among U.S. high school students. According to a 2006 article in *Time* magazine, the rate is as high as 30 percent, and headed upward. Because of the high rate of student mobility, precise numbers are difficult to determine, and this figure remains disputed; nevertheless, virtually all researchers agree that the dropout rate is too high, and that it is climbing. A higher rate means that there are fewer people available to perform skilled and technical tasks, and this in itself is a threat to the American economy. Meanwhile, students without even a high school education face an overwhelming challenge in securing employment. Their reduced income means less consumer spending, and that in turn means a slowing of the economy that can rock everyone from McDonald's to Wall Street.

Several potential solutions need to be explored. First, some students may find school more appealing if they can follow a career-oriented path versus the usual academic track. This career-based curriculum might start as early as Middle School. Second, we might seek to motivate some students by allowing them to complete school at their own rate. Those who could do the work and complete a series of tests, projects, or reading/writing requirements faster could graduate at age 16—or even sooner. Finally, we should explore the possibility that some colleges, both two-year and four-year, may be willing to accept students without high school diplomas if they can show other evidence of personal success, such as employment history or a record of volunteer work. Taken together, these creative approaches could cut the dropout rate significantly by letting students "drop in" to a new form of education.

(Information on the dropout rate is from Nathan Thornburgh, "Dropout Nation," in *Time*, April 17, 2006. Vol. 167, No. 16, p. 11.)

Revision of Sample A

Don't Just Sit There and Whine—Do Something!

~~Fix the Traffic Problem!~~

Have you driven on a major city freeway lately? If so, you know how out of control the traffic problem has become. The average commute time one way has expanded from twenty ~~or thirty~~ minutes to as much as two hours per day. As a result of all this time on the road, ~~an hour—or more. Some commuters now spend two to four hours a day on the road. This is ridiculous, people! We need to stop it now.~~

~~The solution is simple. We need fewer cars on the highway.~~ we are using up too much fuel and polluting the air. We are also keeping people from their families and creating more stress. We must reduce the number of cars on our freeway systems, and we must do it now. ~~The problem is exacerbated by our continuing indifference. If we work together, we can solve it. Cooperation is the answer.~~ Several important steps can help.

First, each of us can explore mass transit options, and use them. Employers can help by promoting four-day work weeks and staggering working hours. People object to car pooling, but many won't if there's a tax incentive involved. If we write to our legislators, we can make this happen. Finally, once we're on those traffic-snarled freeways, we can practice simple courtesy, allowing cars in when they clearly need to enter. Studies of so-called "synchronicity" show that a courteous approach keeps traffic flowing faster than fighting for position. As a final step, we should provide financial incentives for people who choose to live close enough to their work that they can commute on foot or by bicycle. These steps have something in common. They all show a serious desire to solve the problem, not just sit in traffic and whine about it!

Sample C: Whole Class Revision

Clear statement of the problem? Clear proposed solution? Strong thesis?

Exotic pets are tempting. It's exciting to imagine a giraffe in the back yard or a tortoise in the garden. People may want to own an orangutan or alligator or snake when they see it on television or discover it for sale somewhere. With the advent of the Internet, exotic pets are far easier to locate and obtain, even in places where their purchase is illegal. Unfortunately, such pets seldom behave exactly as their owners predicted, and it is not always convenient to keep them.

It is important to educate people about various kinds of animals and whether they do or do not make good pets. When this does not happen, it can be difficult to return the animals to the wild. This leads to difficulties both for pets and their current—or previous—owners!

Sample D: Revising with Partners

Clear statement of the problem? Clear proposed solution? Strong thesis?

Despite protests from teachers, public speakers, and others, many users are reluctant to turn off cell phones. Why? Are they so desperate to maintain an ongoing communication with friends and family that they cannot "disconnect" for even a few minutes? It is rude to carry on a conversation that makes it hard for other people to listen. It is also rude to speak so loudly that people in the immediate area are forced to be part of the conversation, like it or not.

Perhaps we simply should not allow cell phones in classrooms and theaters or other places where listening is imperative and where cell phone use is likely to interfere with the ability of others to learn or to enjoy a performance. It seems extreme, but something must be done. Until we come up with a better solution, some users simply cannot be entrusted with cell phones.

Suggested Revisions of C and D

Sample C: Whole Class Revision

Choose Your Pet Wisely (title added)

but owning one can become inconvenient for the owner, and may prove tragic for the pet itself.

Exotic pets are tempting. It's exciting to imagine a giraffe in the back yard or a tortoise in the garden. People may want to own an orangutan or alligator or snake when they see it on television or discover it for sale somewhere. With the advent of the Internet, exotic pets are far easier to locate and obtain, even in places where their purchase is illegal. Unfortunately, ~~such pets seldom behave exactly as their owners predicted, and it is not always convenient to keep them.~~ **once the giraffe grows up, it consumes the shrubbery, the snake outgrows its terrarium, the alligator becomes too dangerous to approach, and the orangutan becomes hard to handle. Science Illustrated sums it up this way: "Adorable at first, within a few years the apes grow into much larger, difficult-to-manage animals with the strength of several grown men" (p. 56).**

Domesticated animals such as cats, dogs, rabbits, or guinea pigs make the best pets.

~~It is important to educate people about various kinds of animals and whether they do or do not make good pets.~~ When **people find themselves with a pet they cannot manage,** ~~this does not happen,~~ it can be difficult to return **it** ~~the animals~~ to the wild. This leads to difficulties both for pets and their current—or previous—owners! **In the case of the baby orangutan, for instance, it is not enough simply to let it go. A baby orangutan spends up to nine years with its mother, learning what to eat or not eat. Its diet includes over**

400 plants. One of them is the durian, an Asian fruit that "looks more like a weapon from the Middle Ages than a meal" (p. 58). Handling this and other foods, and a thousand other lessons, can only be taught by the mother orangutan—not by a human pet owner.

Things humans can do are to respect laws forbidding the adoption of exotic pets, and reporting any violations. People who care deeply can also support foundations that sponsor rehabilitation of former pets. The Nyaru Menteng Orangutan Training Center in Borneo is one example.

Information for this revision is taken from "Learning to Be an Orangutan," in *Science Illustrated.* March/April 2008, pp. 54–59.

Sample D: Revising with Partners

Cell Phone Courtesy (title added)

Cell phone use has grown dramatically in recent years. Unfortunately, so has cell phone abuse! It's annoying, but we can foster courtesy if we're creative. Abuse is any use that infringes on the ability of others to speak or listen. For example, despite protests from teachers, public speakers, and others, many users are reluctant to turn off cell phones during lectures or concerts. ~~Why? Are they so desperate to maintain an ongoing communication with friends and family that they cannot "disconnect" for even a few minutes?~~ It is rude to carry on a conversation that makes it hard for other people to listen. It is also rude to speak so loudly that people in the immediate area are forced to be part of the conversation, like it or not. So, what can be done? Several things, actually.

~~Perhaps we simply should not allow cell phones in classrooms and theaters or other places where listening is imperative and where cell phone use is likely to interfere with the ability of others to learn or to enjoy a performance. It seems extreme, but something must be done. Until we come up with a better solution, some users simply cannot be entrusted with cell phones.~~ First, we can continue to verbally remind cell phone users to turn their phones off at certain times. Some people need a visual reminder, though, such as a poster or illuminated red cell phone. In certain circumstances, such as professional performances, reasonable fines for cell phone use may be warranted. Some performers have suggested "cell phone proofing" theaters—and that's another possibility. Anyone who has tried to read or carry on a conversation in an airport or bus station can appreciate the need for some "cell phone free" spaces to which non-users can retreat. Finally, we might consider installing a special voice monitor (such as a blinking light on each cell phone) to let users know when their voices are exceeding tolerable volume levels for bystanders. That way, we make rudeness visible, and we give cell phone users (including ourselves) every chance to be courteous!

Handling Tricky Agreements (Part 2)

Lesson **10**

Trait Connection: **Conventions**

Introduction (Share with students in your own words—or as a handout.)

In the last editing lesson, we considered two situations that can make the issue of subject-verb agreement tricky:

Situation 1: Words Coming Between the Subject and Verb

Molly, who passed out once when she had to have stitches, nevertheless *hopes* (not *hope*) to become a doctor one day.

Situation 2: Compound Subjects with *and, or, nor*

Monday and Tuesday *are* Irving's days off.

All weekdays or every other Saturday *is* fine for lunch.
(The word *Saturday* is closer to the verb, so *is* is correct.)

Neither Wilbur nor his pet squirrels *are* welcome in my newly carpeted house. (The word *squirrels* is closer to the verb, so *are* is correct.)

Now it's time to consider two more tricky subject-verb situations:

Situation 3: Sentences with a "Be" Verb

When a sentence contains a "be" verb (*is, are, was, were*), that verb must agree with the sentence subject (the noun that comes first), not with the complement (the noun that comes *after* the verb). Don't let this terminology confuse you. Some examples will help:

The primary <u>problem</u> *is* forest fires burning out of control.

Problem is the sentence subject. It's singular, so it takes a singular verb, *is*. *Fires*, though plural, is the complement, not the subject; the complement is a noun that comes *after* the verb and tells us more about the subject. The subject, *problem*, needs to go with the verb, *is*. Let's see now what happens if we turn this around, making *Forest fires* the subject.

Forest fires burning out of control *are* the primary problem.

Forest fires is now the sentence subject. It's plural, so it takes a plural verb, *are*. In this sentence, *primary problem* is the complement. If you feel confused by all this subject-complement talk, just remember this: The verb always, *always* matches the subject of the sentence—*the thing the sentence is about.*

Situation 4: Special Cases

Some words look plural, but are considered singular in meaning: *measles, mumps, mathematics, economics, news.*

The news *is* grim tonight. (Not *The news are grim.*)

Economics *is* a fascinating but rather difficult major.

Mathematics *is* foundational to business management.

Other words are used as plurals, even though they refer to just one object: *scissors, pants, trousers.*

The scissors *are* in the drawer. (Not *The scissors is in the drawer.*)

Your pants *have* been pressed. (Not *Your pants has been pressed.*)

Warm-Up

Following is a short warm-up based on the kinds of examples we just shared with you. If you have any difficulty with this warm-up, review the opening examples again, or consult your handbook (*Write Source* or another of your choice) under "subject-verb agreement." (Answers appear on the following page.)

1. Our main concern (*is, are*) the graduation requirements.
2. The graduation requirements (*is, are*) our main concern.
3. Economics (*is, are*) Mike's major. Mathematics (*is, are*) his minor.
4. The scissors (*was, were*) behind the masking tape.
5. Long, difficult tests (*is, are*) a problem for many students.
6. One problem for many students (*is, are*) difficult tests.

Teaching the Lesson (General Guidelines for Teachers)

1. Use our examples or your own to illustrate ways of handling tricky subject-verb agreements.
2. Ask students to complete the six sentences in the Warm-Up, and check to see if anyone has difficulty. If they do, you may wish to provide further examples and/or refer students to the appropriate section of whatever handbook you use in your classroom.
3. Ask students to keep our examples handy for easy reference, and also to have a handbook available in case they need more information on subject-verb agreement.
4. Share the editing lesson on the following page. Students should read the passage *both silently and aloud*, looking and listening for correct subject-verb agreement. Some verbs are correct as is, so they must read carefully.
5. Some students may find it helpful to underline the sentence subject first, then check the verb.
6. Ask students to edit individually first, then check with a partner.
7. When everyone is done, ask them to coach you as you edit the same copy. You may wish to discuss the reasons for each correction as you go.
8. When you finish, read your edited copy aloud, answering any additional questions students may have. Then compare your edited copy with our suggested text on page 105.
9. For students who have any difficulty with this activity, review the Warm-Up sentences, answering any questions. Then, repeat the practice, this time reading aloud with students as they work. Help them identify the sentence subject in each case; *then* ask them to match it with the verb, providing feedback *as you go*.

Editing Goal: Correct 7 mismatched verbs.
Follow-Up: Check for subject-verb agreement in your own work.

Answers to Warm-Up

1. Our main concern *is* the graduation requirements.
2. The graduation requirements *are* our main concern.
3. Economics *is* Mike's major. Mathematics *is* his minor.
4. The scissors *were* behind the masking tape.
5. Long, difficult tests *are* a problem for many students.
6. One problem for many students *is* difficult tests.

Editing Practice

Correct any verb that does not agree with the sentence subject.
HINT: You may find it easier if you identify and underline the sentence subjects *first*.

For some first-year college students, the biggest challenge is grades. Tests is the hardest thing for others. Finding the right major also presents problems. Many freshmen begin the year majoring in business administration. Some change majors, however, when they discover that in business, mathematics is one of the requirements. Economics are another. Often, their primary objection are the textbooks—which tend to be long, and sometimes dry! Technical lectures is a problem as well—not to mention the homework! Studying for six or seven hours a night are enough to wear anyone out. No wonder so many students do not discover the right major until well into their sophomore year. By then, dealing with grades and tests have become more routine. The good news are that many students stick with business administration, and go on to run their own companies.

Edited Copy

7 verbs corrected
Sentence subjects underlined

For some first-year college students, the biggest challenge is grades. Tests ~~is~~ are the hardest thing for others. Finding the right major also presents problems. Many freshmen begin the year majoring in business administration. Some change majors, however, when they discover that in business, mathematics is one of the requirements. Economics ~~are~~ is another. Often, their primary objection ~~are~~ is the textbooks—which tend to be long, and sometimes dry! Technical lectures ~~is~~ are a problem as well—not to mention the homework! Studying for six or seven hours a night ~~are~~ is enough to wear anyone out. No wonder so many students do not discover the right major until well into their sophomore year. By then, dealing with grades and tests ~~have~~ has become more routine. The good news ~~are~~ is that many students stick with business administration, and go on to run their own companies.

Revising Organizational Architecture

Lesson 11

Trait Connection: **Organization**

Introduction

Ernest Hemingway said, "Prose is architecture, not decoration." The underlying architecture of any writing is its organization; that's what holds it together and gives it shape and form. As we have seen in the last two revision lessons, organization is partly about pattern: chronological, visual, comparison-contrast, problem-solution, and so on. Organization is also about structure, and its key elements include an effective lead, good order, sound transitions, and a satisfying conclusion. In this lesson, you'll look systematically at these four critical elements, and revise those that need attention. Then you'll give each piece an appropriate title. By the way, we're just considering the skeleton of the writing at this point—the bones, if you will. You may think a piece needs expansion, in addition to good architecture. That's fine. You don't need to do the expansion this time around, but make a marginal note, raising a question for the writer (who might be you) to answer later.

Teacher's Sidebar . . .

The purpose of this lesson is to expand students' organizational focus by asking them to deal with four key elements (*lead, order, transitions,* and *conclusion*)—plus an appropriate *title*. In addition, they are asked to briefly consider whether any points of the discussion or story require *expansion*, and to note that in the margin. This is an advanced revision lesson that deals with many elements at one time. Encourage students to read each piece more than once in order to maximize the effectiveness of the revision. Please note that not *every* organizational element in a given piece may call for revision. Students must use their own judgment.

Focus and Intent

This lesson is intended to help students:

- Recall the key elements that make up strong organization.
- Practice revising for more than one thing at a time.
- Revise a piece systematically by reviewing (1) lead, (2) order, (3) transitions, (4) conclusion, (5) title, and (5) need for expansion.

Teaching the Lesson

Step 1: Looking at the Bookends

Organizationally, nothing is more important than the bookends: lead and conclusion. Following are the lead and conclusion from several pieces of literature with which your students may be familiar. Ask them to rate the effectiveness of each on a scale of 1 to 10, and to describe what the lead and conclusion tell us about each book—or at least, what questions they raise.

1. *To Kill a Mockingbird* by Harper Lee

   Lead

   When he was nearly thirteen, my brother Jem got his arm badly broken at the elbow.

   Effectiveness: 1 ——————————— 5 ——————————— 10

   Conclusion

   He [Atticus Finch] turned out the light and went into Jem's room. He would be there all night, and he would be there when Jem waked up in the morning.

   Effectiveness: 1 ——————————— 5 ——————————— 10

2. *Animal Farm* by George Orwell

   Lead

   Mr. Jones, of the Manor Farm, had locked the hen-houses for the night, but was too drunk to remember to shut the popholes.

   Effectiveness: 1 ——————————— 5 ——————————— 10

   Conclusion

   The creatures outside looked from pig to man, and from man to pig, and from pig to man again; but already it was impossible to say which was which.

   Effectiveness: 1 ——————————— 5 ——————————— 10

3. *Bad Boy* by Walter Dean Myers

   Lead

   Each of us is born with a history already in place.

   Effectiveness: 1 ——————————— 5 ——————————— 10

   Conclusion

   I am in a world of book lovers and people eager to rise to the music of language and ideas. All in all it has been a great journey and not at all shabby for a bad boy.

   Effectiveness: 1 ——————————— 5 ——————————— 10

4. *Stargirl* by Jerry Spinelli

   Lead

   When I was little, my uncle Pete had a necktie with a porcupine painted on it.

   Effectiveness: 1 ——————————— 5 ——————————— 10

   Conclusion

   Last month, one day before my birthday, I received a gift-wrapped package in the mail. It was a porcupine necktie.

   Effectiveness: 1 ——————————— 5 ——————————— 10

- *To Kill a Mockingbird* by Harper Lee. 1960. Harper Perennial Classics edition published 2006. New York: Harper Perennial Classics.
- *Animal Farm* by George Orwell. 2003 (anniversary edition). New York: Harcourt.
- *Bad Boy* by Walter Dean Myers. 2001. New York: HarperCollins.
- *Stargirl* by Jerry Spinelli. 2000. New York: Alfred A. Knopf.

Step 2: Making the Reading-Writing Connection

Following is a very short piece from the March/April 2008 edition of *Science Illustrated*. It is titled "Watch Your Tone in Thailand." As you read through this piece, ask yourself, "Do the lead and conclusion hold the piece together—like bookends? Does the title work? Does everything seem in order?"

> *Linguists refer to the Thai language as a tonal language, because the pitch and pattern of speech affect word meanings. Thais distinguish among five tones: even, low, falling, high and rising. Words spelled exactly the same can have wildly different meanings depending on their pronunciation. The word "na," for instance, can mean "thick," "face," or "rice paddy," based on whether the tone rises, falls, or stays constant. Vowel length can also change word meaning. The tonal character of Thai makes it a challenging language for some to learn. And although there is a standard method for translating the Thai alphabet into English, not everyone follows it. That's why in tourist brochures and guidelines for Thailand, you'll often find the same place name spelled many different ways.*
>
> (From "Watch Your Tone in Thailand," in *Science Illustrated.* April/May 2008. Ed. Mark Jannot. Copenhagen, Denmark: Bonnier Publications, p. 87.)

Does the title work well? Would you change anything about—or add anything to—the lead or conclusion? Read through the piece again slowly to appreciate the transitions, sentence to sentence. You should be able to find a way in which every single sentence links back to the one before it. Suppose that as a writer you were asked to expand this brief commentary into a two-page article on the Thai language. What additional information should be included in your expansion (e.g., additional examples of confusing words)? It would be a good idea, as part of your planning, to make a marginal note indicating *each expansion possibility.*

Step 3: Involving Students as Evaluators

Ask students to review Samples A and B, reviewing all the components of architectural organization we have discussed: title (if there is one), lead, order, transitions, and conclusion. Have students work together, considering each element in turn and making marginal notes. Ask them to identify the stronger piece, and to discuss what could be done to revise the other.

Discussing Results

Most students should find Sample A stronger. Writer A has a relevant title, and a good lead and conclusion. Elements seem in order and are held together by sound transitions. By contrast, Writer B has no real lead or conclusion—or title, for that matter. At least one sentence seems out of order. One possible revision of Sample B is provided.

Step 4: Modeling Revision

- Share Sample C (*Whole Class Revision*) with students. Read the original aloud.
- Ask students to review the key elements of architectural organization one by one (lead, order, transitions, conclusion, title), and to say whether each is strong. (Most students should say *three elements or more need work.*)
- Give students time to discuss the piece with partners.
- Then, as a class, go through the piece one element at a time, revising as you go. (Feel free to invent information or add details from your own knowledge.) How should it begin? Is anything out of order? Do any transitions need work? How should it end? Do you want to offer the writer any marginal notes about expanding any parts of the discussion?
- Give the piece a new title.
- Read the final revision aloud to hear the difference.
- If you wish, compare your revision to ours, keeping in mind that your revisions need not match ours. You will notice that in our revision, we cut some details that did not seem relevant to the main discussion about how destructive squirrels can be. It was also important to connect the paragraph on predators to this main discussion. Notice that this section is moved and marked as a new paragraph.

Step 5: Revising with Partners

Share Sample D (*Revising with Partners*). Ask students to follow the basic steps you modeled with Sample C. *Working with partners,* they should:

- Read the passage aloud.
- Systematically consider the key elements of organization: lead, order, transitions, conclusion—and title.

- Take time to discuss each element, identifying any weaknesses and considering how best to revise to make the piece stronger.
- Revise each element that needs work.
- Add marginal notes (to the writer) about any portions of the discussion that call for expansion.
- Give the piece a new title to reflect the revisions.
- Read the revised version aloud to ensure that it has organizational integrity.

Step 6: Sharing and Discussing Results

When students have finished, ask several pairs of students to share their revisions aloud. Did teams identify similar weaknesses in the original? Did they make similar revisions—or is each team's version unique? Which team came up with the most creative title? Be sure to share and compare any marginal notes as well. Then, if you wish, compare your revisions with ours, keeping in mind that we may have made altogether different changes.

Next Steps

- Ask students to review their own work systematically, checking each element of sound organization, and also making marginal notes to guide their own further revision. Talk about how having a revision plan or checklist can make the whole process more manageable.
- Consider the "bookends" of any piece of literature you share as a class—or that your students read independently. Ask them to point out favorites. Sometimes the lead and conclusion—as in *Stargirl*—seem closely connected. What does this suggest about the author's internal organization?
- *For an additional challenge:* Many authors not only capture a primary theme of a book between the lead and conclusion bookends, but are able to achieve this organizational structure within individual chapters as well, beginning and ending each chapter in a way that reflects content or theme. Ask students who are ready for a challenge to explore the literature they know and love for such a book. (*Hint:* Look for a book in which the individual chapters are titled.) Then invite them to share their findings with the class. Discuss how organization helps a reader navigate a book—just the way a good map can guide any person through a city, shopping mall, or store.

Sample A

Lead and conclusion?
Order?
Transitions?
Good title?

Look Up! It's Superfrog!

If you think frogs can't fly, take another look. Some—like the Wallace's flying frog of Southeast Asia—have such large feet and such extensive webbing between their toes, that their feet act like small parachutes when the frogs leap. These four-inch creatures are named after Alfred Russel Wallace, a British natural historian who first discovered them in the nineteenth century.

Their performance is nothing short of Olympic. When the flying frogs want to take off, they simply leap like any frog, but spread their toes as far as they can—and let small wind currents do the rest. Frogs are incredibly light creatures, and their webbed "foot wings" keep them aloft for an amazing distance—as much as 50 feet. That is enough to help them catch insects that may have felt safe just seconds before. It's also enough to help them elude predators like snakes (none of which can fly, so far as scientists know). Pound for pound, it's an effort that leaves virtually every other creature (excepting the flea) in the proverbial dust.

Information for this sample is taken from "World of Science: When Frogs Fly," in *Science Illustrated.* March/April 2008. Copenhagen, Denmark: Bonnier Corporation, p. 87.

Sample B

Lead and conclusion? Order? Transitions? Good title?

It's interesting to learn that we have more than one television set per person in America. Choosing a television is different from choosing a car, but maybe it shouldn't be!

Older televisions use more energy than newer models with the exception of plasma TVs, which are notorious for the amount of energy they consume. A mid-sized LCD may be the most energy efficient.

Altogether, television viewing accounts for a fairly large percentage of total energy consumption in the United States. What is more, the things people think of first when they choose a television tend to be size and picture quality. Even cost is a distant third.

How many hours a day do you spend watching television? If you're a typical consumer, your viewing has probably doubled in the past ten years. In terms of energy consumption, we should be headed in the other direction.

Revision of Sample B

Big Screen = Big Energy Consumption

~~It's interesting to learn that~~ We currently have more than one television set per person in America. ~~Choosing a television is different from choosing a car, but maybe it shouldn't be.~~ and are watching more than twice as much television as we were a decade ago. In terms of energy consumption, we should be headed in the other direction.

How many do we have per person?

Older televisions use more energy than newer models with the exception of plasma TVs, which are notorious for the amount of energy they consume, or that a ~~A~~ mid-sized LCD may be the most energy efficient.

move down

Altogether, television viewing accounts for a fairly large percentage of total energy consumption in the United States. ~~What~~ Energy consumption is not the first thing people think of ~~is more, the things people think of first~~ when they choose a television, however; most buyers are far more concerned with ~~tend to be~~ size and picture quality. ~~Even cost is a distant third.~~ Maybe we should choose televisions more the way we choose cars, thinking at least partly of energy efficiency. Then we'd appreciate knowing that

What percentage? Say more.

~~How many hours a day do you spend watching television? If you're a typical consumer, your viewing has probably doubled in the past ten years. In terms of energy consumption, we should be headed in the other direction.~~ When both television screen size and average viewing time grow smaller, we'll know we're making progress.

Sample C: Whole Class Revision

Lead and conclusion?
Order?
Transitions?
Good title?

The Western gray squirrel warns other grays of predators in the area with a loud chirping noise that can be heard from quite a distance. Its main predator is the coyote, but squirrels are also eaten by wolves, bobcats, and even mountain lions (who will go after squirrels if larger prey eludes them). A few squirrels are killed by automobiles or by forest fires.

Squirrels can be highly destructive—both to each other, and to property. During mating season, females become very aggressive, and will wound each other seriously to keep other females away from their nests.

Gray squirrels have been known to kill trees by "circling" them—peeling all the bark from the entire circumference. While they prefer seeds and nuts (high carbohydrate foods that build up the body fat that keeps them warm), they will eat bark if other food is unavailable, and also use it to line their nests. They also attempt to invade attics if there is an opening larger than two inches, and their gnawing can destroy roof rafters.

Sample D: Revising with Partners

Lead and conclusion?
Order?
Transitions?
Good title?

Dental hygienists learn skills by practicing on one another. Sometimes they also participate in free or low-cost clinics, offering cleaning and dental checkup services to volunteers willing to risk a little pain and suffering for the sake of saving money.

Simroid is a new anthropomorphic training tool. It is a robot that is designed to look like a human, and the resemblance is striking. It can also respond like a human. Simroid can blink, grimace in pain—even yell if something goes wrong.

This tool was premiered at the 2007 Tokyo International Robotic Exhibition, where onlookers were awed at how closely it mimics every human response. Simroid can be equipped with teeth of any size, shape, or condition.

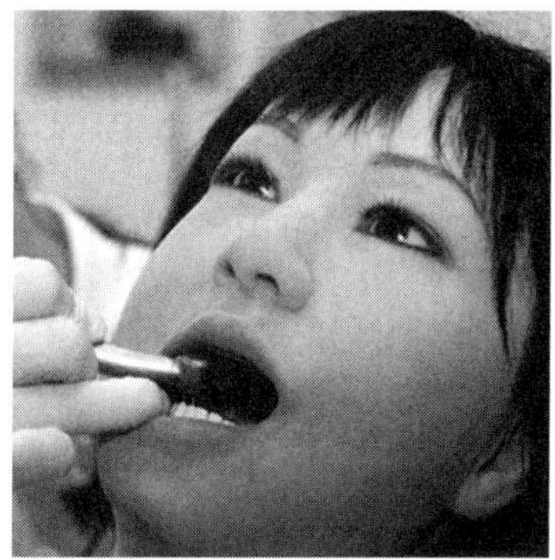

Information for this sample is taken from "Better It Than You," in *Science Illustrated.* March/April 2008. Copenhagen, Denmark: Bonnier Corporation, p. 14.

Suggested Revisions of C and D

Sample C: Whole Class Revision

Don't Feed the Squirrels!

~~The Western gray squirrel warns other grays of predators in the area with a loud chirping noise that can be heard from quite a distance. Its~~

¶ Squirrels are kept in check—somewhat—by predators. Their main predator is the coyote, but squirrels are also eaten by wolves, bobcats, and even mountain lions (who will go after squirrels if larger prey eludes them). A few squirrels are killed by automobiles or by forest fires.

move down

Do you enjoy feeding the squirrels? If so, you're not alone. Gray squirrels are amusing and enjoyable to watch, but if you feed them, you may be sorry.

Start here

Squirrels can be highly destructive—both to each other, and to property. During mating season, females become very aggressive, and will wound each other seriously to keep other females away from their nests.

Aggressive to humans or pets?

Gray squirrels have been known to kill trees by "circling" them—peeling all the bark from the entire circumference. While they prefer seeds and nuts (high carbohydrate foods that build up the body fat that keeps them warm), they will eat bark if other food is unavailable, and also use it to line their nests. They also attempt to invade attics if there is an opening larger than two inches, and their gnawing can destroy roof rafters. The best way to avoid squirrel damage around your home, however, is not to attract them in the first place!

Sample D: Revising with Partners

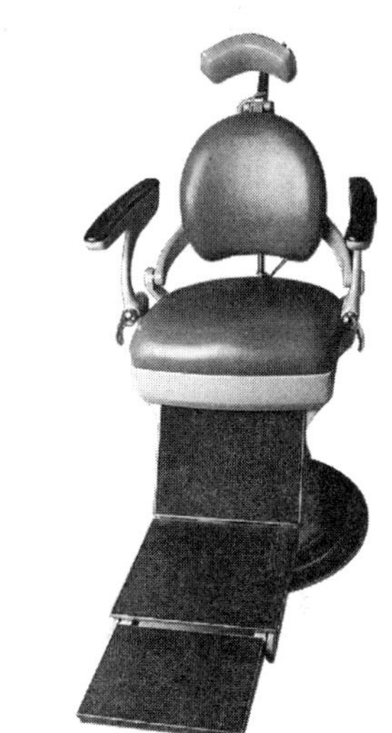

Open Wide, Simroid

Traditionally, dental hygienists ~~learn~~ have learned new skills by practicing on one another. Ouch! Sometimes they also participate in free or low-cost clinics, offering cleaning and dental checkup services to volunteers willing to risk a little pain and suffering for the sake of saving money. Now it seems there is a new option, one that promises more efficient training, with less pain for everyone.

Meet Simroid, ~~Simroid is~~ a new anthropomorphic training tool. Simroid ~~It~~ is a robot that is designed to look and respond like a human dental patient, and the resemblance is striking. ~~It can also respond like a human.~~ Simroid can blink, grimace in pain—even yell if something goes wrong. The robot may actually respond faster and more emphatically than a human patient, alerting the hygienist immediately that something isn't right.

Does Simroid have "skin" and "muscles"?

This tool was premiered at the 2007 Tokyo International Robotic Exhibition, where onlookers were awed at how closely it mimics every human response. Simroid can be equipped with teeth of any size, shape, or condition. This gives hygienists in training a wide range of experience. Now, if we can just get Simroid to go in for our dental checkups, we'll be all set.

When will Simroid be in use?

Handling Tricky Pronouns

Trait Connection: **Conventions**

Introduction (Share with students in your own words—or as a handout.)

We've talked a lot about subject-verb agreement. But we've saved the best challenge for last: *indefinite pronouns*. Are they singular—or plural? And what's an indefinite pronoun anyway? Let's find out.

First, indefinite pronouns are so named because they do not refer to any person *in particular*. In the sentence "Jim forgot his hat" we know that *his* refers to Jim. But in the sentence "Everyone loves ice cream," *everyone* refers to people in general, not to any one person or group of people.

Indefinite pronouns are extremely handy when a writer doesn't have enough information to be specific—or wishes to refer to people or things *in general: <u>Someone</u> dropped a five-dollar bill, <u>Everybody</u> watches television these days, <u>No one</u> wants to get cavities, <u>Everything</u> seemed to be going well.*

Some indefinite pronouns are singular . . .

Many indefinite pronouns are singular and take singular verbs: *anyone, anybody, everybody, nobody, one, no one, everyone, everything, each, somebody, someone, either, neither*:

- It could rain or snow. **Neither** *is* good.
- **Everyone** *is* eligible to win the prize.
- **One** *is* always surprised and pleased by a kind response to anger.

Others are plural . . .

A few indefinite pronouns are plural and take plural verbs: *several, both, few, many*:

- **Many** *love* picnics on sunny days.
- **Few** *enjoy* picnics in the rain.
- **Several** *are* undecided.

Still others can be either . . .

A few can be either, depending on the meaning: *all, any, most, none, some*:

- **Some** of the chicken *is* done.
- **Some** of her relatives *are* flying in from Africa.

- **None** of the money *is* left.
- **None** of the Johnsons *are* related to me.
- **All** the milk *is* sour.
- **All** the voters *have* registered.

What about his or her and their?

If you know whether a person to whom you are referring is male or female, it's easy to know which pronoun to use:

- Bob forgot **his** baseball mitt.
- Erin took **her** mitt with her.

But sometimes you do *not* know. Handle it this way:

- **Someone** [*I don't know who*] forgot **his or her** baseball mitt.

Do NOT write:

- **Someone** forgot **their** baseball mitt.

Why *not?* What's the big deal? The big deal is that *Someone* is singular—one person. It's either *his* (someone's) mitt or *her* (someone's) mitt. It's not *their* mitt unless two (or more) people are sharing a mitt, and in that case, we'd need to write, "Some *people* (more than one) forgot *their* mitt." Here are some more CORRECT examples:

- **Everyone** must bring *his or her* own ticket.
- **No one** likes *his or her* grades to fall.
- **Neither** of the sisters wants *her* poem read aloud.
- **Either** of the twins will share *his* lunch.
- **People** don't like *their* grades to fall. (*People* is plural.)
- **The twins** will share *their* lunch. (*The twins* is plural.)

Key Question

How many people or things are you talking about? One? Or more than one? That will let you know if your verb and pronoun need to be singular or plural.

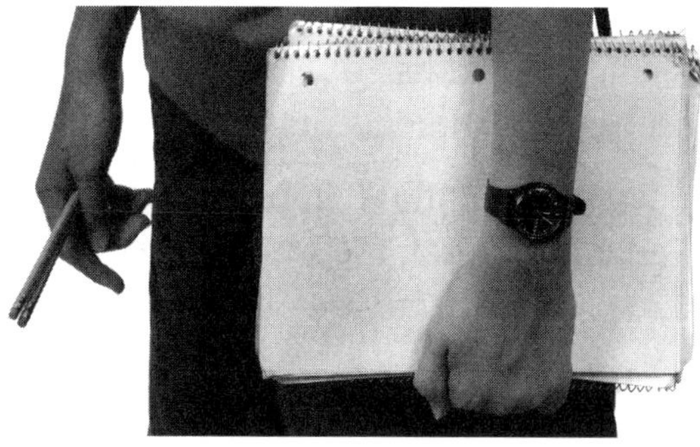

Warm-Up

Following is a short warm-up based on the kinds of examples we just shared with you. If you have any difficulty with this warm-up, review the opening examples again, or consult your handbook (*Write Source* or another of your choice) under "subject-verb agreement." (Answers appear on the following page.)

1. Everyone (*like, likes*) to get a letter in the mail.
2. Many (*enjoy, enjoys*) an occasional email or phone call.
3. None of my friends (*is, are*) good email writers, unfortunately.
4. Everything (*look, looks*) beautiful in the morning sun.
5. Nobody (*want, wants*) a good day to end.
6. A few (*is, are*) especially memorable.
7. Someone left (*his, her, his or her, their*) lunch on the table.
8. Some people like (*his, her, his or her, their*) food spicy.

Teaching the Lesson **(General Guidelines for Teachers)**

1. Use our examples or your own to illustrate ways of handling subject-verb agreements that involve indefinite pronouns.
2. Ask students to complete the eight sentences in the Warm-Up, and check to see if anyone has difficulty. If any do, you may wish to provide further examples and/or refer students to the appropriate section of whatever handbook you use in your classroom.
3. Ask students to keep our examples handy for easy reference, and also to have a handbook available in case they need more information on subject-verb agreement and indefinite pronouns.
4. Share the editing lesson on the following page. Students should read the passage *both silently and aloud*, looking and listening for correct subject-verb agreement and correct use of *his, her, his or her,* and *their*. Some sentences are correct as is, so students must read carefully.
5. Some students may find it helpful to underline sentence subjects. They may also find it helpful to ask the key question: *Is the sentence talking about one person/thing, or more than one?*
6. Ask students to edit individually first, then check with a partner.

7. When everyone is done, ask them to coach you as you edit the same copy.
8. When you finish, read your edited copy aloud, pausing to discuss the reasons for each correction as you go. Then compare your edited copy with our suggested text on page 123.
9. For students who have any difficulty with this activity, review the Warm-Up sentences, answering any questions. Then, repeat the practice, this time reading aloud with students as they work. Help them identify the sentence subject in each case; *then* ask them to match it with the verb, providing feedback *as you go*. Talk about whether indefinite pronouns refer to one person or thing, or more than one.

Editing Goal: Make 12 corrections.
Follow-Up: Check indefinite pronouns in your own work, making sure that all verbs and pronoun references are correct.

Answers to Warm-Up

1. Everyone *likes* to get a letter in the mail. (*Everyone* is singular.)
2. Many *enjoy* an occasional email or phone call. (*Many* is plural.)
3. None of my friends *are* good email writers, unfortunately. (*None* is plural as used in this sentence. Compare: None *is* a good e-mailer.)
4. Everything *looks* beautiful in the morning sun. (*Everything* is singular.)
5. Nobody wants a good day to end. (*Nobody* is singular.)
6. A few are especially memorable. (*A few* is plural.)
7. Someone left his or her lunch on the table. (*Someone* is singular—and we do not know who the person is, or whether that person is male or female. Compare: Some people left *their lunches* on the table.)
8. Some people like their food spicy. (*People* is plural—so *their* is fine in this sentence. Compare: *No one* likes *his or her* food spicy.)

Editing Practice

Correct any verb that does not agree with the sentence subject.
Be sure *his, her, his or her,* and *their* are used correctly.

Everyone need to be careful when disposing of their trash. Many simply litter, tossing trash out at random. Many disposes of their trash in proper receptacles, but without any thought to recycling. Neither approach are good. The truth is, everything made of plastic or paper need to be recycled. Few of us does as much as we could. Some people have lunch at a public park or recreation area, for example, and then throws his or her leftovers close to a river or ocean shore. Each and every bit of refuse add to the pollution problem—especially in ocean waters. When even one person throws their plastic water bottle into the sea, it can remain there for years. Though it may break into tiny particles, it never goes away completely. This is everyone's problem. Each of us need to help solve it. None of us is too busy to recycle. Everyone can and should do his part. And when we see someone recycling properly, we can also applaud their efforts. After all, each of us is responsible for the earth.

Edited Copy

12 corrections

Everyone ~~need~~ needs to be careful when disposing of ~~their~~ his or her trash. Many simply litter, tossing trash out at random. Many ~~disposes~~ dispose of their trash in proper receptacles, but without any thought to recycling. Neither approach ~~are~~ is good. The truth is, everything made of plastic or paper ~~need~~ needs to be recycled. Few of us ~~does~~ do as much as we could. Some people have lunch at a public park or recreation area, for example, and then ~~throws his or her~~ throw their leftovers close to a river or ocean shore. Each and every bit of refuse ~~add~~ adds to the pollution problem—especially in ocean waters. When even one person throws ~~their~~ his or her plastic water bottle into the sea, it can remain there for years. Though it may break into tiny particles, it never goes away completely. This is everyone's problem. Each of us ~~need~~ needs to help solve it. None of us is too busy to recycle.* Everyone can and should do his or her part. And when we see someone recycling properly, we can also applaud ~~their~~ his or her efforts. After all, each of us is responsible for the earth.

**None of us* <u>*are*</u> *too busy to recycle* is also correct.

Revising the Memoir Voice

Lesson **13**

Trait Connection: **Voice**

Introduction

A writing voice, like a speaking voice, must shift slightly to suit the occasion. You have one voice for speaking to your best friend, and perhaps another for a parent, an adult you don't know, an infant, and so on. We moderate our speaking voices without even thinking about it. When it comes to writing, though, we need a minute to choose the right voice, asking, *Why am I writing this, and who's going to read it?* Your voice is unique, of course, and something of *you* comes through in the writing no matter what your audience or purpose. But it would be odd indeed if you used the same voice in a note to a friend that you would use in a research report or job application letter. Voice is important to *all* writing because it's a writer's way of forging a connection with a reader. But in a memoir, voice is *vital.* Too much formality or restraint kills the moment. Memoir is personal and autobiographical; it's also intimate and anecdotal in tone. A memoir is a guided tour of life, through a window devised by the writer. Picture yourself comfortably seated on an inviting wooden bench, recounting a favorite memory to someone you know and trust. The voice you're using as you speak has just the right tone for memoir.

Teacher's Sidebar . . .

Memoir is highly personal—and in this lesson, students will rehearse their revision skills on writing that is not their own. They will need to be inventive, but it is helpful to base anecdotal writing on actual events, whether their own experiences or those of someone else. Consider this practice a warm-up. Later, you can expand the power of this lesson by asking students to write their own memoirs—where voice comes naturally because the memory is immediate and personal. In the meantime, as you talk about hitting that "just right note," it may help to share moments from several memoirs. See "Next Steps" for suggestions.

Focus and Intent

This lesson is intended to help students:

- Recognize the "right tone" for memoir.
- Identify characteristics of an appropriate memoir voice.
- Revise a piece that is intended as memoir, but that is told in a restrained way that holds voice in check.

Teaching the Lesson

Step 1: Listening for the Right Note

The voice in memoir comes in part from a writer's willingness to share innermost thoughts and feelings. It also comes—like the voice in a poem—from reflection and insight. Memoir is more than a series of "true confessions." It reveals the writer *through* his or her take on the world. Following are several openings to memoir pieces by various writers. Which ones do you think are on track, confiding in the reader—and which need a more intimate, less standoffish kind of voice? Put a check by those you feel hit the right note.

1. I packed everything I owned into a single suitcase and headed for a remote town in North Dakota. I didn't know a single soul there. I only chose that destination because it was as far as my meager stash of money would take me.

   ___ Right note for memoir

2. My test scores revealed some propensity for science. A counselor suggested a possible career in medical research, and that seemed an alternative worth exploring. Research offers a number of viable options, depending on one's preferences.

   ___ Right note for memoir

3. Who knows what possessed me? I had never in my life been on a stage, and had never sung outside of my own shower. Yet here I was, trying out for a part in a local production of "The Wizard of Oz" as if I'd been doing this sort of insane thing all my life. As if I thought I could actually *sing*. I barely heard the music start—it sounded like some far-off band playing in the park. And I opened my mouth, hoping and praying something more musical than a croak would come out.

   ___ Right note for memoir

4. An X-ray confirmed that my ankle had been broken when I lost my footing on the stairs and subsequently took a fall. Unfortunately, a cast would present some inconvenience, but with practice, I felt I would adjust.

   ___ Right note for memoir

If you are like most readers, you find Examples 2 and 4 a bit formal for memoir. Samples 1 and 3, by contrast, sound as if the writer were talking right to us, having a conversation.

Step 2: Making the Reading-Writing Connection

In her award-winning memoir titled *My Thirteenth Winter*, Samantha Abeel tells the remarkable story of coping with and overcoming a learning disability that was not diagnosed until she was thirteen. As we learn from the book, Samantha is a gifted writer, so verbally adept that she is able to mask her disability, and consequently is often coached to just "try harder." Only she and her family know the truth: that she has never been able to perform even the simplest mathematical tasks, such as telling time, making change—or opening a locker—

I often packed a whole day's worth of books and class work into my backpack, so I didn't need to open my locker at all, and I could avoid the possible embarrassment of not getting it open in time for class. . . . I believed that if anyone found out what I couldn't do or how hard basic things like opening my locker were for me, they would feel like I had been lying to them—they would wonder why I hadn't said anything up until now. They would think that I didn't belong. They would see the smart, wise, well-behaved, talented Sam for who she really was—a terrified, lost, inept girl.

(From *My Thirteenth Winter* by Samantha Abeel. 2003. New York: Scholastic. Pages 48–49.)

Does Samantha Abeel hit the right note for memoir? Do you feel she is confiding in us, as readers, taking us on the guided tour of her personal journey? Identify the moments in this passage that seem most powerful to you.

Step 3: Involving Students as Evaluators

Ask students to review Samples A and B, possibly reading each aloud, and asking which writer hits the right note for memoir. Which voice speaks to readers, inviting them in—and which is less personal, creating a kind of emotional wall? Ask students to discuss what could be done to revise the piece they feel has a less appropriate voice for memoir.

Discussing Results

Most students should find Sample B stronger. Writer A keeps her distance, putting a wall between herself and us, the readers. By contrast, Writer B confides in us, sharing his underlying thoughts, fears, and feelings. One possible revision of Sample A is provided.

Step 4: Modeling Revision

- Share Sample C (*Whole Class Revision*) with students. Read the original aloud.
- Ask students whether this writer hits the right note for memoir. (Most should say *no*.)
- Give students time to discuss the piece with a partner, and to identify moments that would benefit from a more intimate, confiding voice.
- As a class, go through the piece line by line, revising as you go. Feel free to invent information based on actual memories or imagination.
- Give the piece a new title.
- Read the final revision aloud to hear the difference.
- If you wish, compare your revision to ours, keeping in mind that your revision is unlikely to match ours in any way since we have invented other details.

Step 5: Revising with Partners

Share Sample D (*Revising with Partners*). Ask students to follow the basic steps you modeled with Sample C. *Working with partners,* they should:

- Read the passage aloud.
- Talk about whether this writer hits the right note for memoir, and if not, which passages would most benefit from revision.

- Encourage students to use their imaginations in revising, and also to call upon memories of actual experiences, whether their own or those of someone else.
- Revise the piece so that the voice is more suited to memoir. Note that it is fine to rewrite the piece if students find this easier than revising individual moments.
- Give the piece a new title to reflect the revision.
- Read the revised version aloud, listening to the voice and making any final changes to ensure that it is right for memoir.

Step 6: Sharing and Discussing Results

When students have finished, ask several pairs of students to share their revisions aloud. Are the voices similar—or very different? Do the drafts sound, in fact, as if they had been written by different people? Which moments from various pieces do you like particularly well? If you wish, compare your revisions with ours, keeping in mind that our changes are likely to be very different.

Next Steps

- Go back to Samples 2 and 4 under Step 1 and revise them so that the voice better fits memoir.
- Invite students to write a personal memoir. It can be as short as a paragraph—or may run several chapters. Students who wish to do so may choose to share all or part of their memoir with the class.
- Explore the voice of memoir further by checking out any of the following excellent literature:
  - *My Thirteenth Winter* by Samantha Abeel. 2003. New York: Scholastic.
  - **Bad Boy* by Walter Dean Myers. 2001. New York: HarperCollins.
  - **Facing the Lions: Growing Up Maasai on the African Savanna* by Joseph Lemasolai Lekuton. 2003. Washington, D.C.: National Geographic.
  - **In My Hands: Memories of a Holocaust Rescuer* by Irene Gut Opdyke and Jennifer Armstrong. 1999. New York: Random House.
  - **Living Up the Street* by Gary Soto. 1985. New York: Doubleday.
  - **Winterdance: The Fine Madness of Running the Iditarod* by Gary Paulsen. 1994. New York: Harcourt.
- *For an additional challenge:* How does a person's identity influence how he or she writes? Invite students to explore this intriguing question by looking at two pieces—one memoir, one not—by the same writer. Consider, for example, *Monster* and *Bad Boy*, both by Walter Dean Myers. Read *Bad Boy*, Myers' memoir, first; then consider how Myers's own life might have influenced both story and character in *Monster*.

*Indicates a book written for a young adult *through* adult audience. These books may contain mature language or themes.

Sample A

The right voice for memoir?

A Useful Experience

I became employed for the first time at the end of my fourteenth year. It wasn't legal in our state at that time for someone my age to obtain a job. However, because my father worked in construction, he managed to find a place for me. The hours often ran from 6 am to 6 pm. Sometimes we would work later during the summer when we had light. I learned to do a number of different tasks, including framing, putting up sheetrock, and roofing. The jobs all required different skills. I found I was best at framing because I am good at precise measurements. This was a very worthwhile experience from which I gained a real sense of what it was like to hold a job. Initially, my father did not pay me to work since I was still in the learning stage. Later, I earned $5 per hour, and eventually worked my way up to $10 per hour. I also learned some important life skills along with practical skills useful in securing summer employment.

Sample B

The right voice for memoir?

Fish Stories

My first time fishing (actually attempting to catch a fish) was at a remote lake in Northern Michigan. The other guys were all pros. I was the only novice—but I told everyone in the boat I'd been fishing *hundreds* of times with my dad. That wasn't a *complete* lie. I'd actually been out with him in a boat. I just didn't fish—ever. My dad can cast in a way that's pure poetry, and he's always wanted to teach me, but the truth is, I never had the patience for fishing. Never liked getting up early, never liked the smell (not to mention the feel) of fish—didn't even enjoy the late-night fish stories all that much. I went along because every time I said no, my dad looked as if his heart was going to break. For him, fishing is a rite of passage, something you do to become an adult. You can't say no to that—so I went. But I never held a fly rod in my hand or tried to put a fly "just between the rushes and the rocks," as one of the guys was now urging me to do. *How hard could it be?* I thought to myself. I'd seen Dad do it a thousand times. Flick of the wrist, right? Anyone can fish. Any fool can . . . snatch some guy's hat right off his head! Which is exactly what I did with my first cast. I'd made a fool of myself, all right, but mostly I felt relieved. What if I'd hooked his eye? I had to come clean then with the truth about my non-fishing ways, but the guys didn't hold it against me. In fact, they spent most of the day cracking jokes about how I managed to "tell whoppers" without even fishing at all. I hate to admit it, but that attention felt pretty good to me. I decided I was better at lying than I was at fishing, and in fact, I got so good that it would be years before I finally broke this deadly habit.

Revision of Sample A

On the Job Training

~~A Useful Experience~~

I became employed for the first time at the end of my fourteenth year. It wasn't legal

and I soon figured out why. Just because you can get a job is no sign you're employable.

in our state at that time for someone my age to obtain a job. However, because my

It was a bad fit for a teenager who liked to sleep in all morning and party into the night.

father worked in construction, he managed to find a place for me. The hours often ran

much to my horror, even

from 6 am to 6 pm. Sometimes we would work later during the summer when we had

worked every weekend, most evenings, and right through what other kids called "vacation." I protested about the unfairness, but I

light. I learned to do a number of different tasks, including framing, putting up

Looking back, I realize it was a constant struggle for my father to find something I wouldn't botch up too badly, so he'd have to do it over.

sheetrock, and roofing. ~~The jobs all required different skills.~~ I found I was best at

I actually had more patience at this than any of the other guys, and once they figured this out, I was measuring and sawing everything in reach. Having to work a whole lot harder than I wanted to or thought I could turned out to be a

framing because I am good at precise measurements. ~~This was a very~~ worthwhile

took

experience. ~~from which~~ I gained a real sense of what it ~~was like~~ to hold a job.

already costing him money with my mistakes—a fact he cleverly hid from me with kindness and a good sense of humor.

Initially, my father did not pay me to work since I was ~~still in the learning stage.~~

he paid me

Later, ~~I earned~~ $5 per hour, and eventually ~~worked my way up to~~ $10. ~~per hour.~~

I'd like to say I "earned" this wage, but that would be a stretch since, as my dad put it, I spent the first few months "burning through wood faster than a colony of beavers."

I ~~also~~ learned some important life skills ~~along with practical skills useful in securing summer employment~~ that year—such as that being lazy isn't genetic or even viral—it's a choice. Who knew? When I see guys at a construction site, I still wave sometimes. They look, wondering if they should know me—and once in a while they wave back.

Sample C: Whole Class Revision

The right voice for memoir?

My parents lived a normal, quiet life in a moderately sized neighborhood. I grew up with a clear sense of right and wrong. Most of the time, I found decisions about what to say or what to do in various situations fairly straightforward. Afterward, with time to reflect, I would usually feel I had made the appropriate choice.

I can recall only one situation in which the right decision was less than obvious. One of my friends was involved in a shoplifting incident. Though I was initially convinced of this person's innocence, I later had reason to doubt my first impressions. Deciding how to deal with this situation was not as simple as I might have wished. Eventually, the matter was resolved.

Sample D: Revising with Partners

The right voice for memoir?

During my early school years, I was often described as shy. On report cards, instructors often commented on my reluctance to take part in class discussions. I simply was not motivated to do so.

In my middle school years, I decided to run for class president. I campaigned with flyers and posters. When I was not successful, it was a disappointment. To some extent, this experience affected my view of myself. Fortunately, I had good grades. This helped me sustain a positive attitude.

During high school, many of my friends began to drive and to date. My self-confidence had still not returned, unfortunately. Thus, I did not fit into this new life style. I felt reluctant to be in a car by myself, and so made the decision not to get a license until some time in the future. As I was too shy to ask anyone on a date, that portion of my life was also put on hold for a time. It was not until my final year of high school that things finally underwent a significant transformation.

Suggested Revisions of C and D

Sample C: Whole Class Revision

Decisions (title added)

My parents lived a normal, quiet life in a small, suburban ~~moderately sized~~ neighborhood where a barbecue was everyone's idea of excitement. I grew up with a clear sense of right and wrong. I knew the basic rules: Don't hit people, don't take their stuff, tell the truth, clean your room. I wasn't perfect. I was a bully. I tried to tell the truth, but I wasn't above putting some "spin" on it, as they say. ~~Most of the time, I found decisions about what to say or what to do in various situations fairly straightforward.~~ Afterward, with time to reflect, I ~~would usually feel I had made the appropriate choice.~~ always knew if I'd done the right thing, or had just squeaked by without getting caught.

I can recall only one situation in which the right decision was less than obvious. One of my friends got ~~was~~ involved with ~~in a~~ shoplifting—big time. ~~incident. Though I was initially convinced of this person's innocence,~~ At first, I was completely convinced when she said she was innocent. I'd known her since we were five. She couldn't be a thief. ~~I~~ Later I had reason to doubt my first impressions when she began showing me her "new" clothes, phone, iPod, and other "bargains." Deciding how to deal with this situation kept me awake nights. I knew my parents would expect me to speak up. I also knew my best friend would be in serious trouble if I did. ~~was not as simple as I might have wished.~~ I convinced her that if she did not confess, I would have to say something. She looked as if I were betraying her—which in a way, I suppose I was. Eventually, ~~the matter was resolved.~~ She did not speak to me again. I took little comfort from my parents telling me I'd done the right thing. They were probably right, but as I discovered, once you're more than five, being right doesn't always take the pain away.

Sample D: Revising with Partners

Temporarily on Pause (title added)

During my early school years, I was painfully ~~often described as~~ shy. I barely spoke, and when I did, it was a whisper no one but me could hear. On report cards, ~~instructors often commented on my reluctance to take part in class discussions. I simply was not motivated to do so.~~ teachers would write, "Stella needs to raise her hand more." They might as well have saved their breath. I went through my first six years of school in almost total silence.

In my middle school years, I decided to run for class president. What possessed a shy person to make such an idiotic decision I can't say. I campaigned with flyers and posters so I would not have to make speeches. When about half a dozen people voted for me, I thought my heart would crack. My self-confidence plunged. I was a failure. A silent failure. ~~When I was not successful, it was a disappointment. To some extent, this experience affected my view of myself.~~ Fortunately, I had good grades. ~~This helped me sustain a positive attitude.~~ I clung to that, and it helped a little.

During high school, many of my friends began to drive and to date. ~~My self-confidence had still not returned, unfortunately. Thus~~ It was like they were aliens, doing things I was not meant to do. I did not fit into this new life style. I ~~felt reluctant to be in a car~~ was scared to death to drive down the road by myself, and ~~so made the decision not to get~~ to hide my fear, I just told everyone that I would not need a license until some time in the future. I had crushes on three guys, but since ~~As~~ I was too shy to even say hello, much less ask anyone on a date, that portion of my life was also put on hold for a time. Then, in ~~It was not until~~ my final year of high school ~~that things finally underwent a significant transformation.~~ I came out of my cocoon, and everything in my world got tipped on its head.

Putting It All Together (Editing Lessons 8, 10, and 12) Lesson 14

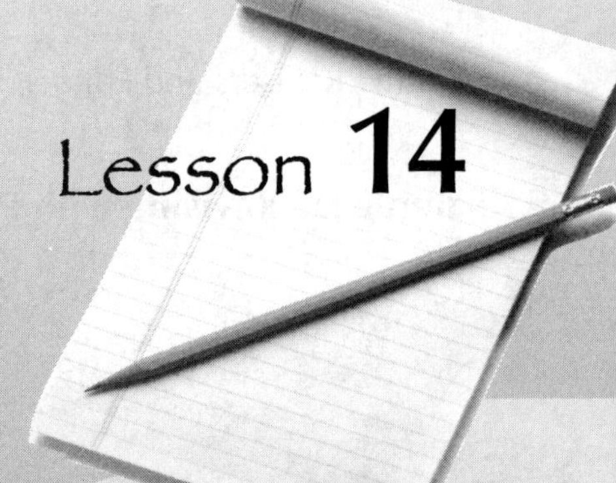

Trait Connection: **Conventions**

Introduction (Share with students in your own words—or as a handout.)

In the last three lessons, we have talked about subject-verb agreement in some rather tricky situations:

1. When words come between subject and verb
   - Amazingly enough, **Ricky**, <u>who has 45 cousins and an endless assortment of relatives and acquaintances</u>, *enjoys* being alone.

2. When the sentence has a compound subject using *and, or, nor*
   - **Burgers and fries** *are* good together.
   - **Neither Pete nor his Uncle Jim** *is* vegetarian.
   - **Either rain or snow** *is* expected by nightfall.

3. When the sentence includes a "be" verb
   - **The main problem** *is* his manners.
   - **Manners** *are* his main problem.

4. In special cases
   - **The news** *is* better today.
   - **Mathematics** *has* always been a challenge for Bill.
   - The **scissors** *are* right behind you.
   - These **trousers** *need* hemming.

5. With tricky pronouns
   - **Everyone** *is* here for the birthday bash.
   - **No one** *likes* a poor loser.
   - **Many** *remain* undecided.
   - **Several** *are* hoping to leave on this plane.
   - **Everyone** *must hold* **his or her** own ticket.
   - **Neither** of the twins *drives* **her** own car.
   - **No one** *expects* **his or her** plans to fall through.

In this lesson, you'll have a chance to put together all you know about these sometimes tricky agreement situations in editing one document. Keep this list of reminders with you as you work. Also feel free to refer to Lessons 8, 10, and 12 or to your handbook for additional help. Remember to read aloud. Many editorial errors occur because writers read hastily. Slow down. Take time to ask, "Is it singular—or plural?" You'll sail right through the text.

Teaching the Lesson (General Guidelines for Teachers)

1. Begin by reviewing the various subject-verb agreement situations covered in Lessons 8, 10, and 12. Make sure *all* situations are clear in students' minds, and that they understand the overall concept of agreement itself: singular nouns with singular verbs, plural nouns with plural verbs.
2. Take time to review indefinite pronouns that are singular (*everyone, everybody, no one, nobody, everything, each, either, neither*, etc.), plural (*both, several, many, few*), and those that can be either (*some, none, all*). If you wish, make and post a list for reference during editing. Even practiced editors benefit from reminders.
3. Encourage students to review Lessons 8, 10, and 12 on their own—and to refer to them as they work on this lesson. Also provide handbooks (recommended: *Great Source: New Generation*).
4. Share the editing lesson on the following page. Students should read the passage silently (prior to doing any editing), then once more aloud (pencil in hand), looking *and listening* for agreement, always asking, "Is it singular—or plural?"
5. Ask them to work individually first, then check with a partner.
6. When everyone is done, ask them to coach you as you edit the same copy, making any changes you and they decide are important. Discuss and/or explain changes as you go. When you finish, compare your edited copy to the one on page 139.

Editing Goal: Correct any errors in agreement.
Correct any faulty pronoun references.
Follow-up: Correct subject-verb disagreement in your own work.

Editing Practice

Correct any verbs that do not match their subjects.
Check for correct use of *his, her, his or her,* and *their.*

The news in the Simon family, traveling across the country via phone, e-mail, and text messages, have been gigantic! Uncle Freddie and Aunt Flo, a wonderful couple, is celebrating their 50th wedding anniversary—with a luau in Hawaii. Everyone in the whole family, including about 60 cousins, are invited. Plans has been a challenge, however! Neither Freddie nor Flo are a meat eater. Fortunately, both Freddie and Flo eats rice, fish—and of course, poi, a traditional food at any luau. Twin cousins, Lori and Madison, are planning the dessert. Each of them runs their own bakery, so it should be no problem! Everybody has their own idea what the cake might look like. But Madison, who in the course of her lifetime has personally baked and decorated more than a thousand birthday cakes and almost five thousand wedding cakes, guarantee that this cake will be the "surprise of the century." Most expenses are covered, though each guest must purchase their own airline ticket. One last-minute problem have been the slow responses from some guests—who get so excited they forget to say they're coming. And of course, Aunt Flo has been fussing over her new outfit. "The fabric is gorgeous and the scissors is flying!" she says, as her new dress comes together. No one knows exactly what to expect at the party, but everyone are excited. Several members of the family is staying on for a few days to enjoy the Hawaii sunshine. Many, sad to say, needs to leave when the party concludes. Freddie and Flo says, "If you think this is great, just wait until our 100th!"

Edited Copy

13 verbs corrected
3 pronouns corrected

The news in the Simon family, traveling across the country via phone, e-mail, and text messages, ~~have~~ has been gigantic! Uncle Freddie and Aunt Flo, a wonderful couple, ~~is~~ are celebrating their 50th wedding anniversary—with a luau in Hawaii. Everyone in the whole family, including about 60 cousins, ~~are~~ is invited. Plans ~~has~~ have been a challenge, however! Neither Freddie nor Flo ~~are~~ is a meat eater. Fortunately, both Freddie and Flo ~~eats~~ eat rice, fish—and of course, poi, a traditional food at any luau. Twin cousins, Lori and Madison, are planning the dessert. Each of them runs ~~their~~ her own bakery, so it should be no problem! Everybody has ~~their~~ his or her own idea what the cake might look like. But Madison, who in the course of her lifetime has personally baked and decorated more than a thousand birthday cakes and almost five thousand wedding cakes, ~~guarantee~~ guarantees that this cake will be the "surprise of the century." Most expenses are covered, though each guest must purchase ~~their~~ his or her own airline ticket. One last-minute problem ~~have~~ has been the slow responses from some guests—who get so excited they forget to say they're coming. And of course, Aunt Flo has been fussing over her new outfit. "The fabric is gorgeous and the scissors ~~is~~ are flying!" she says, as her new dress comes together. No one knows exactly what to expect at the party, but everyone ~~are~~ is excited. Several members of the family ~~is~~ are staying on for a few days to enjoy the Hawaii sunshine. Many, sad to say, ~~needs~~ need to leave when the party concludes. Freddie and Flo ~~says~~ say, "If you think this is great, just wait until our 100th!"

Revising the Book Jacket Voice

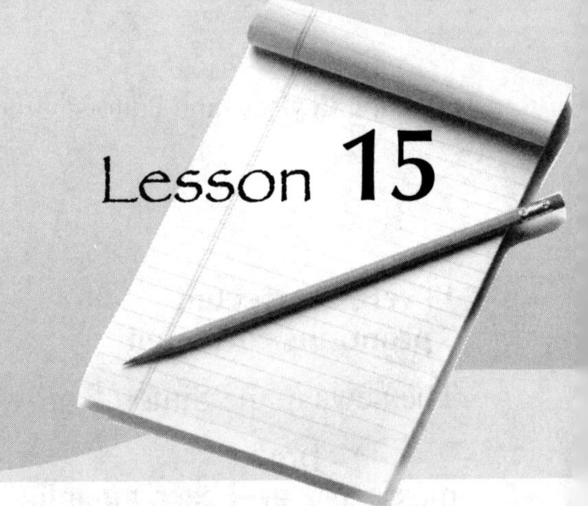

Lesson **15**

Trait Connection: **Voice**

Introduction

Have you ever wondered whether to read a book or not—and used the copy on the book jacket (inside the front cover) to help you decide? If so, then you owe a debt to an unsung writer, usually someone within the publishing company who is assigned the task of reading the book, looking at the author's own description, and coming up with a concise but persuasive paragraph that will get readers hooked. Book jacket copy is challenging to write. The writer must know the book well and be able to share intriguing highlights without giving too much away: It's a summary with important questions left unanswered. He or she must also know the intended audience well, and consider what is likely to appeal to them. Finally, the writer must use a voice that is persuasive and passionate. After all, if this writer doesn't sound excited about the text, why should you be? In this lesson, you'll have a chance to challenge yourself by writing book jacket copy that will sell books.

Teacher's Sidebar . . .

For this lesson, we have endeavored to focus on texts with which many eighth grade students are familiar. If your students do not know a particular book, however, give them time to become familiar with it. They should feel free to not only read or skim the book, but also to read reviews or analyses online or elsewhere. (This is what the professionals do, after all.) Even the current book jacket copy is fair game—so long as they *do not copy it.* "Use it, but don't plagiarize it" is the motto. (You'll have that copy, too, so you'll know the difference.) Our drafts and revisions are all originals—nothing borrowed. Theirs should be the same. Remember, this lesson focuses on *voice*—which means that nothing short of the writer's personal views and beliefs will do. (Also, if you prefer to substitute a different text for any part of this lesson, feel free to do so.)

Focus and Intent

This lesson is intended to help students:

- Recognize the right persuasive voice for book jacket copy.
- Identify the salient features of a good book jacket summary.
- Revise book jacket copy so that it is more likely to result in sales of the book.

Teaching the Lesson

Step 1: Making a Sale

Book jacket copy is important to the publisher because it can result in sales. From a strictly financial point of view, there is no more valuable "real estate" than the inside flap of the book jacket. As a warm-up for this lesson, choose two or three books (fiction or nonfiction, young adult or adult) that most of your students have not read. These may come from your school library or your own collection. Read just the book jacket copy—nothing from the book itself—and ask these questions:

1. What genre is this? (mystery, courtroom drama, nonfiction science, memoir, true life adventure, etc.)
2. What audience is this book intended for? Are you part of that audience?
3. What questions does the writer raise that might make you want to read the book?
4. Would you buy this book?

Based on Question 4, reread the most successful text(s), and see if you can identify three, four, or more features that are "must have's" for a book jacket. Make a list and keep it posted throughout the lesson.

Step 2: Making the Reading-Writing Connection

In 2008, Newberry Honor winner Gary D. Schmidt (author of *The Wednesday Wars* and *Lizzie Bright and the Buckminster Boy*) published a book titled *Trouble.* The book tells the story of Henry Smith, whose older brother Franklin is struck by a pickup truck—a truck in which a young Cambodian man, Chay Chouan, is riding. Henry and Franklin had been planning a mountain climbing trip, and now their dream is shattered in an instant. The incident sparks significant racial tensions throughout the town. Here is an excerpt from the book jacket:

> *Caught between anger and grief, Henry does the only thing he feels he can: he sets off for Mt. Katahdin, which he and Franklin had planned to climb together. One July morning, he leaves for Maine with his best friend and the loveable stray, Black Dog, in tow. But when they encounter Chay Chouan on the road, fleeing demons of his own, Henry learns that turning a blind eye to Trouble only brings Trouble closer . . . .*
>
> (From *Trouble* by Gary D. Schmidt. 2008. New York: Clarion Books. Front book jacket.)

What questions does this short bit of text raise? What do you predict will happen? Why does the writer capitalize the word "Trouble"? Has the book jacket writer persuaded you to buy the book?

Step 3: Involving Students as Evaluators

Ask students to review Samples A and B, considering all the elements they identified as essential to good book jacket copy. Have them work together, discussing each text and making marginal notes. Ask them also to identify the piece they think is more likely to intrigue readers and to discuss ways of improving the weaker copy.

Discussing Results

Most students should find Sample A stronger. Writer A tells just enough to get readers hooked without telling too much, and uses a persuasive tone designed to build excitement. Writer B, by contrast, simply summarizes the text, giving readers very little reason to want to know more.

Step 4: Modeling Revision

- Share Sample C (*Whole Class Revision*) with students. Read the original aloud.
- Ask students whether this writer hits the right persuasive tone for good book jacket copy (Most should say *no.*)
- Give students time to discuss the piece with a partner, and to identify missing or weak features that could be strengthened to give this book jacket copy some punch.
- Then, as a class, go through the piece line by line, revising as you go. Those students most familiar with the text can be editorial advisors, and can suggest what should be included or excluded.
- Note that book jacket text does not have a title as such—because that could create confusion with the title of the book itself. Instead, book jackets usually have a lead-in line: one sentence that captures something interesting at the heart of the book. For example, the lead-in for the fairy tale "The Three Little Pigs" might be "*Sometimes, good construction is a life and death decision* . . ." Write a lead-in line for your copy.
- Read the final revision aloud, asking, "How many people would buy or read this book?"
- If you wish, compare your revision to ours, keeping in mind that your revision need not match ours.

Step 5: Revising with Partners

Share Sample D (*Revising with Partners*). Ask students to follow the basic steps you modeled with Sample C. *Working with partners,* they should:

- Read the passage aloud.
- Talk about whether this writer uses a strong persuasive voice appropriate for book jacket copy, and, if not, how the passage could best be revised.
- Encourage students to consider everything they know about the book in writing their copy—including online (or other) reviews. *Everything* is fair *except* copying the current book jacket text (if any is available).
- Revise the piece so that the voice is persuasive and speaks to readers.
- Give the piece a lead-in line that will hook readers from the start.
- Read the revised version aloud, listening to the voice, and making any final changes to make sure the book has the best sales edge possible.

Step 6: Sharing and Discussing Results

When students have finished, ask several pairs of students to share their new book jacket copy aloud. Which teams—according to the class as a whole—came up with the most effective pitch to readers? Which moments from various pieces do you like particularly well? If you wish, compare your revisions with ours, keeping in mind that our changes are likely to be very different.

Next Steps

- As a class, create book jacket copy for a short story, fable, or fairy tale everyone knows well. Working with a short piece offers good practice in what a good book jacket writer needs to emphasize.
- Textbooks are generally purchased by a school district and given to students, who have little or no say about the choice. What if students *did* have a say, though? Write copy for a textbook jacket that would persuade *students* (not teachers or administrators) to purchase it—if they had to do so individually. Think carefully about which features of a textbook you would emphasize for your peers. Talk about how this task differs from writing book jacket copy for a memoir or novel.
- Talk about how book jacket copy is different from or similar to content for a movie trailer. Does the writer of copy for a movie trailer focus on the same kinds of things as the writer of book jacket copy? How is the task different?
- Collect favorite book jackets and create a display. You may find some your students think they can improve upon—and this offers excellent practice. Recommended:
    - *Trouble* by Gary D. Schmidt. 2008. New York: Clarion Books.
    - **Birdland* by Tracy Mack. 2003. New York: Scholastic.
    - *Escape! The Story of the Great Houdini* by Sid Fleischman. 2006. New York: HarperCollins.
    - *No More Dead Dogs* by Gordon Korman. 2000. New York: Hyperion.
    - **Puppies, Dogs, and Blue Northers* by Gary Paulsen. 1996. New York: Harcourt Brace.
    - *Stargirl* by Jerry Spinelli. 2000. New York: Alfred A. Knopf.
    - *The Wednesday Wars* by Gary D. Schmidt. 2007. New York: Clarion Books.
    - **The Winter Walk* by Loretta Outwater Cox. 2003. Anchorage, AK: Alaska Northwest Books.
- *For an additional challenge:* Invite students to *re*-write book jacket covers for any favorite book of their choice. The challenge is to improve upon the original by making the book even more enticing to readers. Some may wish to share their writing with the publisher of the book; addresses can be found online.

*Indicates a book written for a young adult *through* adult audience. These books may contain mature language or themes.

Sample A

A strong book jacket voice? Likely to sell books?

Aesop's Fables

Come inside. Rediscover the beauty, the joy, the comedy, and the wisdom of the world's most beloved Grecian story teller, the legendary Aesop. Each of these fifteen stories offers a simple, but captivating plot, animal "characters" that allow us to look at ourselves in the mirror, and a moral that captures each story's theme. From *The Tortoise and the Hare* to *The Lion and the Mouse*, these tales are timeless—and ageless, as enjoyable to adults as to the youngest readers. Updated illustrations bring the tales to life for a new generation of readers.

Sample B

A strong book jacket voice? Likely to sell books?

No More Dead Dogs (by Gordon Korman)

Wallace Wallace is the main character in Gordon Korman's very funny novel about a middle school student who tries hard to tell the truth. Wallace gets in trouble when he is too honest in his book report. He winds up in detention, and this leads to a whole series of events, most of which are extremely funny. Throughout the book, Wallace Wallace never loses his sense of humor or his determination to be an honest person. Much of the book takes place in the classroom, in the lunchroom, or on the football field. If you enjoy plays, and you love to laugh, don't miss this comical book.

Revision of Sample B

No More Dead Dogs (by Gordon Korman)

Who knew "Old Shep, My Pal" was a musical??!! (New lead-in line)

Middle school student Wallace Wallace is ~~the main character in Gordon Korman's very funny novel about a~~ determined to tell the truth, the whole truth, and nothing but—beginning with his book report on Old Shep, My Pal. Unfortunately, Wallace is not fond of the book. Anything but. His outspoken honesty about this tired, corny tale lands him ~~middle school student who tries hard to tell the truth. Wallace gets in trouble when he~~ ~~is too honest in his book report. He winds up~~ in detention, where the class is rehearsing a production of "Old Shep, My Pal" that is even worse than the book! Wallace Wallace to the rescue. From the moment he suggests one small revision to one line, his fate is sealed. He winds up re-staging the whole production, with hysterical results. As lights come up, rock music plays, and stuffed animals fly, ~~and this leads to a whole series of events, most of which are extremely funny. Throughout the book~~ Wallace ~~Wallace never loses~~ retains his sense of humor ~~or~~ and his ~~determination to be an honest person.~~ commitment to honesty. ~~Much of the book takes place in the classroom, in the lunchroom, or on the football field. If you enjoy plays, and you love to laugh, don't miss this comical book.~~ If you've ever gotten into trouble for telling the truth, you'll enjoy this zany, comical tale of revision gone wild!

Sample C: Whole Class Revision

A strong book jacket voice? Likely to sell books?

Of Mice and Men (by John Steinbeck)

Of Mice and Men by John Steinbeck is the story of two men, George and Lennie, and their friendship. They are itinerant farm workers, moving from one vegetable field to another, with a hand-to-mouth existence. George is small, but quick and alert. Lennie, by contrast, is huge and powerful, but struggles to comprehend the world. Thus, George becomes Lennie's guardian. Throughout the book, George struggles to help Lennie cope with life and behave appropriately. As a reader, you will find yourself caught up in their story, hoping for them to make their dream of a little farm all their own come true. Lennie wants nothing more than just to tend the rabbits on the farm—and remain George's friend. Will it happen? As Steinbeck leads us through their adventures, we meet many other characters, some lonely and some cruel, all of whom will play a part in pushing this story to its sad but inevitable conclusion.

Sample D: Revising with Partners

A strong book jacket voice? Likely to sell books?

Animal Farm (by George Orwell)

The animals on Manor Farm are tired of their lives. They have their own view of the world, and in this tale by George Orwell, they plot a revolution that will put the animals in charge instead of the humans. At first things go very well. The animals come up with a series of rules (*All animals are equal, No animals shall wear clothes, No animal shall kill another four-legged animal*) that seem to make perfect sense. They live in harmony for a time. Then, the pigs begin to think they are superior to the other animals. Gradually, they take over, and soon, the animals are hardly better off than they were before. The book is sometimes funny, and sometimes serious. You will find yourself laughing at the characters—or sometimes hating them! And the ending is one that will stay in your mind for a long, long time.

Suggested Revisions of C and D

Sample C: Whole Class Revision

Of Mice and Men (by John Steinbeck)

Lennie just wants to live on a farm and tend the rabbits. Is that so much to ask? (New lead-in line) ~~*Of Mice and Men* by John Steinbeck is the story of two men~~ George and Lennie, an unlikely pair, have formed a fast ~~and their~~ friendship. ~~They are~~ Itinerant farm workers, they move ~~moving~~ from one vegetable field to another, with a hand-to-mouth existence. George is small, but quick and alert. Lennie, by contrast, has enormous power, but lacks the intellect to control it. ~~is huge and powerful, but struggles to comprehend the world. Thus, George becomes~~ As Lennie's guardian, ~~Throughout the book~~ George struggles to help Lennie cope with life and keep his strength in check. Together, they share a dream: a little farm all their own, where Lennie can tend the rabbits. As the book rushes headlong toward its chilling, inevitable conclusion, we find ourselves desperately wanting to call out to Lennie and George, to warn them of what's coming. ~~behave appropriately. As a reader, you will find yourself caught up in their story, hoping for them to make their dream of a little farm all their own come true. Lennie wants nothing more than just to tend the rabbits on the farm — and remain George's friend. Will it happen? As Steinbeck leads us through their adventures, we meet many other~~ Set against the backdrop of the Salinas Valley, with a rich cast of characters, some lonely and some cruel, ~~all of whom will play a part in pushing this story to its sad but inevitable conclusion.~~ Steinbeck's story of dreams, loyalty, love, and friendship still tugs at the hearts of readers everywhere. It's a tiny book with enormous power.

Sample D: Revising with Partners

Animal Farm (by George Orwell)

A world run by animals would be kind and gentle—wouldn't it? (New lead-in line)

enslavement, and under the direction of pigs Snowball and Napoleon,

The animals on Manor Farm are tired of ~~their lives. They have their own view of~~

oust the wretched humans and put the animals in charge.

~~the world, and in this tale by George Orwell,~~ they plot a revolution that will ~~put the~~

it appears to be a brilliant plan, designed to promote freedom and good will.

~~animals in charge instead of the humans.~~ At first, ~~things go very well.~~ The animals

come up with a series of rules (*All animals are equal, No animals shall wear clothes,*

reflect their new enlightened state of harmony and tolerance.

No animal shall kill another four-legged animal) that seem to ~~make perfect sense.~~

But gradually, adopt a

~~They live in harmony for a time. Then,~~ the pigs ~~begin to think they are~~ superior ~~to the~~

attitude, behaving disarmingly like the humans they replaced. In a book that is by turns comical and horrifying, Orwell explores the chilling consequences of power.

~~other animals. Gradually, they take over, and soon, the animals are hardly better off~~

~~than they were before. The book is sometimes funny, and sometimes serious. You will~~

this is one

~~find yourself laughing at the characters—or sometimes hating them!~~ And ~~the~~ ending

linger

~~is one~~ that will ~~stay~~ in your mind for a long, long time.

Lesson 16

The Terrible Twos

Trait Connection: **Conventions**

Introduction (Share with students in your own words—or as a handout.)

When it comes to editing, it's the little things that often cause the most trouble. One of the peskiest little concerns involves deciding whether a word is actually two words, or just one. Is it *everyone* or *every one? Nobody* or *no body?* Is *no one* two words? In this lesson, we'll clear up some of those mysteries.

Before we get started, here's an overriding rule to keep in mind: Conventions serve ideas, and not the reverse. Think *meaning first*—what is it you want to say? Then it becomes easier to choose the right form of a word or expression.

1. ***No one* and *none***

   No one is always written as two words. It is always singular, whether it means "nobody" or "no single one":

   > *No one* is planning to take this course again.
   >
   > *No one* hat fits every head.

   None means "not a single one," and it can be singular or plural—depending on how it is used. You need to use your editor's judgment on this one:

   > She has invited many people. *None* are coming, though. (plural)
   >
   > He bought three cell phones. *None* is currently working. (singular)

2. ***Everyone* versus *every one, Everybody* versus *every body***

   Everyone is written as one word when it means "all" or "the whole group." It is written as two words when it means "every single one":

   > *Everyone* came to the dance.
   >
   > *Every one* of my roses wilted by morning.

   The same rule holds true for *everybody*—and *every body*. The first means "everyone" or "all." The second means "every single body":

   > *Everybody* loves ice cream—or almost *everybody*, at any rate.
   >
   > *Every body* is different and some require more maintenance than others.

3. ***Nobody*** **and** ***no body, anybody*** **and** ***any body***

Nobody is written as one word when it means "not a single person." It is written as two words when it means "not a single body":

Nobody enjoys being embarrassed.

No body can sustain itself without food or water for long.

Similar distinctions hold true for *anybody* and *any body, somebody* and *some body:*

Anybody who studies will do better on the test.

Any body of water over ten acres is a lake, not a pond.

Somebody left the door open.

The map shows *some body* of water east of the peninsula.

Two more pests . . .

As long as we are talking about one word versus two, here's a reminder about two-word expressions that adult editors (including those who write for the news) continue to confuse. Leapfrog ahead of them by mastering these:

All right is two words: *It is* ***all right*** *with me if we leave now.*
(You will see *alright* on the news ticker, but don't be fooled; it's not word.)

A lot is also two words: *That seems like* ***a lot*** *of salad to eat.*
(You will also see *alot* a lot. Make a face, and vow not to write it yourself.)

Warm-Up

Following is a short warm-up based on the kinds of examples we just shared with you. If you have any difficulty with this warm-up, review the opening examples again, or consult your handbook (*Write Source: New Generation* or another of your choice) under "indefinite pronouns" or the expressions "*all right* and *a lot*." (Answers appear on the following page.)

1. (*Everyone, Every one*) of my e-mails bounced back!
2. (*Everyone, Every one*) is looking forward to graduation.
3. (*Anyone, Any one*) can dance well with enough practice.
4. I think you could sing (*anyone, any one*) of these songs.
5. It is (*alright, all right*) with me if we eat later.
6. That looks like (*alot, a lot*) of data to memorize.
7. None of us (*is, are*) happy about the election.

Teaching the Lesson (General Guidelines for Teachers)

1. Use our examples or your own to illustrate appropriate uses of indefinite pronouns—as well as the ever-troublesome *a lot* and *all right*.
2. Ask students to complete the seven sentences in the Warm-Up, and check to see if anyone has difficulty. If any do, you may wish to provide further examples and/or refer students to the appropriate section of whatever handbook you use in your classroom.
3. Ask students to keep our examples handy for easy reference, and also to have a handbook available in case they need more information on indefinite pronouns.
4. Share the editing lesson on the following page. Students should read the passage *both silently and aloud*, looking and listening for meaning before deciding whether the correct form of each pronoun is used. Some sentences are correct as is, so students must read carefully. Also remind them to look for *a lot* and *all right*—both should consistently be written as two words.
5. Ask students to edit individually first, then check with a partner.
6. When everyone is done, ask them to coach you as you edit the same copy. You may wish to discuss the reasons for each correction as you go.
7. When you finish, read your edited copy aloud, answering any additional questions students may have. Then compare your edited copy with our suggested text on page 155.
8. For students who have any difficulty with this activity, review the Warm-Up sentences, answering any questions. Then, repeat the practice, this time reading aloud with students as they work. Help them focus on the meaning of each sentence before making a decision.

Editing Goal: Make 20 corrections.
Follow-Up: Check indefinite pronouns in your own work, making sure that forms are correct. Remember to write *a lot* and *all right* as two words.

Answers to Warm-Up

1. *Every one* of my e-mails bounced back! *(Every single one of them)*
2. *Everyone* is looking forward to graduation. *(All the people)*
3. *Anyone* can dance well with enough practice. *(Any person)*
4. I think you could sing *any one* of these songs. *(Any single one you choose)*
5. It is *all right* with me if we eat later. *(Alright is nonstandard.)*
6. That looks like *a lot* of data to memorize. *(Alot is nonstandard.)*
7. None of us (is, are) happy about the election. (Either is correct, depending on subtleties of meaning: *Not even one person among us* ***is*** *happy*, or *Not even a few of us* ***are*** *happy*.)

Editing Practice

Correct indefinite pronouns so that the right form is used.
Correct any verbs that do not match the subjects.
Watch for the correct forms of *all right* and *a lot*.

Graduation is only a few months away, and every body are excited. Everyone of the teachers are involved in planning a special awards ceremony, and noone wants to miss it. Of course, it will require alot of work, but no body seems to mind. In fact, the principal has commented how gratifying it is that everyone are willing to help out. No one is required to help, of course, but it is alright for any one to volunteer. At this point, no one know who will be giving the commencement speech. It could be anyone of several well-qualified speakers. Everyone of them would make a strong impression. Following the ceremony itself, a dance will be held in the conference center adjoining the gym. Everyone is invited to attend. In addition, any one who wishes to do so may sing. Of course, not everybody feel confident enough to do that! But, if anyone of the students wants to try it, the opportunity is there! Surely, some one will volunteer. It may take alot of courage, but nobody of students have ever been more courageous than this one!

Edited Copy

20 corrections

Graduation is only a few months away, and ~~every body are~~ everybody is excited. ~~Everyone~~ Every one of the teachers ~~are~~ is involved in planning a special awards ceremony, and ~~noone~~ no one wants to miss it. Of course, it will require ~~alot~~ a lot of work, but ~~no body~~ nobody seems to mind. In fact, the principal has commented how gratifying it is that everyone ~~are~~ is willing to help out. No one is required to help, of course, but it is ~~alright~~ all right for ~~any one~~ anyone to volunteer. At this point, no one ~~know~~ knows who will be giving the commencement speech. It could be ~~anyone~~ any one of several well-qualified speakers. ~~Everyone~~ Every one of them would make a strong impression. Following the ceremony itself, a dance will be held in the conference center adjoining the gym. Everyone is invited to attend. In addition, ~~any one~~ anyone who wishes to do so may sing. Of course, not everybody ~~feel~~ feels confident enough to do that! But, if ~~anyone~~ any one of the students wants to try it, the opportunity is there! Surely, ~~some one~~ someone will volunteer. It may take ~~alot~~ a lot of courage, but ~~nobody of students have~~ no body of students has ever been more courageous than this one!

Revising with Multiple Voices

Lesson 17

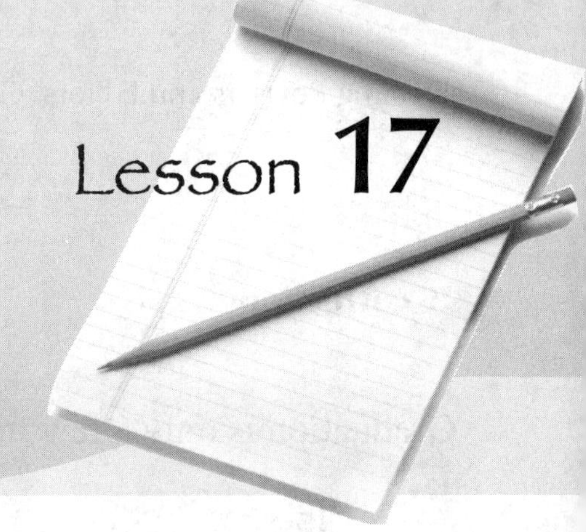

Trait Connection: **Voice**

Introduction

One of the things that makes each voice unique is that we all see the world differently. It is fair to say that no two people, however close their bond of friendship, however deep their rapport, ever see things *exactly* the same way. So in some respects, voice is about attitude and perspective. Small wonder then that one of the most interesting and enlightening ways to explore voice is by looking at the world through multiple perspectives. If you have ever read a book in which the speaker changes from chapter to chapter, then you have encountered this approach. The challenge for the writer, of course, is to get inside the hearts and minds of these different speakers in order to make each point of view—and each voice—sound authentic. If you're the sort of person who can see the world through the eyes of a friend, teacher, parent, grandparent, or neighbor, then you're ready for the challenge.

Teacher's Sidebar . . .

What makes the multiple-voice approach work is to respect diversity. The writer must "let go" of his/her own perspective for a time, and allow each character to have a strong voice—as if he or she were a real person. This can be more difficult than it sounds! But if the writer's own voice dominates, the characters may wind up sounding like clones of one another. This is why prewriting is so important to this lesson. To set up the writing well, students need to discuss the situation, identify possible characters who would be involved—who would have a "stake" in the situation—and explore their probable thoughts and feelings. They must then allow each character a *true voice,* a passionate expression of a point of view that may or may not agree with the writer's own.

Focus and Intent

This lesson is intended to help students:

- Understand how voice shifts with perspective.
- Practice seeing the world from different perspectives.
- Revise a single-perspective piece so that it is re-told in three diverse voices.

Teaching the Lesson

Step 1: Seeing Through Other Eyes

Identify a situation from your own recent experience or that of one of your students in which there are at least three "players," all of whom would have different perspectives. Examples might be:

1. Traffic is tied up, causing tempers to flare.
2. Someone attempts to return a faulty item to a merchant.
3. Someone is injured during a soccer/baseball/football game.
4. Someone receives a phone call at a bad time.
5. Parents argue with a son or daughter—and a sibling tries to intervene.

These are only examples. *Any* situation involving several people—each with a different "take" on things—will do. Once you have identified the situation on which you wish to focus, pick three key players, each of whom would likely see the situation differently. Create two lines of *silent monologue* for each character; in other words, get inside the person's head, and capture, from first person perspective, what that person is thinking. This may be very different from what the person would *say* in the situation. Here's an example, based on a 16-year-old taking a driver's test—reluctantly.

> **Lily:** *I wish I were somewhere else. Anywhere else. I hate driving! I feel so stupid. I can't parallel park. I don't need a stupid license anyway. Why is my mom making me do this!!??*
>
> **Officer:** *My God, I think she's actually killed the engine. I can't believe this. This is a first. I can't pass her now no matter <u>what</u> else she does. Why is she even here? I'm so blooming tired of this job . . . "Uh, you want to try restarting the car?"*
>
> **Mom:** *What kind of a kid doesn't want to get her license? What's <u>wrong</u> with her anyway? Just please let her pass, at least. If she doesn't, I'll have to keep driving her everywhere. I need a life of my own. It's time to grow up—isn't it? Isn't that what every teenager wants—to grow up? Why does she make such a big deal out of everything? And how did I wind up with a kid who is nothing in the world like me????*

Can you tell from this short example what each character is thinking and how he or she is feeling? Multiple voices gain power when each voice is revisited. This is why chapter books told in multiple voices are so powerful. The reader is introduced to a voice early on—then cycles back to it down the road. By the end of the book, each reader usually has a favorite character, the one whose voice most closely resonates with his or her own.

Step 2: Making the Reading-Writing Connection

Paul Fleischman's book *Seedfolks* has become a classic. In this book, thirteen very different voices (young, old, from many cultures) tell the story of an inner city garden, on Cleveland's Gibb Street, that transforms a neighborhood and the people who live there. It all begins with Kim, a young girl from Vietnam who wants to show her now-dead father that she, too, can be a farmer; she, too, can plant things and make them grow. As Kim plants her first seeds, she has no idea that she is being watched—by Ana, an older woman who has followed the changing history of the neighborhood for many years, and who wonders why people need television when there is so much people-watching to be done. Here are brief snippets of each voice:

> *I dug six holes. All his life in Vietnam my father had been a farmer. Here our apartment house had no yard. But in that vacant lot he would see me. He would watch my beans break ground and spread, and would notice with pleasure their pods growing plump. He would see my patience and my hard work. I would show him that I could raise plants, as he had. I would show him that I was his daughter. (From "Kim," p. 3)*
>
> *Down in the lot, a little black-haired girl, hiding behind that refrigerator. She was working at the dirt and looking around suspiciously all the time. Then I realized. She was burying something . . . And after twenty years typing for the Parole department, I just about knew what she'd buried. Drugs most likely, or money, or a gun. The next moment, she disappeared like a rabbit. (From "Ana," p. 6)*
>
> (From *Seedfolks* by Paul Fleischman. 2004. New York: HarperTeen.)

What do we learn about these two people from this short introduction? How do multiple perspectives, such as those in Fleischman's book, enrich our understanding of what is true or real? Though this lesson focuses on voice, the use of multiple perspectives is also a powerful organizational strategy. In Fleischman's book, the garden is like the hub of a wheel; it is the center that links all the voices together. What else can you think of that could, like the garden, serve as a focal point to link multiple perspectives and voices?

Step 3: Involving Students as Evaluators

Ask students to review Samples A and B, considering whether each writer has made the voices sufficiently different to create multiple perspectives. Ask them to work together, discussing the situation and how each character would *really feel.* Ask them also to identify the piece they think more authentically captures different voices, and to discuss ways of creating greater diversity within the weaker copy.

Discussing Results

Most students should find Sample A stronger. Writer A creates characters that sound distinct from one another, and truly hold diverse perspectives. Writer B, by contrast, creates three characters that are virtually indistinguishable from one another. One possible revision of Sample B is provided.

Step 4: Modeling Revision

- Share Sample C (*Whole Class Revision*) with students. Read the original aloud. Notice that in this example, students have one voice provided—they need to invent the others.

- Ask students whether the writer has created an authentic voice for the first character. (Most should say *no*.)
- Give students time to discuss the situation with a partner, identifying two additional characters who might have a stake in this situation, and talking about how each of them would *really feel*.
- As a class, revise the first voice. Ask students to recite the actual thoughts they believe this character would have, and record the best suggestions.
- Brainstorm the two additional characters you think would provide sufficiently diverse points of view to make this multiple-voice piece interesting. There are no right or wrong answers to this, and the characters you choose need not match the ones we chose.
- Invent internal monologue for the two characters you have added. If you wish, you can ask volunteers to "play the parts" of the three characters, voicing their thoughts aloud.
- You may find that after you finish creating characters 2 and 3, you want to make changes to character 1. Each voice influences the others, and with each revision, the voices tend to become more distinctive.
- Read your final revision aloud, making any last-minute changes that lend the voices authenticity and bring out differences among the characters.
- If you wish, compare your revision to ours, keeping in mind that your characters are likely to be quite different from ours.

Step 5: Revising with Partners

Share Sample D (*Revising with Partners*). Ask students to follow the basic steps you modeled with Sample C. *Working with partners,* they should:

- Read the passage aloud.
- Talk through the situation first, before writing *anything* on paper—and ask themselves who else would have a stake in this situation, and what different points of view each might have.
- Consider the authenticity of the first voice, and begin the revision with that.
- Revise Voice 1 to make it an authentic reflection of that character's thoughts, beliefs, motivations, and feelings.
- Add Voices 2 and 3. (Consider asking students to "voice" the part of each character.) Then go back to make additional changes to all three voices, as the characters begin to emerge clearly.
- Give the characters names or some form of identity.
- Read the revised version aloud, listening to the diverse voices, and making any final changes to help underscore the distinctiveness of each voice. They should sound very different from one another.

Step 6: Sharing and Discussing Results

When students have finished, ask several pairs of students to share their mini-dramas aloud. Some teams may choose to work together so that different students can "perform" the voices, giving the piece additional authenticity. Since student teams will have created many different voices, you can also perform a larger voice collage with different characters from several teams. After listening, ask the class as a whole to identify characters that particularly stand out. If you wish, compare your revisions with ours, keeping in mind that our characters and voices are likely to be very different.

Next Steps

- Extend any piece written for this lesson by letting characters "speak" more than one time. Hearing multiple voices two or even three times each deepens readers'/listeners' understanding of who each character is.
- Look for literature written in a multiple-voice format. Which pieces do you and your students consider particularly effective? You may want to perform some aloud; you may wish to hand pick excerpts from each "performance" to make this manageable. Recommended:
  - **Seedfolks* by Paul Fleischman. 2004. New York: HarperTeen.
  - *Bull Run* by Paul Fleischman. 1995. New York: HarperTrophy.
  - *Flipped* by Wendelin Van Draanen. 2003. New York: Alfred A. Knopf. (Only two voices, but very well done.)
  - **Whirligig* by Paul Fleischman. 2004. New York: Laurel Leaf.
  - **Witness* by Karen Hesse. 2001. New York: Scholastic.
- *For an additional challenge:* Some books are not written in a multi-voice format, but allow for creative expansion in this format. Students may select any book they like especially well, and try creating voices for characters who do not speak out directly. *Hint:* Don't take on the whole book; focus on one small scene in which several characters interact. Recommended:
  - **The Book Thief* by Markus Zusak. 2005. New York: Alfred A. Knopf.
  - *The Breadwinner* by Deborah Ellis. 2000. Toronto: Groundwood.
  - *Number the Stars* by Lois Lowry. 1998. New York: Lauren Leaf.
  - *Out of the Dust* by Karen Hesse. 1999. New York: Scholastic.
  - *Soldier's Heart* by Gary Paulsen. 2000 (reprint edition) New York: Laurel Leaf.
  - **Tuesdays with Morrie* by Mitch Albom. 2002. New York: Broadway.

  *Indicates a book written for a young adult *through* adult audience. These books may contain adult language and themes.

Sample A: New Job

Authentic voices?
Diverse voices?

Situation in a Nutshell
Carla is applying for a job she needs badly—working as a hospital receptionist. It pays $15 per hour, and the hours are 4 p.m. to midnight. Carla is a single mother with two children: Eloise, who is thirteen, and Nora, who is only six months old. The only way she can make this work is for Eloise to babysit Nora—for free—during her working hours.

Carla: *This has to work. Please—you have to see how perfect I am for this job! See how I'm smiling? See how calm I am? Oh, I know I'm going to face the wrath of Eloise later, but what can I do? She's thirteen, and that's old enough to take on responsibility for the good of the family. It's a lot to ask, sure, but for once in her life, she has to not be selfish.*

Interviewer: *This woman looks downright desperate. Good grief—get a grip. She is very fidgety. What is she so afraid of? I see on her resume she has children—always a problem. Her smile seems so forced. Not a happy person no matter how she tries to fake it. Our hospital patients are not going to be comfortable with her. How many more questions do I need to ask to be polite before I can get rid of her?*

Eloise: *Nora, why do you have to be so small? Why do you have to be so helpless? Why do you have to cry every waking second of your life? Mom, when are you coming home? Do you even care about us? I have a mountain of homework to do, and I might like to see my friends—sometime. This is so unfair. I need a life. I'm not the one with a six-month-old baby! Why can't she just take the baby with her?? This is unfair, unfair, unfair!!!*

Sample B: Dropping Out

Authentic voices?
Diverse voices?

Situation in a Nutshell
Rob is thinking of dropping out of school to work full time—just as his friend Mick did. He has finished ninth grade and feels he could complete his high school equivalency later and get a GED certificate. His parents, Margaret and David, are hoping Rob will not only finish high school, but go on to college, then law school, as Rob's father did.

Rob: *I think this could be a good plan for me. School isn't working all that well anyway. My grades could be better. I need to try going in a different direction. If things go wrong, I can get a GED later.*

Rob's dad: *At least he could talk to a counselor before making this decision. I think he'll be sorry if he makes this decision. I wish I knew what to say to convince him.*

Mick: *This isn't the right decision, but I don't like to be the one to tell him. Working isn't better than being in school. The hours are longer and the pay isn't all that great. I don't know—maybe I should say something.*

Revision of Sample B

Man, I need out. My grades are in the tank. I can't keep telling my parents I'm getting A's. At least with a job I'll have some money coming in. Right now, I feel like the world's Number One failure. Working can't be worse than this.

Rob: ~~I think this could be a good plan for me. School isn't working all that well anyway. My grades could be better. I need to try going in a different direction.~~ If things go wrong, I can always get a GED later.

Is he out of his mind? What is it with kids today? Someone please tell me! He'll regret this the rest of his life, and unfortunately, so will I! But, does he think of that?

Rob's dad: ~~At least he could talk to a counselor before making this decision. I think he'll be sorry if he makes this decision.~~ I wish I knew the magic words that would ~~what to say to~~ convince him. I know he'll come to his senses. This kid was born to be an attorney!! He has the right attitude, the right temperament—and the grades.

Rob, you freaking idiot! Way to rock everyone's world, buddy! You think you'll be happy working here, stocking shelves with those scrawny muscles of yours? Give me a break. Lousy hours. Crummy pay.

Mick: ~~This isn't the right decision, but I don't like to be the one to tell him. Working isn't better than being in school. The hours are longer and the pay isn't all that great.~~ I don't know—maybe I ~~should say something~~ need to haul you to work with me for a few days so you can see the light. Rob, my buddy, wake up. Who am I going to hire as my attorney if you don't hang in? Right, dude? You'll make a lousy drop-out.

Sample C: Whole Class Revision

Authentic voices?
Diverse voices?

Situation in a Nutshell
Amy wants to try out for a school singing competition. Her friends are waiting for her decision. Amy is unsure whether to take the big step and sing in front of everyone. What if her voice isn't really that good? On the other hand, what if she misses a big opportunity?

Amy: *I am not sure I can do this. Singing in the shower is one thing. Singing in front of the whole world is something else. Maybe I should just forget it.*

Voice 2:

Voice 3:

Sample D: Revising with Partners

Authentic voices?
Diverse voices?

Situation in a Nutshell
An author is visiting a school where one of her books has been banned. Her other books have all been best sellers, well received by students and parents alike. She is planning to give a talk to the students about her life as an author. Some of the students (along with parents and teachers) agree with the book ban. Many do not.

Author: *It's wrong to ban books. No voice should be suppressed. How do I talk openly about book banning to people who have not read my book?*

Voice 2:

Voice 3:

Suggested Revisions of C and D

Sample C: Whole Class Revision

Singing in Public

Amy: I ~~am not sure I can do this.~~ don't know how I got myself into this mess. Singing in the shower is one thing. Singing in front of the whole world is something else. ~~Maybe I should just forget it.~~ If I don't do it, though, they're going to say I'm a coward. Besides, what if I'm really good? Really, really good? American Idol good? I'm not that good, though. And the thing is, if my voice cracks, I will pass out, right there on the stage. Seriously, there's no way to go through with this.

~~Voice 2~~ Regie (a friend): No one likes a show-off. Who does she think she is, the next American Idol or something? Who told her she could sing—her mother? Ears, prepare for pain. Oh, and if she gets a standing O or something, then what? Can we even live with her after that? Why is every one of my friends a total narcissist? I would never embarrass her this way. Why is she doing this to me, her best friend on Earth? People just don't care who they hurt.

~~Voice 3~~ Ms. Morgan (a teacher): I was so afraid she wouldn't do this, that she would just chicken out and go hide in a corner or something. With that voice. That incredible voice. She has no idea how really good she is. Even though I tell her every day. If I could sing like that, I wouldn't care if I was good at one single other thing. I was afraid Regie was going to talk her out of it. Why doesn't Regie just put a big sign around her neck: "Hey everyone—I'm consumed with jealousy." Come on, Amy—you can do this.

Sample D: Revising with Partners

Author of Banned Book

Author: ~~It's wrong to ban books. No voice should be suppressed. How do I talk openly about book banning to people who have not read my book?~~ Why do people ban books? Why do they want to silence anyone's voice? Have they even read my book? Do they even know what the message is? I am not an evil person, out to corrupt children. I am a writer, but I have to write what I believe—don't I? It feels as if they've banned me. When I step out on that stage, will they see me for what I really am? I'm not an evil force. I'm just a person who wants kids to love books.

A Student
~~Voice 2~~: I'm thrilled she's coming, no matter what anyone says about her. I love her books—all of them. I've read every single one. I don't understand the point of banning books when we can get them anyway. Isn't book banning like trying to stop people from thinking? Isn't that what Fahrenheit 451 was about? Is it about protecting people, or about control? We're grown up! Let us decide for ourselves!

A Parent
~~Voice 3~~: Why are they inviting this woman to the school when they know how we feel? At least how some of us feel? It isn't right to ignore our feelings. They call us "book burners." That's very cruel. It hurts. These kids are our children. We love them. It should be our choice. Not everything is fit for children's eyes—or children's minds. They'll know too much too soon as it is. In a few years, they'll be much more ready to understand some things.

Sorting Out the Sound-Alikes

Lesson **18**

Trait Connection: **Conventions**

Introduction (Share with students in your own words—or as a handout.)

Words that sound alike—or *almost* alike—but have different meanings (sometimes called *homophones* or *homonyms*) are easy to confuse, especially if you are writing quickly. A good computer program may catch such errors, changing *their* to *there* at the right moment, for example. Computers are far from infallible, however, so even if you are composing on a keyboard, you still need to go back and reread what you have written—with a good editor's eye.

In this lesson, you'll have a chance to test your editor's eye, making sure that the word given matches the intended meaning. Following are a few sound-alike demons that cause trouble for many writers. There are many others. Remember that the best way to ensure you're using the right word is to think carefully about *meaning*. Using conventions carefully is just one more way of making your meaning clear.

Troublesome Sound-Alikes

there, their,* and *they're

- Dan's house is over **there.**
- Jason is **their** favorite cousin.
- **They're** [They are] not staying for the barbecue.

to, too,* and *two

- She hopes **to** become a doctor.
- It's **too** hot for comfort today.
- We'd like to go, **too**.
- I won't spend over **two** dollars for one scoop of ice cream.

accept, except (These do not sound *exactly* alike.)

- I was happy to **accept** his invitation.
- Everyone loved the book **except** Emily.

affect, effect

- Practicing daily could **affect** our standing in the play-offs. (verb meaning influence)
- Her dark look had no **effect** on me. (noun meaning impact, result)
- A rash of complaints might **effect** a change in airline policy. (verb meaning bring about)

aisle, isle

- Please keep your feet out of the **aisle**.
- She lives on a gorgeous, enchanted **isle**.

allusion, illusion (These do not sound *exactly* alike.)

- Stacy's report included several **allusions** to the book *To Kill a Mockingbird*. (An allusion is a reference.)
- Palmer was under the **illusion** that he was every girl's dream. (An illusion is a misguided idea or mistaken belief.)

already, all ready

- Sue has only been in Europe a month, and is **already** lonesome. (one "l," one word, means *even at this point*)
- Are you **all ready** for spring to come? (two "l's," two words, means *totally prepared*)

Warm-Up

Following is a short warm-up based on the kinds of examples we just shared with you. If you have any difficulty with this warm-up, review the opening examples again, or consult your handbook (*Write Source: New Generation* or another of your choice) under "homophones." (Answers appear on page 171.)

1. I hope (*there, their, they're*) going to remain over (*there, their, they're*) on (*there, their, they're*) own side of the field.
2. Brad says he hopes (*to, too, two*) have at least (*to, too, two*) more chances (*to, too, two*) win at Lacrosse, (*to, too, two*).
3. Though Chance appreciated the nomination, he felt he could not (*accept, except*).
4. No one (*accept, except*) Rachel was willing to go off the high dive.
5. The hot weather had minimal (*affect, effect*) on beach use.
6. I couldn't let her cutting remarks (*affect, effect*) my good mood.
7. The only way to (*affect, effect*) change is to speak up for it.
8. Just as we looked up, a group of pirates sailed round the (*aisle, isle*).
9. The bride floated down the (*aisle, isle*), her face aglow.
10. I believe he was making an (*allusion, illusion*) to our earlier conversation.
11. Julie was under the (*allusion, illusion*) that she would be part of the new band.
12. Tyler is (*already, all ready*) to coach the football team.
13. The team has (*already, all ready*) won three games.

Teaching the Lesson (General Guidelines for Teachers)

1. Use our examples or your own to illustrate appropriate uses of confusing sound-alike words. You may wish to spend time pointing out the correct pronunciation for words (*allusion, illusion*) that sound *similar*, but not identical.
2. Ask students to complete the 13 sentences in the Warm-Up, and check to see if anyone has difficulty. For any students who do, you may wish to provide further examples and/or refer students to the appropriate section of whatever handbook you use in your classroom.
3. Ask students to keep our examples handy for easy reference, and also to have a handbook available in case they need more information on homophones or homonyms.
4. Share the editing lesson on the following page. Students should read the passage *both silently and aloud*, thinking about meaning before deciding whether a given word is correct. No options are provided (as they were in the warm-up), so students must read carefully—more than once.
5. Ask students to edit individually first, then check with a partner.
6. When everyone is done, ask them to coach you as you edit the same copy, discussing/explaining choices as you go.
7. When you finish, read your edited copy aloud, answering any additional questions students may have. Then compare your edited copy with our suggested text on page 172.
8. For students who have any difficulty with this activity, review the Warm-Up sentences, answering any questions. Then, repeat the practice, this time reading aloud with students as they work. Encourage them to focus on the *meaning* of each sentence before making a decision.

Editing Goal: Make 26 corrections.
Follow-Up: Check sound-alike words in your own work, making sure that you have chosen the correct word to convey the intended meaning.

Answers to Warm-Up

1. I hope *they're* going to remain over *there* on *their* own side of the field.
2. Brad says he hopes *to* have at least *two* more chances *to* win at Lacrosse, *too.*
3. Though Chance appreciated the nomination, he felt he could not *accept.*
4. No one *except* Rachel was willing to go off the high dive.
5. The hot weather had minimal *effect* on beach use.
   (noun, meaning *impact*)
6. I couldn't let her cutting remarks *affect* my good mood.
   (verb, meaning *influence*)
7. The only way to *effect* change is to speak up for it.
   (verb, meaning *bring about*)
8. Just as we looked up, a group of pirates sailed round the *isle.*
   (*little island*)
9. The bride floated down the *aisle,* her face aglow. (*walkway*)
10. I believe he was making an *allusion* to our earlier conversation.
    (*reference*)
11. Julie was under the *illusion* that she would be part of the new band.
    (*mistaken belief*)
12. Tyler is *all ready* to coach the football team. (*prepared*)
13. The team has *already* won three games. (*even at this point*)

Editing Practice

Check all sound-alike words to make sure the word matches the intended meaning.

The shark is among the most effective predators ever too inhabit the ocean. They're sleek shape, replaceable teeth, and thick skins qualify them as matchless hunters. There well-developed sensory system enables them too detect even small amounts of blood in the water. For this reason, their able too quickly locate fish in distress—and dispatch them. This has a favorable affect on the ecology of the ocean, and keeps other fish populations in balance, to.

The shark has few enemies—accept for people. Commercial fishing has all ready had a major affect on the overall shark population. Even without necessarily meaning two do so, fishermen catch large numbers of sharks annually in there nets. Because shark meat sometimes goes by a different label, though, many diners are under the allusion they are eating salmon (or something similar) when their actually consuming shark meat. Menus usually describe the popular dish "fish and chips" without any illusion too sharks, but sometimes, shark meat is the main ingredient!

Few people are willing too except sharks as swimming companions. Scientists are all ready working on a shark repellant, but so far, their unable too identify any ingredient that has a significant affect on the sharks themselves. It may be years before such a product is already for consumers, but once developers come up with the right formula, their going too make a lot of swimmers happy!

Edited Copy

26 corrections

The shark is among the most effective predators ever ~~too~~ to inhabit the ocean. ~~They're~~ Their sleek shape, replaceable teeth, and thick skins qualify them as matchless hunters. ~~There~~ Their well-developed sensory system enables them ~~too~~ to detect even small amounts of blood in the water. For this reason, ~~their~~ they're able ~~too~~ to quickly locate fish in distress—and dispatch them. This has a favorable ~~affect~~ effect on the ecology of the ocean, and keeps other fish populations in balance, ~~to~~ too.

The shark has few enemies—~~accept~~ except for people. Commercial fishing has ~~all ready~~ already had a major ~~affect~~ effect on the overall shark population. Even without necessarily meaning ~~two~~ to do so, fishermen catch large numbers of sharks annually in ~~there~~ their nets. Because shark meat sometimes goes by a different label, though, many diners are under the ~~allusion~~ illusion they are eating salmon (or something similar) when ~~their~~ they're actually consuming shark meat. Menus usually describe the popular dish "fish and chips" without any ~~illusion too~~ allusion to sharks, but sometimes, shark meat is the main ingredient!

Few people are willing ~~too except~~ to accept sharks as swimming companions. Scientists are ~~all ready~~ already working on a shark repellant, but so far, ~~their~~ they're unable ~~too~~ to identify any ingredient that has a significant ~~affect~~ effect on the sharks themselves. It may be years before such a product is ~~already~~ all ready for consumers, but once developers come up with the right formula, ~~their~~ they're going ~~too~~ to make a lot of swimmers happy!

Revising to Create Atmosphere

Lesson **19**

Trait Connection: **Word Choice**

Introduction

Words aren't just about meaning. They're also about mood and atmosphere. The smallest descriptive words offer readers a preview of coming events—just as a dark and somber stage set portends ominous drama, while bright lights and colors suggest comedy and optimism. Ray Bradbury's classic *Fahrenheit 451* opens with these words: "It was a pleasure to burn. It was a special pleasure to see things eaten, to see things blackened and *changed*" (p. 3). These words suggest we'd better brace ourselves for something grim. Who or what is being *eaten?* And why does someone take *pleasure* in it? These dark questions haunt us before we have even figured out what is happening. Gary D. Schmidt sets a different kind of stage altogether with the description of his living room in *The Wednesday Wars*: "I walked past the Perfect Living Room, where no one ever sat because all the seat cushions were covered in stiff, clear plastic" (p. 6). How much do we learn about Holling's family just from this one line? What's the most telling word in this description? And if you walked into a theater and saw the "Perfect Living Room" as a stage set, what sort of play would you expect? In this lesson, you will set the stage for readers by choosing words that create mood and atmosphere. Two things are critical: First, you need to know what sort of mood or atmosphere you're going for. Second, the words you choose must work together. Otherwise, you'll create a potpourri of moods the reader will find confusing.

Teacher's Sidebar . . .

It doesn't take a hundred words to create mood. Bradbury's words "eaten" and "blackened" are enough to make us tense up. Schmidt's words "perfect" and "stiff" get us ready to enjoy ourselves (perhaps at the expense of Holling's very proper family). Encourage students to use resources such as a book of synonyms or an online thesaurus to find two or three "just right" words to set the emotional stage. Used sparingly, powerful words have more impact.

Quotations from the introduction are taken from:

- Ray Bradbury. *Fahrenheit 451*. 1991 (2nd ed). New York: Random House.
- Gary D. Schmidt. *The Wednesday Wars*. 2007. New York: Clarion Books.

Focus and Intent

This lesson is intended to help students:

- Understand the power of words to create mood or atmosphere.
- Identify the particular mood suggested by a specific word or phrase.
- Revise the language of a piece to create or enhance a particular mood.

Teaching the Lesson

Step 1: Playing with Mood

Share the following example from Laure Halse Anderson's novel *Speak*:

> *I stand in the center aisle of the auditorium, a wounded zebra in a National Geographic special, looking for someone, anyone, to sit next to. A predator approaches: gray jock buzz cut, whistle around a neck thicker than his head. Probably a social studies teacher, hired to coach a blood sport (p. 5).*
>
> (Anderson, Laurie Halse. 1999. *Speak*. New York: Farrar, Straus & Giroux.)

Read the example more than once, and talk first about the mood or atmosphere it creates. Who is the speaker? Where is she—and how does she see herself and her surroundings? See if you can identify the specific words that create this mood. What if these words were eliminated—or changed? Try rewriting this piece to give it a light, cheerful tone—just by changing some key words. In so doing, you will identify the most powerful words in this passage. If the emotional "weight" of words could be measured in pounds, which would be the heaviest words in this passage?

Step 2: Making the Reading-Writing Connection

Harper Lee's novel *To Kill a Mockingbird* contains a very moody stage-setting passage that is so powerful it was adapted as the opener for the film based on Lee's book. Likely you have heard it, read it, or both—but to appreciate Harper Lee's careful word choice, see if you can fill in the blanks:

> *Maycomb was an old town, but it was a __1__ old town when I first knew it. In rainy weather, the streets turned to red slop; grass grew on the sidewalks, the courthouse __2__ in the square. Somehow, it was hotter then: a black dog __3__ on a summer's day; bony mules hitched to Hoover carts flicked flies in the sweltering shade of the live oaks on the square. Men's stiff collars __4__ by nine in the morning. Ladies bathed before noon, after their three-o'clock naps, and by nightfall were like teacakes with frostings of __5__ and sweet talcum. (pp. 5–6)*
>
> (From *To Kill a Mockingbird* by Harper Lee. 1960, renewed 1988. New York: HarperPerennial.)

If you know Harper Lee's book well, you may have found this easy—but even then, it is helpful to understand the mood, the feeling she means to create. On this "stage," people move slowly. They take their time. They notice things. The oppressive heat slows them down—and perhaps makes them see and experience life a little differently. Lee chose these words to go in the blanks: (1) *tired*, (2) *sagged*, (3) *suffered*, (4) *wilted*, and (5) *sweat*. Did you recall (or guess) the words correctly—or if not, did you fill in the blanks with words that create a similar mood? On a scale of 1 to 10, how precise do you think Harper Lee's word choice is? To appreciate it fully, read the passage aloud again, with the correct words inserted—then, if possible, view the first part of the film to see how well director Robert Mulligan's vision reflects the original description.

Step 3: Involving Students as Evaluators

Ask students to review Samples A and B, considering whether each writer has effectively chosen words that create a definitive atmosphere or mood. Have them work together, discussing the probable intention of the writer and underlining words or phrases that offer possibilities of reinforcing the intended mood. Ask them also to identify the piece they think creates a strong, consistent mood, and to discuss ways of improving the weaker piece.

Discussing Results

Most students should find Sample B stronger. Writer B creates a definitive mood, whereas Writer A creates no particular atmosphere at all. This stage set could suggest anything from comedy to dark drama—we cannot yet tell. One possible revision of Sample A is provided.

Step 4: Modeling Revision

- Share Sample C (*Whole Class Revision*) with students. Read the original aloud.
- Ask students whether the writer has created a definitive atmosphere or mood. (Most should say *no*.)
- Give students time to discuss the piece with partners, brainstorming various possibilities for defining the mood and identifying the one they feel fits the circumstance best.
- As a class, discuss "stage-setting" possibilities, and choose the mood or atmosphere you want to go for. Underline key words or phrases that you wish to revise to reinforce your chosen mood. *Caution:* Don't feel obligated to choose too many. If your word choice is strong, you won't need a dozen revisions; three to five may be sufficient.
- Revise the piece line by line, reading aloud as you go. When you come to the end, feel free to go back and revisit any word choices you feel can be further refined. Also feel free to change or delete any portion of the original.
- Read your final revision aloud, making any last-minute changes that enhance the atmosphere.

- If you wish, compare your revision to ours, keeping in mind that your revisions—and even your chosen atmosphere—may be quite different from ours. In addition, for the sake of showing possibilities, we have added more revisions than you need to make.

Step 5: Revising with Partners

Share Sample D (*Revising with Partners*). Ask students to follow the basic steps you modeled with Sample C. *Working with partners,* they should:

- Read the passage aloud.
- Talk about stage-setting possibilities and the mood or atmosphere they wish to create.
- Underline words or passages that provide opportunities to define the mood or atmosphere of the piece.
- Revise the original line by line, making at least three strong changes, but not overwhelming the reader with "moody" language.
- Revisit early changes to see if anything can be further improved.
- Read the final revision aloud, with as much voice as possible, listening to the power of the words. They should create a definitive mood.
- Imagine this scene filmed. What would the lighting be like? How would the opening scene look? What kind of music would be playing? Would the film be black and white—or in color? How would each of these decisions further influence the chosen mood?

Step 6: Sharing and Discussing Results

When students have finished, ask several pairs of students to share their revisions aloud. After listening, ask the class as a whole to identify the mood they hear and feel, and to specify words or phrases that create it. Ask the class to also imagine one or two of the revisions on film, and to describe how it might look. Do their visions match those of the student revisers? If you wish, compare your revisions with ours, keeping in mind that our changes are likely to be very different.

Next Steps

- Atmospheric language is important in many kinds of description, and often finds its way into informational writing, as well as fiction, biography, memoir, history, and poetry. Look for descriptions that set the stage for factual information to follow—as in this introductory piece from Sy Montgomery's informational text, *Quest for the Tree Kangaroo*: "Here the trees are cloaked in clouds. The ground is carpeted with thick green moss. In the cloud forests of Papua New Guinea, ferns grow into trees—trees like those the dinosaurs knew. Moss and ferns, vines and orchids, hang from branches like the beards of wise old wizards" (p. 7). With words like *cloaked, carpeted, beards*, and *wizards*, Montgomery takes us into another world, and another time—which is precisely his intent. How could words like these make a reader more receptive to the writer's informational message?

- Ask students to review their own writing for opportunities to create mood or atmosphere. Remind them to consider carefully the mood they wish to create. It must suit the text, absolutely. But in addition, like author Sy Montgomery in the preceding example, they may wish to think about the impact on the reader. Do they want the reader tense? Relaxed? Laughing? Sympathizing with a character? Words can play with readers' feelings in powerful ways.
- Look and listen for atmospheric passages in the literature you share aloud. Recommended:
    - *The Wednesday Wars* by Gary D. Schmidt. 2007. New York: Clarion.
    - **Speak* by Laure Halse Anderson. 1999. New York: Farrar, Straus & Giroux.
    - **Birdland* by Tracy Mack. 2003. New York: Scholastic.
    - **The Book Thief* by Marcus Zusak. 2005. New York: Alfred A. Knopf.
    - **Fahrenheit 451 by Ray Bradbury*. 1953 (renewed 1981). New York: Random House.
    - **The Old Man and the Sea* by Ernest Hemingway. 1952 (renewed 1980). New York: Scribner.
    - *Quest for the Tree Kangaroo* by Sy Montgomery. 2006. Boston: Houghton Mifflin.
- *For an additional challenge:* Consider a lesson recommended by middle school teacher Barbara Andrews. Ask students to identify favorite expressions, and create a collection. Then ask them to "adapt" one of these expressions to their own writing by changing it slightly. For example, consider the earlier quotation from *To Kill a Mockingbird*, notably the expression "the courthouse sagged in the square." Imagine that expression with a different *building* (or other object)—and a different *verb*—but one equally unexpected: e.g., "Corn stalks relaxed in the twilight." This lesson offers an opportunity to borrow "strategy" without plagiarizing.

*Indicates a book written for a young adult *through* adult audience. These books may contain adult language and themes.

Sample A

What's the mood?
The right words
for the mood?

Warrior

The young man stood in the sun. He knew what was expected, and what he must do. The hunting and killing of lions had been a tradition for his people for many generations. Still, success was far from inevitable. He was by himself, a long way from his village and his family.

This was the way of things: Once he set out on the hunt, he had to come back victorious. To run was not an option. To opt out of the hunt was not an option.

His eyes moved carefully over the grass as he walked barefoot over the dry earth. Suddenly, something was different. The cattle were milling about in a restless manner. Perhaps they sensed something. They began to call to one another, softly at first, then louder. The warrior felt the spear in his right hand, his fingers curling firmly around it.

Sample B

What's the mood?
The right words
for the mood?

Conspiracy

It was a plot. She tried. She tried not to see it as a conspiracy, but the hairs around her face were dancing, laughing. "You can't trap us," they taunted. Twisting, squirming, they wound themselves into a fierce knot of protest that stood defiantly on top of her head. This was not the way to go to a job interview. She wanted cooperative hair. Not this mane of rebellion. "How will they expect me to manage an office," she thought miserably, "if I cannot even manage my appearance?" As if offended by her very thoughts, her hair asserted itself, spiking off to the left. It seemed to be attempting to escape from her head. Sighing, she clamped a hat over it, and headed out the door.

Revision of Sample A

Warrior

The young man ~~stood in~~ soaked up the heat and strength of the sun. He knew what was expected, and what he must do.

The hunting and killing of lions had been a tradition for his people for many generations. Still, success ~~was far from inevitable.~~ came only to those strong in heart, mind, and body. He was ~~by himself, a long way~~ alone now, cut off from his village and his family.

This was the way of things: Once he set out on the hunt, he had to come back victorious. To run was ~~not an option.~~ to admit defeat. To ~~opt out of~~ forsake the hunt was ~~not an option.~~ to betray his people.

His eyes ~~moved carefully over~~ searched the grass ~~as he walked barefoot over~~ even as his bare feet felt for the softest vibrations on the dry earth. Suddenly, something was different. The cattle were milling about ~~in a restless manner. Perhaps they sensed something.~~ restless and confused, as if they could smell death coming. They ~~began to call~~ bellowed to one another, softly at first, then ~~louder.~~ with urgency. The warrior ~~felt~~ grasped the spear in his right hand, his fingers ~~curling firmly~~ tightening around it.

Sample C: Whole Class Revision

What's the mood?
The right words
for the mood?

Blind Date

Aaron stood on the front porch, wondering why he had agreed to this. His brother had told him how much fun blind dates were. "You'll have a good time," Keith had told him. Yes, of course. Maybe he could just run away. He looked down. He had forgotten to change his shoes. He still had on his gym shoes! They looked a little worn.

Already, he could feel moisture on his back. The fabric of his trousers felt rough. Reflexively, he ran his hands through his hair. What *was* that? Had he used too much gel? His hair felt odd. He hoped Sheila wouldn't touch his hair. She wouldn't do that on a first date, though—would she? Was he recalling her name correctly?

He could hear footsteps moving toward him on the other side of the door. Pretty soon, if he didn't leave, it would be too late. They were coming closer . . . the door was opening . . .

"Hello," he said, trying to smile.

Sample D: Revising with Partners

What's the mood?
The right words
for the mood?

Fishing

They'd been three months out fishing. It was mail call. Derek felt hopeful. He hadn't had a letter in a long while, and thought there might be something for him today. He studied the face of the mail clerk, watching his lips form the names—Stevens, Murphy, Johanssen, Huang, Arliss . . . his name wasn't on the list.

He turned and walked away, noticing the wet planking on the ship where they had hauled in the last catch. For a time, he stood at the railing, leaning on it, just looking out across the waves, trying to picture his family back home. He could see the house in his mind. The front porch had a light tucked just under the eave, and he could picture it perfectly, as if he were standing right there. Then, the image faded a bit.

After a while, the sky clouded over, and the wind picked up. He shivered a bit in the cold, and went below to his bunk.

Suggested Revisions of C and D

Sample C: Whole Class Revision

Blind Date

Aaron ~~stood~~ rocked back and forth on the front porch, wondering why he had agreed to this. His brother had ~~told him~~ regaled him with lies about how much fun blind dates were. "You'll have ~~a good time,"~~ the time of your life," Keith had told him. ~~Yes, of course.~~ Yeah, right. Maybe he could just run away —or evaporate into the atmosphere. He looked down. He had forgotten to change his shoes. He still had on his stupid gym shoes! They looked ~~a little worn~~ as if he'd been wading through a swamp.

Already, he could feel ~~moisture on~~ little rivers of sweat making their way down his back. The fabric of his trousers ~~felt rough.~~ was tickling his legs with a thousand twitchy little fingers. Reflexively, he ran his hands through his hair. What *was* that? Had he used too much gel? His hair felt ~~odd.~~ bristly and broom-like—almost crisp. He hoped Sheila wouldn't touch his hair. It might actually break! She wouldn't do that on a first date, though—would she? ~~Was he recalling her name correctly?~~ Hang on—was Sheila even her name? How about Shelly? Sharon???

He could hear footsteps ~~moving toward~~ closing in on him on the other side of the door. Pretty soon, if he didn't leave, ~~it would be too late. They~~ his fate would be sealed. The invisible feet were coming closer . . . the door was opening to swallow him alive . . .

~~"Hello,"~~ "Help," he ~~said, trying to~~ squeaked, stretching his lips into an imitation smile. "I mean, *hello.*"

Sample D: Revising with Partners

Fishing

dreary / a stab of hope and tried to suppress it.

They'd been three months out fishing. It was mail call. Derek felt ~~hopeful.~~ He hadn't

what felt like years.

had a letter in ~~a long while, and thought there might be something for him today.~~ He

leathery, pinched / as his thin lips squeezed out

studied the face of the mail clerk, ~~watching his lips form~~ the names—Stevens,

of the lucky.

Murphy, Johanssen, Huang, Arliss . . . his name wasn't on the list.

for the first time how weary and worn / looked, hosed down after

He turned and walked away, noticing the wet planking ~~on the ship where~~ they had hauled in the last catch. For a time, he stood at the railing, leaning on it, just

neverending / almost call up a picture of

looking out across the waves, trying to picture his family back home. He could ~~see~~ the

beckoned him with

house in his mind. The front porch ~~had~~ a light tucked just under the eave, and he could

see himself stepping right up to the door. / just as the door opened,

~~picture it perfectly, as if he were standing right there.~~ Then, the image ~~faded a bit.~~

floated off on the waves.

As he stood there, / clouds bunched into a fist / clawed at his face.

~~After a while,~~ the ~~sky clouded over,~~ and the wind ~~picked up.~~ He ~~shivered a bit~~

shrank deeper into his jacket,

~~in the cold,~~ and went below to his bunk.

To Capitalize or Not to Capitalize . . .

Lesson **20**

Trait Connection: **Conventions**

Introduction (Share with students in your own words—or as a handout.)

Winnie the Pooh, as fans of A. A. Milne know well, has His Own Rules for capitalization. On Eeyore's birthday, for example, he is quite worried about his friend and points out to Piglet that "poor Eeyore is in a Very Sad Condition, because it's his birthday, and nobody has taken any notice of it, and he's very Gloomy . . ." (A. A. Milne, *Winnie the Pooh*, 1950 reprint edition, New York: H. Wolff, p. 76). Pooh, of course, is the Sort of Character who can get by with this charming and whimsical capitalization of all Personally Important Words. The Rest of Us, however—the rest of us, that is—have to go by the rules. What *are* they, anyway?

Capitalization can be a very confusing prospect indeed. It helps if we remember, though, that *most* capitalization—sentence beginnings aside—is for the purpose of identifying something as a proper name. We name things all the time, of course: *There's my* ***house****, Sit in this* ***chair****, Where's the* ***dog****?* But these are common, *everyday noun* sorts of names—unlike, say, Harry, or Queen Elizabeth, or *The Old Man and the Sea*, or Disneyland. A proper name, such as your *own* name, refers to a one-of-a-kind, *particular* person, place, or thing. And it is those names that require capitals. Here are some distinctions that may help.

A Brief Capitalization Guide

1. Capitalize names and titles:

   - She attends the **University of Colorado**.
   - Here comes **Professor Hall** from the **Anthropology Department**.
   - She lives in **Windsor Castle**.
   - I'm enrolled in **Physics 101**.
   - I enjoy **Math 2**.

   But . . .

   - She attends *the university*. (a kind of institution, not a name)
   - Here comes our *professor,* who teaches *anthropology*. (occupation and course of study, not names)

- She lives in a *castle*. (a kind of building, not the castle name)
- I study *physics*. (a subject, not a course name)
- I enjoy *math*. (a subject, not a course name)

2. Capitalize *President* when referring to the current U.S. President, or a *particular* U.S. President:

    - Here comes the **President**.
    - The **President's** plane has arrived.
    - Countless people found **President Kennedy** inspiring.

    But the word *president* is not otherwise capitalized *unless* it is part of someone's title . . .

    - Harriet is *the president* of our travel club.
    - Charles is *the president* of his corporation.
    - Not all U.S. *presidents* were great speakers. (presidents in general)
    - We received a memo from *President Lewis* about the new parking policy. (part of a title)

3. Capitalize names of languages, nationalities, and races:

    - I study **English**.
    - Phyllis speaks **French, German, and Greek**.
    - Many of our students are **African American** or **Asian**.

4. Capitalize names of states, countries, and *regions of the country or world*:

    - Have you ever lived in **Florida** or **Texas**?
    - Our **French Club** is visiting **France** next summer.
    - Lia is touring the **West**; Raoul is visiting friends in **Eastern Europe**.
    - The **Midwest** experiences many tornadoes, while **Northern California** has scarcely a one.
    - That fabric is imported from the **Middle East**.

    But, do not capitalize *directions* . . .

    - Head *west* for two miles to find the fairgrounds. (versus *She lives in the West*—a region of the country)
    - The storm is moving *northeast* to *southwest*. (versus *Weather is unpredictable in the Northeast*—a region of the country)

5. Capitalize names of days, months, and holidays:

    - I'll meet you **Tuesday**.
    - My favorite months are **October** and **November**.
    - They're gone from **Thanksgiving** right through **New Year's Day**.

But . . . seasons and times of the month, week, or day are not capitalized unless they form part of a name:

- Ralph and I love the winter because we ski.
- We're always busy during the summer.
- I'll see you next weekend.
- By morning, we'll know the election results.
- We hope to see you during our city's **Fall Concert Series**.

6. Capitalize brand names but not references to *kinds* of products:

- Hand me the **Saran Wrap**.
- I need a **Kleenex**.
- Did you turn off the **Xerox** machine?
- Sarah doesn't drink **Coke**.

But . . .

- Hand me the cellophane wrap.
- I need a tissue.
- Did you turn off the copy machine?
- Sarah doesn't drink soda.

7. Capitalize Mom and Dad (or similar references to relatives) *only* when they are used as names:

- I think **Mom** promised to pick us up. (You could substitute a proper name for "Mom": *I think **Ellen** promised to pick us up*)
- I need to ask **Dad** about borrowing the car.
- Have you seen **Uncle Ted**?
- I can't believe **Grandma** still skydives!

But . . .

- I think my mom promised to pick us up. (not used as a name)
- I need to ask my dad about borrowing the car.
- Have you seen Bruce's uncle?
- I can't believe your grandma still skydives!

Key Question

Is it the *proper name* of a *particular* person, place, or thing? Is it a *title?* A *brand name?* Or—does it refer to a *broad general category* of people, places, or things? This key question should help you in deciding when capitals are needed.

Teaching the Lesson (General Guidelines for Teachers)

1. Use our examples or your own to illustrate appropriate uses of capitalization to set off specific proper names.
2. Ask students to keep our examples handy for easy reference, and also to have a handbook available in case they need more information on capitalization. Recommended: *Great Source: New Generation*.
3. Share the editing lesson on the following page. Students should read the passage *both silently and aloud*, asking the Key Question: *Is it a specific proper name referring to a one-of-a-kind person, place, or thing, or is it a generic reference to a category?* Some capitals (31) are missing. Other words (25) are capitalized when they should not be.
4. Ask students to edit individually first, then check with a partner.
5. When everyone is done, ask them to coach you as you edit the same copy, discussing/explaining choices as you go.
6. When you finish, read your edited copy aloud, answering any additional questions students may have. Then compare your edited copy with our suggested text on page 190.
7. For students who have any difficulty with this activity, review the *Brief Capitalization Guide*, answering any questions. Also make sure students have access to a good handbook and know how to find the information they need. Then, repeat the practice, this time reading aloud with students as they work. Encourage them to ask whether each noun in question is really a name—or is a generic reference. *You may wish to do the activity one paragraph at a time, thus limiting the number of corrections students must make at any one time.*

Editing Goal: Make 56 corrections.
Follow-Up: Check for accurate capitalization in your own work.

Editing Practice

Correct errors in capitalization. Triple underscore (≡) letters that *should* be capitalized but *are not*. Draw a slash (/) through those that *are* capitalized but should *not be*.

Students and Faculty of south Hampton university have varied plans for the coming summer vacation. Some History Students are headed to various regions in europe, while many of those from the anthropology department are headed to the south pacific. (Those from psychology 101 will remain on Campus an additional month to take a special Psychology course. Boo hoo. Pass the kleenex.) One of the Professors is planning a Tour through eastern Europe. Several are joining Europe unlimited Tours, inc., which is headed to northern italy in august. They have spent most of early may xeroxing copies of maps and itineraries.

Most of the students are visiting friends and relatives within the u.s. They are lonesome for Mothers, Fathers, Grandparents—even siblings that they have not seen for over ten months. Let's hope families will have enough Ice Tea and coke for all those Summer picnics and visits to State Fairs.

A few Seniors are headed on a Bike Tour of the United States. They will begin in the midwest, then head West for a time, dipping into the southwest, and finally heading north again. The bike tour begins in June and continues through early august. The students plan to see mount Rushmore, with the sculptures of the four Presidents, and the grand canyon. They will take time for White Water Rafting on the Colorado river. The tour—known as the bike America tour—concludes with a ride through the breathtaking redwood forest of northern California and a giant Fireworks display to mark independence day. What a way to spend Summer!

Edited Copy

25 capitals changed to lower case (/)
31 capitals added (≡)

Students and Faculty of south Hampton university have varied plans for the coming summer vacation. Some History Students are headed to various regions in europe, while many of those from the anthropology department are headed to the south pacific. (Those from psychology 101 will remain on Campus an additional month to take a special Psychology course. Boo hoo. Pass the kleenex.) One of the Professors is planning a Tour through eastern Europe. Several are joining Europe unlimited Tours, inc., which is headed to northern italy in august. They have spent most of early may xeroxing copies of maps and itineraries.

Most of the students are visiting friends and relatives within the u.s. They are lonesome for Mothers, Fathers, Grandparents—even siblings that they have not seen for over ten months. Let's hope families will have enough Ice Tea and coke for all those Summer picnics and visits to State Fairs.

A few Seniors are headed on a Bike Tour of the United States. They will begin in the midwest, then head West for a time, dipping into the southwest, and finally heading north again. The bike tour begins in June and continues through early august. The students plan to see mount Rushmore, with the sculptures of the four Presidents, and the grand canyon. They will take time for White Water Rafting on the Colorado river. The tour—known as the bike America tour—concludes with a ride through the breathtaking redwood forest of northern California and a giant Fireworks display to mark independence day. What a way to spend Summer!

Revising the Documentary Voice-Under

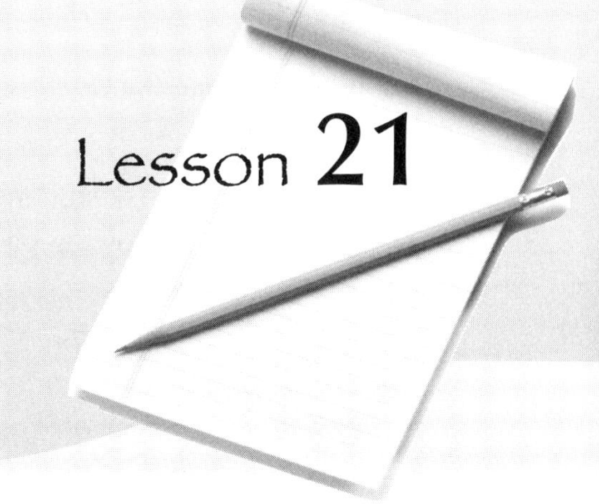

Lesson 21

Trait Connection: **Word Choice**

Introduction

Precise nouns and strong verbs form the skeleton of all writing. But verbs, which pack an energetic punch, are particularly important to film scripts. Film is about motion, and a good voice-under (the voice you hear as you watch the images on-screen) must reflect action and drama. Revising to make verbs more powerful takes more than simply replacing one word or phrase with another: *Our team throttled the opposition* versus *Our team held off the opposition*. While *throttled* is a big improvement over *held off*, revising in this slow-paced word-by-word manner can take a very long time. In this lesson, you'll combine three strategies that are all designed to work together to give verbs center stage: condensing, using verbs in multiples, and eliminating (or at any rate, *minimizing*) modifiers. Get ready to unleash some power.

Teacher's Sidebar . . .

Encourage students to imagine that their revisions will become the voice-under scripts for a documentary video. As they write, they should try to picture what will appear on-screen, and create a script that will give that video dramatic flair.

Focus and Intent

This lesson is intended to help students:

- Recognize nouns and verbs as the underlying structure of strong writing.
- Identify several strategies for strengthening verb power.
- Revise a documentary script to give it power.

Teaching the Lesson

Step 1: Going for a Triple Play

Strategy 1

Putting rocks in your pocket can inhibit movement—and the more rocks, the harder it is to move. Weighing writing down with unneeded words works much the same way. Ask students to engage in a brief competition to see which of them can shorten the following passage the most *without compromising any of the central meaning:*

> *Behavioral psychologists study human behavior. One example might be looking at how human beings use their hands as they speak, and whether men and women differ in the way they gesture to accentuate their speech. To study this, a behavioral psychologist will observe equal numbers of men and women as they speak, and carefully record each and every time that each speaker touches his or her face, hair, or clothing, as well as each time that the speaker gestures in the air or touches a nearby object, such as a book or table. (93 words)*

See if your students can slice this passage by *at least one third.*

Strategy 2

In the following expressions, the writer relies on an adverb to bolster the power of a weak verb. Ask students to brainstorm as many strong verbs as they can think of to replace each *weak verb-adverb* combo:

- Move slowly ______________________________
- Talk loudly ______________________________
- Touch lightly ______________________________
- Work hard ______________________________
- Go quickly ______________________________

Strategy 3

If one verb adds energy and power, think what three or four within a single sentence can do for both force and imagery. Consider this sentence from *To Kill a Mockingbird.* The narrator, Scout, has bundled herself into an old tire, and asked her brother Jem to push her down the road. She describes the experience this way:

> *The tire bumped on gravel, skeetered across the road, crashed into a barrier and popped me like a cork onto pavement. (*From *To Kill a Mockingbird by* Harper Lee. 1988. New York: HarperPerennial, p. 42*)*

Ask students to identify the verbs and to discuss why a writer might use four different verbs to describe this situation. (Why wouldn't just one—e.g., *bumped*—do?) Then, ask students to create an imitative sentence on any topic—such as their own experience navigating the hallways of your school. Their original sentences must include *a minimum of three verbs.*

Sample responses to these warm-up activities appear at the end of "Next Steps," p. 195.

Step 2: Making the Reading-Writing Connection

Verbs matter in all writing, but nowhere is their power felt more strongly than in a scene where both action and intensity matter. In her best-selling historical narrative *Seabiscuit*, author Laura Hillenbrand offers readers a moment-by-moment replay of what is widely regarded as the greatest horse race in history. It is November 1,

1938, and a nation hungry for heroes is riveted to the rivalry between two thoroughbreds: an unbeaten Triple Crown champion, the legendary War Admiral—and the relative "upstart" Seabiscuit, a much smaller horse with a far shorter résumé. Here is one small glimpse of that famous two-horse match, with both horses heading into the backstretch:

> *The horses stretched out over the track. Their strides, each twenty-one feet in length, fell in perfect synch. They rubbed shoulders and hips, heads snapping up and reaching out together, legs gathering up and unfolding in unison. The poles clipped by, blurring in the riders' peripheral vision . . . The track rail hummed up under them and unwound behind.*
>
> (From *Seabiscuit* by Laura Hillenbrand. 2001. New York: Random House, p. 272)

Count the verbs—you may be surprised by the number in this small passage. Which do you think are especially strong? (You may wish to read Hillenbrand's full account of the race, start to finish: pp. 270–274. The number of verbs within the complete passage is equally impressive.) Now go back and look for adjectives and adverbs. You will see that they are used sparingly. How often does Hillenbrand use more than one verb in a single sentence?

Step 3: Involving Students as Evaluators

Ask students to review Samples A and B, considering whether each writer has made the most of potential verb power—and has written a piece that would make an effective voice-under for a documentary. Ask them to work together, underlining passages that work well, and making marginal notes about passages that could be eliminated or revised.

Discussing Results

Most students should find Sample A stronger. Writer A creates a concise account in which verbs dominate. By contrast, Sample B is wordy and over-reliant on modifiers, never allowing verbs to show off their full power. One possible revision of Sample B is provided.

Step 4: Modeling Revision

- Share Sample C (*Whole Class Revision*) with students. Read the original aloud.
- Ask students whether the writer has made maximum use of verb power, and whether the piece as is would make an effective documentary voice-under. (Most should say *no*.)
- Give students time to discuss the piece with a partner, talking through each of the three strategies from this lesson in turn: condensing, minimizing modifiers (both adjectives and adverbs), and using multiple verbs within a single sentence.
- As a class, discuss revision possibilities, and work through the strategies one at a time, asking students to envision the images that might accom-

pany this text. Begin by crossing out any words that are not needed, rephrasing as necessary to smooth the flow.

- Next, see if any modifiers can be eliminated—perhaps by strengthening a verb.
- Finally, try working more than one verb into at least one sentence.
- When you finish, read your final revision aloud, making any last-minute changes that enhance the power of the text.
- If you wish, compare your revision to ours, keeping in mind that your revision is likely to be quite different from ours.

Step 5: Revising with Partners

Share Sample D (*Revising with Partners*). Ask students to follow the basic steps you modeled with Sample C. *Working with partners,* they should:

- Read the passage aloud.
- Talk about revision possibilities, imagining the video that might accompany this text.
- Begin by condensing, crossing out words or phrases that are not needed.
- Reduce the number of modifiers by strengthening some of the verbs.
- Bolster the power by working two, three, or more verbs into at least one sentence.
- Read the final revision aloud, with as much voice as possible, listening to the power of the verbs, and making any last-minute changes.

Step 6: Sharing and Discussing Results

When students have finished, ask several pairs of students to share their revisions aloud. After listening, ask the class as a whole to talk about which revisions most sound like authentic voice-under script. Did any of the teams manage to use as many verbs as Laura Hillenbrand? If you wish, compare your revisions with ours, keeping in mind that our changes are likely to be very different.

Next Steps

- Ask students to revise a piece of their own writing, using the strategies identified in this lesson.
- Consider the books your students have read that (like *Seabiscuit*) have been translated into film. What impact might verbs have on a film maker's ability to capture something on the screen? Would a piece with weak verbs be more difficult to turn into a film?
- Send for a video script your students can analyze. Notice how spare the language is—how it avoids repetition and relies heavily on verbs. Ask how many of your students have considered a career doing such writing.

- Look and listen for strong, multiple verbs in the literature you share aloud. Recommended:
  - **Seabiscuit* by Laura Hillenbrand. 2001. New York: Random House.
  - *Aleutian Sparrow* by Karen Hesse. 2003. New York: Aladdin.
  - **The Book Thief* by Marcus Zusak. 2005. New York: Alfred A. Knopf.
  - **Fahrenheit 451* by Ray Bradbury. 1953 (renewed 1981). New York: Random House.
  - **Secretariat: The Making of a Champion* by William Nack. 2002. New York: Da Capo Press.
  - *Team Moon: How 400,000 People Landed Apollo 11 on the Moon* by Catherine Thimmesh. 2006. Boston: Houghton Mifflin.
  - **Winterdance* by Gary Paulsen. 1994. Orlando: Harcourt Brace.
- *For an additional challenge:* Ask students to create a voice-under script for an actual video—and to produce the video. View it as a class, and talk about how the words and video need to complement each other.

*Indicates a book written for a young adult *through* adult audience. These books may contain adult language and themes.

Suggested Responses to "Going for a Triple Play," p. 191

Strategy 1

Do men and women differ in how they gesture as they speak? To find out, behavioral psychologists observe speakers of both sexes, recording each time a speaker touches his or her face, hair, or clothing; gestures in the air; or touches a nearby object, such as a book or table. (50 words—down from 93)

Strategy 2

- Move slowly **inch, creep, tiptoe, slide, slip, dawdle, plod, lag, trail**
- Talk loudly **scream, yell, holler, shout, clamor, shriek, squall, roar, bellow**
- Touch lightly **finger, tap, caress, brush, stroke, pat, bump**
- Work hard **labor, toil, slave, grind, stress, strain, struggle**
- Go quickly **dash, tear, bolt, zoom, whisk, thunder, scurry, skedaddle, abscond**

Strategy 3

Original from *To Kill a Mockingbird*:

The tire bumped on gravel, skeetered across the road, crashed into a barrier and popped me like a cork onto pavement.
(From *To Kill a Mockingbird by* Harper Lee. 1988. New York: HarperPerennial, p. 42)

Possible imitative sentence:

The forward ripped down the field, danced by frustrated blockers, slipped and slogged through the mud, and smacked the ball into the net.

Sample A: Everest

Wordy?
Too many modifiers?
More than one verb per sentence?

Mt. Everest is widely regarded as the highest mountain on Earth, soaring 29,028 feet from base to summit. (Mauna Kea in Hawaii is taller measured from its base on the ocean floor—but does not stretch as far above sea level as Everest.) The mountain stands guard on the border between Nepal and Tibet, beckoning admirers and daredevils alike. Many take the dare. Each year, climbers ranging from experienced mountaineers to novices pay $25,000 to risk everything for a chance at glory. Most succumb to cold or buckle under the physical strain, and retreat before ever approaching the far heights. Near the peak, oxygen plummets to precarious levels, temperatures transform snow to ice, and raging winds pierce even the most protective clothing. More than 200 people have slid to their deaths—or yielded to the harsh conditions. Some bodies remain, to this day, where they fell.

Sir Edmund Hillary of New Zealand guided a successful expedition to the top of Everest in 1953—and is generally honored as the first climber to plant his foot on its summit. Many other attempts have followed. In 1996, several expeditions brought climbers to within striking distance of the top—but that year marked the single deadliest year in Everest's history, with fifteen people losing their lives on the mountain. Journalist Jon Krakauer was part of one expedition that year, and his experience inspired him to write the book *Into Thin Air*—a book that has aroused climbing fever among climbers throughout the world.

Sample B: Boy Soldiers

Wordy?
Too many modifiers?
More than one verb per sentence?

Most people study the Civil War, at least briefly, and in doing so, many may picture in their minds grizzled soldiers in their forties, fifties, or sixties. While many were no doubt soldiers of such age, or older, the truth is that many soldiers of the Civil War were boys between the ages of fourteen and sixteen. Some may even have been younger. Recruiters were desperate for enlistees, after all, and did not necessarily take great care with their enlistment procedures. It was easy for a boy seeking adventure to be accepted as a soldier at that difficult time. Some estimates place the number of young soldiers (under sixteen) at somewhere between a quarter and half million.

In an age before telecommunication, many of the soldiers kept diaries or journals. They were writers. From their writings and from their letters home, we have learned much about what they experienced. For most (if not all) of them, the experience of war was very different from what they had anticipated, with death, loneliness, heartache, and bloodshed around every corner. Still, in the midst of suffering and upheaval, these young men made a record of their experiences, writing about their raggedy clothing, meager food, inadequate medical care, enduring friendship, and the personal resilience that kept them hanging together—a record that remains with us to this day through their writing.

Information for this sample is taken in part from *The Boys' War* by Jim Murphy. 1990. New York: Clarion Books.

Revision of Sample B

~~Most people study~~ The Civil War may call up images of ~~at least briefly, and in doing so, many may picture in their minds~~ grizzled soldiers in their forties, fifties, or ~~sixties. While many were no doubt soldiers of such age, or~~ older, but many soldiers who fought and died on Civil War battlefields ~~the truth is that many soldiers of the Civil War~~ were boys sixteen or younger. ~~between the ages of fourteen and sixteen. Some may even have been younger.~~ Recruiters ~~were~~ desperate for enlistees, welcomed anyone who would put on a uniform, disregarding proper ~~after all, and did not necessarily take great care with their~~ enlistment procedures and happily handing out ammunition and a haversack to any ~~It was easy for a~~ boy seeking adventure. Somewhere between a quarter and a half million ~~to be accepted as a soldier at that difficult time. Some estimates place the number of young~~ soldiers (under sixteen) ~~at somewhere between a quarter and half million~~ would march headlong into a world of horror and death. Fewer would march back.

Luckily for us, they recorded their adventures in ~~In an age before telecommunication, many of the soldiers kept~~ diaries, ~~or~~ journals, ~~They were writers. From their writings and from their~~ or letters home. ~~we have learned much about what they experienced. For most (if not all) of them, the~~ They documented ~~experience of war was very different from what they had anticipated, with~~ death, loneliness, heartache, and bloodshed in words that shock our sensibilities still. Yet even as they suffered, starved, bled, and mended one another, they took time to capture the tiniest details ~~around every corner. Still, in the midst of suffering and upheaval, these young men made a record of their experiences, writing~~ about their raggedy clothing, meager food, inadequate medical care, and enduring friendship. Their ~~and the~~ personal resilience ~~that kept them hanging together—a record that remains with us to this day through their writing~~ resounds in every line—and today transports us back to a time they preserved for us.

Sample C: Whole Class Revision

Wordy?
Too many modifiers?
More than one verb per sentence?

Last Haul

Fishermen always eagerly await the final catch of any fishing trip. If it's a good haul, they can finish their fishing voyage and return to port for three welcome months of rest. If the nets are empty, they must remain at sea for several more days. They might even have to remain out for several more weeks, depending on how long it takes them to find another productive fishing spot.

The wind and cold make hauling in the heavy nets harder. The ropes become slippery and hard to handle. The fish are heavy, and workers must work hard to haul the nets up onto the deck.

When at last they haul the last of the fish on board, they weigh the catch. If the weight is sufficient, everyone is extremely happy.

Then, a whole series of tasks begins. First, workers load the fish into a giant receptacle that takes them through the ship's processing plant. They are sorted first to make sure they are all healthy. Just before sorting, they are cleaned. Then after sorting, they are rinsed again. They must also be scaled and filleted. Finally, the fish are frozen. Giant packs of frozen fish remain in the ship's freezer until it returns to port. Those frozen fish are worth a small fortune on the American market. Many Americans eat fish from Canadian or Alaskan waters—though few appreciate the time and trouble required to catch and prepare them.

Sample D: Revising with Partners

> Wordy?
> Too many modifiers?
> More than one verb per sentence?

The Fence Effect

Eco-scientists are increasingly intrigued by the impact of something known as the so-called Fence Effect on small mammals such as voles. This phenomenon is based on the observation that animals (such as voles) within a fenced area tend to experience a population surge followed by a population crash. The surge and crash are related to the fact that the animals are fenced in and cannot escape. Even if predators are capable of entering the area, the surge and subsequent crash are still observed. Providing the animals with food inside the area of confinement does not appear to affect the surge or crash either.

Some scientists speculate that the Fence Effect may be the result of social behavior on the part of the animals. Aggressive animals cannot escape and this eventually has a devastating effect on the population. In addition, when space is limited, female voles may attack and kill the young of other females. This also precipitates the eventual crash. Scientists still are not sure how large the fenced area would need to be before the Fence Effect would no longer be observed.

> **Information for this sample is based in part on Barry Shell, *Sensational Scientists: The Journeys and Discoveries of 24 Men and Women of Science*. 2005. Vancouver: Raincoast Books. Pages 91–97.**

Suggested Revisions of C and D

Sample C: Whole Class Revision

Last Haul

Fishermen ~~always~~ eagerly await the final catch of any fishing trip. ~~If it's~~ A good haul ~~they can finish their fishing voyage and return~~ sends the ship sailing back to port for three welcome months of rest. ~~If the nets are empty, they must remain at sea for several more days. They might even have to remain out for several more weeks, depending on how long it takes them to find~~ Empty nets leave fishers battling the sea for as long as it takes to search out another productive fishing spot.

The wind and cold ~~make hauling in~~ force fishers to scrap for every inch as they haul in the heavy nets. ~~harder. The ropes become slippery and hard to handle. The fish are heavy, and workers must work hard to haul the nets up onto the deck.~~ Slick ropes cut their hands and break their grip—but not their determination.

~~When at last they haul the last of the fish on board, they weigh the catch. If the weight is sufficient, everyone is extremely happy.~~ Workers gather round as the catch is loaded onto the scales. They hold their breath awaiting the result—then cheers explode as weary fishers realize it's been a good haul.

~~Then, a whole series of tasks begins.~~ Everyone pitches in to finish the final tasks. First, on-deck workers load the fish into a giant receptacle that ~~takes them through~~ whisks them off to the ship's processing plant. ~~They are sorted first to make sure they are all healthy. Just before sorting, they are cleaned. Then after sorting, they are rinsed again. They must also be scaled and filleted.~~ Workers below deck are waiting to sort, rinse, clean, scale, and fillet the fish. Finally, ~~the fish are frozen. Giant packs of frozen fish remain in the ship's freezer until it~~ they pack them into giant packs to be frozen until the ship returns to port. Those frozen fish ~~are worth~~ will pull in a small fortune on the American market, ~~Many Americans eat~~ where people are all too happy to eat fish from Canadian or Alaskan waters—though few appreciate the time and trouble required to catch and prepare them.

Sample D: Revising with Partners

The Fence Effect

Eco-scientists are increasingly intrigued by the impact of something known as the ~~so-called~~ Fence Effect. ~~on~~ When small mammals such as voles are confined ~~This phenomenon is based on the observation that animals (such as voles)~~ within a fenced area, ~~tend to experience a~~ their population first explodes, and then dwindles to almost nothing. Scientists believe the population surges, then crashes, because ~~surge followed by a population crash. The surge and crash are related to the fact that~~ the animals are fenced in and cannot escape. ~~Even if~~ Releasing predators into ~~are capable of entering~~ the area does not prevent the initial population explosion. ~~the surge and subsequent crash are still observed. Providing~~ Furthermore, feeding the animals ~~with food inside the area of confinement does not appear to affect the surge or crash either~~ will not sustain the population, so long as they are confined.

Some scientists ~~speculate that~~ think the animals' own social behavior may trigger the Fence Effect. ~~may be the result of social behavior on the part of the animals~~ Aggressive animals that cannot escape ~~and this eventually has a devastating effect on the population~~ turn on the less aggressive members of the colony and kill them. In addition, when space is limited, female voles may attack and kill the young of other females. ~~This also precipitates the eventual crash~~ Internal warfare eventually wipes out the entire population. Scientists ~~still are not sure how large~~ wonder how far the fenced area would need to ~~be~~ stretch before the Fence Effect would ~~no longer be observed~~ disappear.

Information for this sample is based in part on Barry Shell, *Sensational Scientists: The Journeys and Discoveries of 24 Men and Women of Science*. 2005. Vancouver: Raincoast Books. Pages 91–97.

Putting It All Together Lesson 22

(Editing Lessons 12, 16, 18, and 20)

Trait Connection: **Conventions**

Introduction (Share with students in your own words—or as a handout.)

Whew. Those last three lessons have been fairly intense, with many editorial corrections in each lesson. We have focused on five areas of confusion that require even experienced editors to slow down and concentrate on meaning so that they can make careful choices about:

1. One-word and two-word pronouns
   - **No one** appreciates sloppy editing.
   - **None** are objecting, however.
   - **Someone** is at the door.
   - **Anyone** can become good at checkers.
   - **Any one** of your sisters might be Helen's bridesmaid.
   - Almost **everyone** loves chocolate.
   - **Every one** of my chocolates has been eaten!
2. All right and a lot
   - It is **all right** (NOT *alright*) with me if we stay at the beach.
   - Jim has **a lot** (NOT *alot*) of studying to do.
3. Correct verbs with indefinite pronouns
   - **Everyone** *is* excited about the dance.
   - **Everybody** *likes* to think he or she is right.
   - **Many** *are* undecided.
   - **A few** *have* made up their minds.
4. Sorting out sound-alikes
   - It is **their** turn.
   - **They're** saying the ball is right **there**, behind the tree.
   - It is **too** hot **to** go into the city.
   - Do you want to come, **too**?
   - Everyone decided to **accept**—**except** for Rudy.
   - We're **already** late, so I hope you are **all ready** to leave.

5. Capitals
    - I have to say that **Psych 101** is my toughest course.
    - I enjoy studying *psychology*, however.
    - I heard **Professor Forbes** has moved to the **English Department**.
    - I heard that one of the *professors* moved to a different *department*.
    - When you visit the **West**, don't miss the **Pacific Ocean**.
    - If you head *west*, you'll come to the *ocean*.

Please review all or part of Lessons 12, 16, 18, and 20 for additional examples. Feel free to keep those lessons plus your handbook nearby for additional help and reference as you work through this lesson. Remember to read aloud and to ask, "What is the intended meaning?" When you have a question about a capital, ask, "Is it a proper name or title—or only a category or description?" For this lesson, you will need to look for a wide range of problems. *Slow down*. Read silently—then out loud. It helps to go through any copy *more than once*. All professional editors do this. It is very likely that on your second time through you will catch *at least* one or two more problems you missed in your first reading.

Teaching the Lesson (General Guidelines for Teachers)

1. Begin by reviewing all or any part of the content for Lessons 12, 16, 18, and 20. (We have included Lesson 12 because it deals with singular and plural indefinite pronouns, and this is hard to separate from the pronoun forms themselves.) Answer any questions that students may have.
2. Encourage students to keep their work from these lessons handy as they do the editing for this lesson. Also provide handbooks and be sure students know how to use them to find the information they need (recommended: *Great Source: New Generation*).
3. Share the editing lesson on the following page. Students should read the passage silently (prior to doing any editing), then once more aloud (pencil in hand), looking *and listening* for problems. They will find a wide range of errors, so it is important to read slowly and carefully. For students who find this much editing challenging, *do just one paragraph at a time, dividing the lesson into four parts.*
4. Ask them to work individually first, then check with a partner.
5. When everyone is done, ask them to coach you as you edit the same copy, making any changes you and they decide are important. Discuss and/or explain changes as you go. When you finish, compare your edited copy to the one on page 206.

Editing Goal: Correct 42 errors.

Follow-Up: Read your own work silently and aloud to check for errors.

Editing Practice

Read silently and aloud to check for errors.

Mrs. Frawley's class, english 210, is working on a Take-Home Examination too be completed by the end of the Term. Every one is a little apprehensive, though their is really no reason too fret. Mrs. Frawley assures the class that there already for any question she can throw at them. "Every body in here are going to pass this test, I guarantee you!" she tells them.

A few students remains skeptical. Some are convinced they cannot pass, even though they have read the books on which the exam is based, *Of mice and men* by John Steinbeck and *To Kill a Mockingbird* by harper Lee. "Don't be such worry warts!" Mrs. Frawley sputters. "The whole English department is rooting for you!"

If any one can pass this test, it's Charles. He has all ready demonstrated his skill on previous tests. He studies alot, and is a member of a local Book Club. Besides, English is his favorite subject—next to math. He aces most tests, and gets A's on everyone of them. "Their is nothing hard about the test itself," says Charles. "It's the stress that gets two you and effects your memory."

One helpful thing is that every one is allowed to bring their own book too the test. That way, their able too look up favorite quotations. Extra Credit is given for any direct illusions to things characters in the books say or do. If the class does well, there scheduled for a Field Trip too sunnyville park, a local amusement center. That should be enough two motivate most students—accept those who suffer from motion sickness.

Edited Copy

42 corrections

Mrs. Frawley's class, english 210, is working on a Take-Home Examination ~~too~~ to be completed by the end of the Term. ~~Every one~~ Everyone is a little apprehensive, though ~~their~~ there is really no reason ~~too~~ to fret. Mrs. Frawley assures the class that ~~there already~~ they're all ready for any question she can throw at them. ~~"Every body~~ "Everybody in here ~~are~~ is going to pass this test, I guarantee you!" she tells them.

A few students ~~remains~~ remain skeptical. Some are convinced they cannot pass, even though they have read the books on which the exam is based, *Of mice and men* by John Steinbeck and *To Kill a Mockingbird* by harper Lee. "Don't be such worry warts!" Mrs. Frawley sputters. "The whole English department is rooting for you!"

If ~~any one~~ anyone can pass this test, it's Charles. He has ~~all ready~~ already demonstrated his skill on previous tests. He studies ~~alot~~ a lot, and is a member of a local Book Club. Besides, English is his favorite subject—next to math. He aces most tests, and gets A's on ~~everyone~~ every one of them. ~~"Their~~ "There is nothing hard about the test itself," says Charles. "It's the stress that gets ~~two~~ to you and ~~effects~~ affects your memory."

One helpful thing is that ~~every one~~ everyone is allowed to bring ~~their~~ his or her own book ~~too~~ to the test. That way, ~~their~~ they're able ~~too~~ to look up favorite quotations. Extra Credit is given for any direct ~~illusions~~ allusions to things characters in the books say or do. If the class does well, ~~there~~ they're scheduled for a Field Trip ~~too~~ to sunnyville park, a local amusement center. That should be enough ~~two~~ to motivate most students—~~accept~~ except those who suffer from motion sickness.

Editing Practice

Read silently and aloud to check for errors.

Mrs. Frawley's class, english 210, is working on a Take-Home Examination too be completed by the end of the Term. Every one is a little apprehensive, though their is really no reason too fret. Mrs. Frawley assures the class that there already for any question she can throw at them. "Every body in here are going to pass this test, I guarantee you!" she tells them.

A few students remains skeptical. Some are convinced they cannot pass, even though they have read the books on which the exam is based, *Of mice and men* by John Steinbeck and *To Kill a Mockingbird* by harper Lee. "Don't be such worry warts!" Mrs. Frawley sputters. "The whole English department is rooting for you!"

If any one can pass this test, it's Charles. He has all ready demonstrated his skill on previous tests. He studies alot, and is a member of a local Book Club. Besides, English is his favorite subject—next to math. He aces most tests, and gets A's on everyone of them. "Their is nothing hard about the test itself," says Charles. "It's the stress that gets two you and effects your memory."

One helpful thing is that every one is allowed to bring their own book too the test. That way, their able too look up favorite quotations. Extra Credit is given for any direct illusions to things characters in the books say or do. If the class does well, there scheduled for a Field Trip too sunnyville park, a local amusement center. That should be enough two motivate most students—accept those who suffer from motion sickness.

Edited Copy

42 corrections

Mrs. Frawley's class, english 210, is working on a Take-Home Examination ~~too~~ to be completed by the end of the Term. ~~Every one~~ Everyone is a little apprehensive, though ~~their~~ there is really no reason ~~too~~ to fret. Mrs. Frawley assures the class that ~~there already~~ they're all ready for any question she can throw at them. ~~"Every body~~ "Everybody in here ~~are~~ is going to pass this test, I guarantee you!" she tells them.

A few students ~~remains~~ remain skeptical. Some are convinced they cannot pass, even though they have read the books on which the exam is based, *Of mice and men* by John Steinbeck and *To Kill a Mockingbird* by harper Lee. "Don't be such worry warts!" Mrs. Frawley sputters. "The whole English department is rooting for you!"

If ~~any one~~ anyone can pass this test, it's Charles. He has ~~all ready~~ already demonstrated his skill on previous tests. He studies ~~alot~~ a lot, and is a member of a local Book Club. Besides, English is his favorite subject—next to math. He aces most tests, and gets A's on ~~everyone~~ every one of them. ~~"Their~~ "There is nothing hard about the test itself," says Charles. "It's the stress that gets ~~two~~ to you and ~~effects~~ affects your memory."

One helpful thing is that ~~every one~~ everyone is allowed to bring ~~their~~ his or her own book ~~too~~ to the test. That way, ~~their~~ they're able ~~too~~ to look up favorite quotations. Extra Credit is given for any direct ~~illusions~~ allusions to things characters in the books say or do. If the class does well, ~~there~~ they're scheduled for a Field Trip ~~too~~ to sunnyville park, a local amusement center. That should be enough ~~two~~ to motivate most students—~~accept~~ except those who suffer from motion sickness.

Editing Practice

Read silently and aloud to check for errors.

Mrs. Frawley's class, english 210, is working on a Take-Home Examination too be completed by the end of the Term. Every one is a little apprehensive, though their is really no reason too fret. Mrs. Frawley assures the class that there already for any question she can throw at them. "Every body in here are going to pass this test, I guarantee you!" she tells them.

A few students remains skeptical. Some are convinced they cannot pass, even though they have read the books on which the exam is based, *Of mice and men* by John Steinbeck and *To Kill a Mockingbird* by harper Lee. "Don't be such worry warts!" Mrs. Frawley sputters. "The whole English department is rooting for you!"

If any one can pass this test, it's Charles. He has all ready demonstrated his skill on previous tests. He studies alot, and is a member of a local Book Club. Besides, English is his favorite subject—next to math. He aces most tests, and gets A's on everyone of them. "Their is nothing hard about the test itself," says Charles. "It's the stress that gets two you and effects your memory."

One helpful thing is that every one is allowed to bring their own book too the test. That way, their able too look up favorite quotations. Extra Credit is given for any direct illusions to things characters in the books say or do. If the class does well, there scheduled for a Field Trip too sunnyville park, a local amusement center. That should be enough two motivate most students—accept those who suffer from motion sickness.

Edited Copy

42 corrections

Mrs. Frawley's class, english 210, is working on a Take-Home Examination ~~too~~ to be completed by the end of the Term. ~~Every one~~ Everyone is a little apprehensive, though ~~their~~ there is really no reason ~~too~~ to fret. Mrs. Frawley assures the class that ~~there already~~ they're all ready for any question she can throw at them. ~~"Every body~~ "Everybody in here ~~are~~ is going to pass this test, I guarantee you!" she tells them.

A few students ~~remains~~ remain skeptical. Some are convinced they cannot pass, even though they have read the books on which the exam is based, *Of mice and men* by John Steinbeck and *To Kill a Mockingbird* by harper Lee. "Don't be such worry warts!" Mrs. Frawley sputters. "The whole English department is rooting for you!"

If ~~any one~~ anyone can pass this test, it's Charles. He has ~~all ready~~ already demonstrated his skill on previous tests. He studies ~~alot~~ a lot, and is a member of a local Book Club. Besides, English is his favorite subject—next to math. He aces most tests, and gets A's on ~~everyone~~ every one of them. ~~"Their~~ "There is nothing hard about the test itself," says Charles. "It's the stress that gets ~~two~~ to you and ~~effects~~ affects your memory."

One helpful thing is that ~~every one~~ everyone is allowed to bring ~~their~~ his or her own book ~~too~~ to the test. That way, ~~their~~ they're able ~~too~~ to look up favorite quotations. Extra Credit is given for any direct ~~illusions~~ allusions to things characters in the books say or do. If the class does well, ~~there~~ they're scheduled for a Field Trip ~~too~~ to sunnyville park, a local amusement center. That should be enough ~~two~~ to motivate most students—~~accept~~ except those who suffer from motion sickness.

Revising with One-Syllable Words

Lesson 23

Trait Connection: **Word Choice**

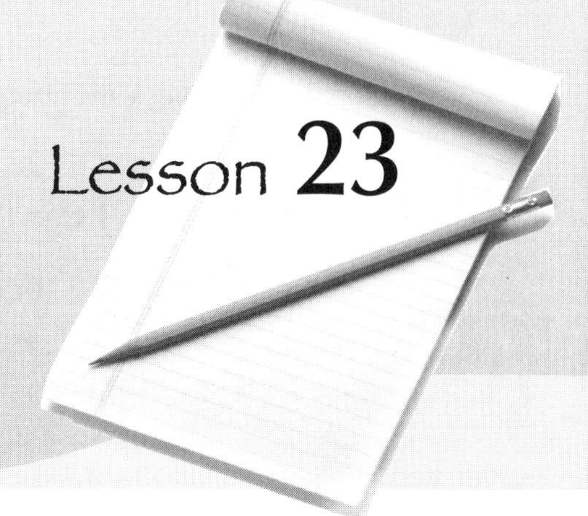

Introduction

Hold the phone. One-syllable words? Wouldn't that be a task for younger writers? Actually, no. Writing a complex message using only one-syllable words is extremely challenging. Two things have to happen. First, as a writer and *reader*, you have to understand the message at the most basic level. This requires interpretation, and sometimes inference as well. Second, you need to stretch for the right words, the words that will convey your message clearly. Just because a word has only one syllable, that doesn't mean it isn't capable of conveying a sophisticated meaning. Here's a hint to guide you through this lesson: Don't go with the first word that pops into your head. Take time to think. Reach for words that will speak to your readers. You'll be surprised how often those are the one-syllable words!

Teacher's Sidebar . . .

Students will most surely not be writing in one-syllable words from this point forward. But within the bounds of this lesson, it is an excellent exercise. That's because in one-syllable text, there is nowhere to hide. Anyone who has read many political speeches knows that multisyllabic nonsense can be used to camouflage lack of thought and substance. One-syllable text is revealing. It pares the writer's thinking right down to the bone. If a writer really has nothing to say, the simple, unadorned text will give him (or her) away.

Focus and Intent

This lesson is intended to help students:

- Understand that when the message is clear in the writer's mind, he or she can convey it in simple terms.
- Identify a message "buried" in multisyllabic text.
- Revise multisyllabic text to clarify meaning using only one-syllable words.

Teaching the Lesson

Step 1: Decoding

Following are some quotations from well-known authors. The object is not to try to *improve* on their words—but rather, to see if you can understand what they are saying so clearly that you can put the message in *other* words, all one-syllable words, that is. The first one is done for you.

1. *There was only the girl walking with him now, her face bright as snow in the moonlight, and he knew she was working his questions around, seeking the best answers she could possibly give.*

   One-syllable version:

   Just one girl walked with him now, her face bright as snow in the light of the moon, and he knew each thing he asked made her pause to think, as she searched for words that would ease his mind.

2. *Governors allowed the conquered peoples to preserve their laws and customs. For the ruling of so many different peoples no other policy was as sensible as tolerance.*

   One-syllable version:

   ____

   ____

3. *The pigs did not actually work, but directed and supervised the others. With their superior knowledge it was natural that they should assume the leadership.*

   One-syllable version:

   ____

   ____

Sources for quotations:

1. *Fahrenheit 451* by Ray Bradbury. 1982. New York: Random House, p. 7.
2. *The Human Story: Our History from the Stone Age to Today* by James C. Davis. 2005. New York: HarperPerennial, p. 91.
3. *Animal Farm* by George Orwell. 2004 (50th anniversary edition). New York: Signet Classics, p. 35.

Suggested responses for samples 2 and 3 appear at the end of "Next Steps," page 211.

Step 2: Making the Reading-Writing Connection

Finding a passage from literature that is written *exclusively* in one-syllable words is difficult. Writers (unless challenged to do so) do not typically sit down and announce, "Today I'll write only in one-syllable words." Nevertheless, some of our best writers are known for a natural eloquence that comes, in part, from a gift for using simple words well. One such writer is Gary Paulsen. In *Puppies, Dogs and Blue Northers*, Paulsen details his experience of raising sled dogs to run in Alaska's famed Iditarod. His favorite dog—and the team leader—Cookie, has just given birth to pups, one of which was stillborn. Thinking he was being kind, Gary has removed the pup, but Cookie has quietly, secretly retrieved it. When Gary discovers this, he tries once more to remove the pup, but this time finds himself looking right into the eyes of an angry sled dog—and there is no mistaking her message:

> *I will pull your sled,* she said, *and love you and lead the team and save your life and be loyal to all that you are and obey you in all things until I cannot, but if you touch my pup you die.*
>
> (From *Puppies, Dogs and Blue Northers* by Gary Paulsen. 1996. Orlando: Harcourt Brace, p. 20)

Do the words of this passage gain a certain power from the simple, direct language? Paulsen tells us that it is not until four days later that Cookie will let him remove the dead pup, "But even then she growled, this time not at me but at the fates, at all of it. That she would lose a young one—a growl at life." Paulsen's elegant prose reminds us that we do not always need complex words to express complex thoughts.

Step 3: Involving Students as Evaluators

Ask students to review Samples A and B, considering which writer has done the best job of expressing him- or herself simply. Ask them to work together, considering how best to rephrase passages from the more complex sample.

Discussing Results

Most students should find Sample B simpler. Writer A opts for more complexity than is required, given the topic. By contrast, Sample B expresses thoughts simply with very few words of more than one syllable. One possible revision of Sample A is provided.

Step 4: Modeling Revision

- Share Sample C (*Whole Class Revision*) with students. Read the original aloud.
- Ask students whether the writer has managed to convey her message in relatively simple language—one-syllable words, that is. (Most should say *no.*)
- Give students time to discuss the piece with partners, talking through revision possibilities and focusing on the writer's message. What—precisely—is she trying to say?

- As a class, discuss revision possibilities, and work through the revision sentence by sentence, asking students to brainstorm one-syllable possibilities. Use a dictionary or thesaurus to help you find the *best* way to express each thought.
- Translate as much of the text as you can into one-syllable words. If you can do it all, great. Try for a revision with *no more than three words of two syllables or more.*
- When you finish, read your final revision aloud, making any last-minute changes that fine tune meaning without resorting to more complex language. Remember, this isn't *just* about coming up with short words; it's about making the message clear.
- If you wish, compare your revision to ours, keeping in mind that your revision is likely to be quite different from ours.

Step 5: Revising with Partners

Share Sample D (*Revising with Partners*). Ask students to follow the basic steps you modeled with Sample C. *Working with partners,* they should:

- Read the passage aloud.
- Talk about the writer's message: What is he trying to convey to readers?
- Revise sentence by sentence, keeping the primary message in mind, and searching for the best one-syllable words to convey that message. Use a dictionary or thesaurus, if it is helpful.
- Read the final revision aloud, with as much voice as possible, listening for clarity, and making any last-minute changes.

Step 6: Sharing and Discussing Results

When students have finished, ask several pairs of students to share their revisions aloud. After listening, ask the class as a whole to talk about which revisions best captured the message. Which specific words were particularly effective? Did any of the teams manage to translate the entire piece into one-syllable words? If you wish, compare your revisions with ours, keeping in mind that our changes are likely to be different.

Next Steps

- Ask students to periodically practice the one-syllable strategy, using a sample from any textbook, periodical, or newspaper as the original copy. This lesson reinforces skills in both reading and writing with care.
- Invite students to review a sample of their own writing, not with the goal of translating every sentence into one-syllable text, but rather as a check to see if any of the language is unnecessarily inflated. If it is, bring it back down to earth.

- The ability to use simple language to convey extraordinary and profound meaning is not common even in the literary community. So, search for samples to add to this list, and celebrate any you find. Recommended:
  - **Puppies, Dogs and Blue Northers* by Gary Paulsen. 1996. Orlando: Harcourt Brace.
  - **The House on Mango Street* by Sandra Cisneros. 1991. New York: Vintage.
  - **Fahrenheit 451* by Ray Bradbury. 1953 (renewed 1981). New York: Random House.
  - **The Old Man and the Sea* by Ernest Hemingway. 1980. New York: Scribner.
- *For an additional challenge:* Take any complex piece and translate it into text that would be appropriate for a grade one picture book. It is *not* necessary to use one-syllable words exclusively for this exercise; young readers/writers do not want authors to be condescending. What matters is capturing the heart of the message and putting it into words that a beginning reader would find comprehensible, appealing enough to learn and recall, or both. Where in the world of publishing would this "translating" skill be useful?

*Indicates a book written for a young adult *through* adult audience. These books may contain adult language and themes.

Suggested Responses to "Decoding," p. 208

2. *Governors allowed the conquered peoples to preserve their laws and customs. For the ruling of so many different peoples no other policy was as sensible as tolerance.*

   Those who had won the fight and now ruled let those who had lost keep their laws and old ways. Since all new rules are strange to some, it is wise for those who rule vast lands to be fair and just.

3. *The pigs did not actually work, but directed and supervised the others. With their superior knowledge it was natural that they should assume the leadership.*

   The pigs did no real work, but watched to see that the rest would work hard and not shirk. Since they were both wise and smart, it seemed right that they would be the ones to take the lead.

Sample A

Simple?
Can you simplify
it further?

The following was prepared as a recorded message to be read aloud to people on hold.

Bicycle Safety

When biking, it is vital to respect safety regulations. First, always wear a helmet.* Second, select a bicycle appropriate for your size and stature. To assess this, straddle the bike; you should be able to rest comfortably on the tips of your feet. Third, become familiar with the traffic patterns in any area where you plan to ride. And fourth, when crossing any street where vehicles are routinely present, plan to dismount and walk the bike across the intersection, rather than riding it across. Attention to these few requirements will make biking a pleasant recreational experience for everyone!

***Note: It is not necessary to find a substitute for the word *helmet*.**

Sample B

Simple?
Can you simplify
it further?

A New Way In**

A new form of X-ray called *computer tomography** lets scientists* look at fossils* in a whole new way. The new X-rays slice up fossils old as rocks into strips so thin it's just as if they'd been cut with a sharp knife. A fossil that old is frail to be sure, and if it were to be cut with a *real* knife, it would break or turn to dust with the first stroke. The X-ray keeps the fossil in one piece, but still makes each part as clear as if viewed through a lens. Best of all, there is not one scratch, bruise or dent—and a scientist can take in the whole form one slice at a time. What a great way to take our eyes and minds to a world we once had to dream up in our minds.

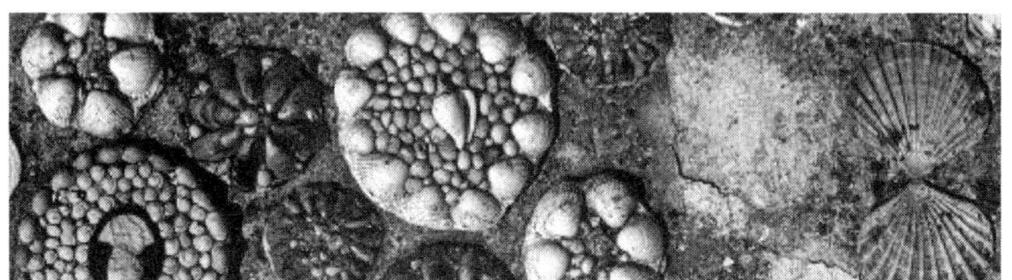

**Computer tomography* is a technical term for which no suitable synonym exists (so far as we know). Similarly, *fossil* and *scientist* have no suitable synonyms, so we have kept those terms. A gold star for you if you can come up with a good substitute for either one!

**Information for this sample is taken in part from "X-Ray Advancement" in *Science Illustrated,* ed. Mark Jannot. March/April 2008. Copenhagen: Bonnier Publications, page 18.

Revision of Sample A

Be Safe When You Bike!
~~Bicycle Safety~~

If you ride a bike, know the rules. ~~When biking, it is vital to respect safety regulations.~~ First, be sure you ~~always~~ wear a helmet when you ride. Second, choose a bike that fits you. To check the fit, do this: Stand up with one leg on each side of ~~select a bicycle appropriate for your size and stature. To assess this, straddle~~ the bike; if you can ~~you should be able to~~ rest both feet on the ground, the bike is the right size. ~~comfortably on the tips of your feet.~~ Third, learn how ~~become familiar with~~ the traffic flows in each place ~~patterns in any area~~ where you plan to ride. And fourth, when you cross a ~~crossing any~~ street where cars or trucks run, ~~vehicles are routinely present,~~ ~~plan to dismount and walk the bike across the intersection, rather than riding it across. Attention to these few requirements will make biking a pleasant recreational experience for everyone.~~ get off and walk your bike. Don't ride in front of cars. In short—know the rules, don't take risks, and have the time of your life.

Sample C: Whole Class Revision

Simple?
Can you simplify
it further?

Creative Thinking

Psychologists* believe that the height of a ceiling* may actually influence creativity. Who knows? Perhaps people subconsciously see the ceiling as an extension of their brain's functioning. Apparently people in a low-ceilinged room have a tendency to fixate on details. On the other hand, persons in a high-ceilinged space have a tendency to engage in more creative and abstract thinking. If further research confirms these initial hypotheses, should such findings have a bearing on how classrooms or offices are constructed? Perhaps architecture will revolutionize problem solving.

*** These words need not be revised. All others are fair game!**

Sample D: Revising with Partners

Simple?
Can you simplify it further?

What Are Our Sleep Requirements?

All animals* seem to engage in some form of rest or inactivity during the day. Even insects* follow biological rhythms that seem to be controlled by natural cycles of light and dark. Evidently, however, such creatures do not experience the deep sleep common to mammals.* During such sleep, mammals lose awareness of their surroundings, something insects do not apparently experience. In addition, deep sleep allows mammals to experience a different kind of brain activity—and this allows them to remain mentally functional. When they do not sleep, this mental alertness is significantly compromised. No one seems certain of the reasons driving our noticeable need for sleep. Some scientists* believe that sleep may be essential for protecting the immune system.* Others feel it is related to digestion since herbivores like cows or horses seem to require far less sleep than carnivores such as bears or lions. Perhaps additional research will resolve such mysteries.

*** These words need not be revised. All others are fair game!**

Suggested Revisions of C and D

Sample C: Whole Class Revision

Raise the Roof! ~~Creative Thinking~~

Could high ceilings help us think? Some psychologists say yes! ~~Psychologists believe that the height of a ceiling may actually influence creativity.~~ Who knows? ~~Perhaps people subconsciously see the ceiling as an extension of their~~ It could be that when we raise the ceiling, we take the lid off for our minds as well! It seems that when the ceiling comes down, we tend to look at the small things. But when the ceiling goes up, the mind can stretch and flex. New thoughts and new ways to see the world flood our brains. ~~brain's functioning. Apparently people in a low-ceilinged room have a tendency to fixate on details. On the other hand, persons in a high-ceilinged space have a tendency to engage in more creative and abstract thinking.~~ If these first thoughts and hopes turn out to be true, ~~further research confirms these initial hypotheses,~~ should ~~such findings have a bearing on how classrooms or offices are constructed? Perhaps architecture will revolutionize problem solving.~~ we all opt for high ceilings in schools—or at work? It could be just the thing! Think of it—a world with no catch or snag or glitch too tough to take on! Just raise the roof and stand back!

Sample D: Revising with Partners

How Much Sleep Do We Need?

~~**What Are Our Sleep Requirements?**~~

need rest of some kind each Like us,

All animals seem to ~~engage in some form of rest or inactivity during the~~ day. ~~Even~~

seem to have a kind of clock that is tuned in to shifts from

insects ~~follow biological rhythms that seem to be controlled by natural cycles of~~ light

to At the same time, it seems that insects do not need that

~~and~~ dark. ~~Evidently, however, such creatures do not experience~~ the deep sleep ~~common~~

must have to thrive. In the midst of such all sense of time and place, while

~~to~~ mammals. ~~During such~~ sleep, mammals lose ~~awareness of their surroundings~~

seem to go "out of it" in quite this way. What's more, lets

~~something~~ insects do not ~~apparently experience. In addition,~~ deep sleep ~~allows~~ mammals

use their brains in a way that "clears their heads" makes

~~to experience a different kind of brain activity~~—and this ~~allows~~ them ~~to remain mentally~~

wake up sharp and "fit to roar." though, they lose their edge.

~~functional~~. When they do not sleep, ~~this mental alertness is significantly compromised~~.

to know for sure just why we need to sleep so much.

No one seems ~~certain of the reasons driving our noticeable need for sleep~~. Some

think that lots of help keep strong. But some

scientists ~~believe that~~ sleep may ~~be essential for protecting~~ the immune system. ~~Others~~

based more on what we eat. Animals that live on plants

feel it is ~~related to digestion since herbivores like cows or horses~~ seem to ~~require~~

get by with

far less sleep than ~~carnivores such as bears or lions. Perhaps additional research will resolve such mysteries.~~ those who crave meat. A horse may sleep a mere hour or two, while a lion will snore right through the whole day. Once we learn just why we need to sleep, we may find a way to spend more time on our feet!

Helping Characters Speak

Lesson 24

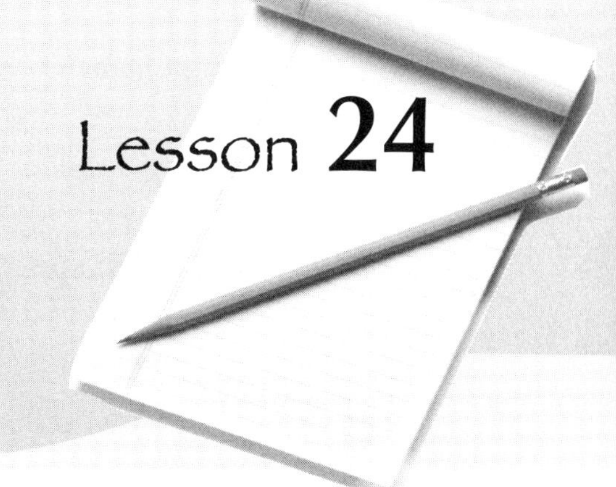

Trait Connection: **Conventions**

Introduction (Share with students in your own words—or as a handout.)

If you've ever read a comic strip or graphic novel, chances are you've noticed a "bubble" used to set off the actual words a character speaks. In most writing, quotation marks work just like that bubble. They mark the beginning—and the end—of what a speaker says. Quotation marks:

- Always come in pairs.
- Always set off *precisely* what the speaker says, and nothing more.
- Surround punctuation that is part of the quotation.

Following are some examples. Pay particular attention to the punctuation: the comma that sets up the quotation and the end punctuation that shows how to read the speech. The speaker might be making a statement, asking a question, or shouting. The punctuation just before the closing quotation marks gives you a clue:

Janet said, "You did some good work on that editing."

"I thought it was good, too," added Erika.

"Oh, did you like it?" Bob asked.

"You missed about a thousand commas!" screamed Marcia (who was *always* in a bad mood).

Notice how the quotation marks effectively "draw a bubble" around just what the speaker says. Notice also that in the first example (Janet speaking), the quotation is *introduced by a comma*. That's because the sentence begins by identifying the speaker—Janet. In the second example, a comma ends the quotation. That comma takes the place of a period because although Erika has finished speaking, the *sentence itself* doesn't really end until the words "said Erika." A period after "I thought it was good, too" would be confusing. The third and fourth examples use a question mark and exclamation point in place of a comma. These marks show how Bob (asking a question) and Marcia (exploding) are expressing themselves.

Special Cases

1. **When speech is interrupted**. When a speaker's words are interrupted *in the middle of a sentence*, the second part of the quotation does not begin with a capital:

   "Hawaii," said Mark, "is one of my favorite places to visit."

   "But," said Janet, "wouldn't you say Florida is fun, too?"

2. **Quoting a single word or phrase**. When the material being quoted is a single word or phrase, no comma is needed to set it up:

   Bob felt rather bad later, recalling how Marcia had accused him of missing "about a thousand commas."

3. **Asking a question *about* a quotation**. Asking a question *about* a quotation is different from asking a question *within* a quotation. In the first situation, the question mark comes *outside* the quotation marks. Notice the difference between these two examples:

   Had Marcia really accused him of missing "a thousand commas"? (The question is *about* the quotation.)

   Marcia asked, "Do you ever proofread your editing?" (Here the question is *part of* the quotation, so the question mark goes inside the quotation marks.)

One last reminder: So long as one person is still speaking, all of that person's speech *can* remain in one paragraph—unless it goes on for a long time, or the speaker changes topics. But every single time someone *new* speaks, the writer *must* begin a new paragraph. That's because it can sometimes get confusing to the reader, who wonders which person is speaking. You may have noticed that not all books offer clues like "said Bob" and "said Fran." When names are missing, paragraphing helps the reader—rather like following a tennis ball back and forth across the net. New paragraphs are marked with this symbol: ¶ Quotation marks are inserted with an inverted caret, and the quotation marks tucked inside, like this: “ ”

Warm-Up

In these warm-up sentences, some quotation marks and other punctuation are missing. See if you can spot all the oversights and insert them as needed:

1. "It's my turn to bat, announced Jake.
2. "I thought," said Robin, that you had been up already."
3. "I can settle this" said the coach. "It was Jake's twin brother John who batted earlier."
4. "Isn't it hard to tell you guys apart" asked Robin.
5. "Batter up" yelled the coach.
6. Had the coach been looking at Jake or John when he yelled "Batter up"

Teaching the Lesson (General Guidelines for Teachers)

1. Use our examples or your own to illustrate appropriate uses of quotation marks and other punctuation to set off speech.
2. Ask students to complete the six warm-up sentences, and respond to any questions that arise. If they are difficult, review the sample sentences, and go through the Warm-Up sentences one at a time, explaining and modeling as you go.
3. Ask students to keep our examples handy for easy reference, and also to have a handbook available in case they need more information on punctuating quotations correctly. (Recommended: *Great Source: New Generation.*)
4. Share the editing lesson on the following page. Students should read the passage *both silently and aloud*, asking whether someone is speaking; if so, who is speaking; and in *what manner* the person is speaking. It is important to read the full text through before beginning to insert punctuation. On the second time through, students should fill in any missing punctuation and also correct any punctuation that is in error. They should also mark new paragraphs.
5. Ask students to edit individually first, then check with a partner.
6. When everyone is done, ask them to coach you as you edit the same copy, discussing/explaining choices as you go.

7. When you finish, read your edited copy aloud, answering any additional questions students may have. Then compare your edited copy with our suggested text on page 224.
8. For students who have any difficulty with this activity, spend some time reviewing your handbook's explanation of quotations. Then, repeat the practice, this time reading aloud with students as they work. Ask them to read aloud, with inflection, *hearing* the speech as they work, and identifying each speaker and the tone he/she wishes to convey. *Divide the lesson into two parts or more if you need to do so.*

Editing Goal: Make 22 corrections. Mark 3 new paragraphs (for a total of 8). Follow-Up: Check for accurate punctuation of quotations in your own work. Make sure to begin a new paragraph each time a new person speaks.

Answers to Warm-Up

1. “It's my turn to bat,” announced Jake.
2. “I thought,” said Robin, “that you had been up already.”
3. “I can settle this,” said the coach. “It was Jake's twin brother John who batted earlier.”
4. “Isn't it hard to tell you guys apart?” asked Robin.
5. “Batter up!” yelled the coach.
6. Had the coach been looking at Jake or John when he yelled “Batter up”?

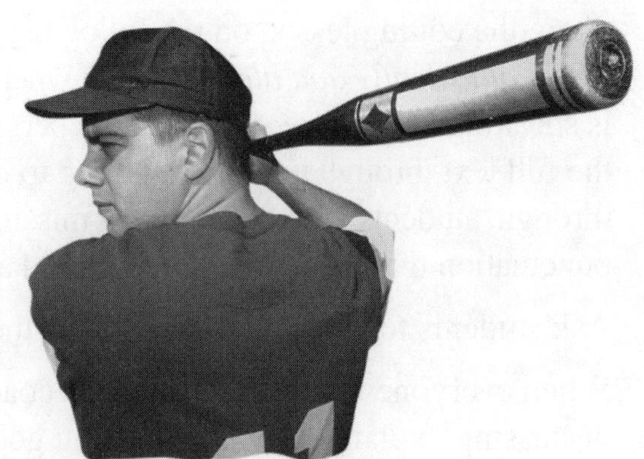

Editing Practice

Correct punctuation in all quotations.
Mark new paragraphs.

Palmer and Shelby were discussing ways each of them liked to pass the time while waiting. "Well, Palmer said, "Let's say you're at the dentist, right? You could like work a crossword puzzle"

Oh, dude! That is so lame!" Shelby answered, laughing out loud. Why wouldn't you just bring along a video game "

"Because, said Palmer "with crossword puzzles, you are actually *learning* something. He could see Shelby was still laughing. It, like, tests your memory and stuff "Oh, right." "No, man, really! Like I saw this show on television and they said that people who do puzzles or take quizzes actually make their brains smarter "

"Yeah, right. If that's true, then why don't you write the puzzles yourself " Shelby asked him?

"Have you ever tried it, Palmer asked Because I *have*, actually. And I have to tell you, it's a LOT harder than it looks. "OK, so I'm impressed, brainiac" Shelby said. Hey, you could *use* that word . . . number fourteen across, starts with a *b*, eight-letter word to describe Palmer the Puzzle Writer . . .

Edited Copy

22 corrections
8 paragraphs total in final copy

Palmer and Shelby were discussing ways each of them liked to pass the time while waiting. "Well," Palmer said, "Let's say you're at the dentist, right? You could like work a cross wordpuzzle."

"Oh, dude! That is so lame!" Shelby answered, laughing out loud. "Why wouldn't you just bring along a video game?"

"Because," said Palmer, "with crossword puzzles, you are actually *learning* something." He could see Shelby was still laughing. "It, like, tests your memory and stuff." ¶"Oh, right." ¶"No, man, really! Like I saw this show on television and they said that people who do puzzles or take quizzes actually make their brains smarter!"

"Yeah, right. If that's true, then why don't you write the puzzles yourself?" Shelby asked him.

"Have you ever tried it?" Palmer asked. "Because I *have*, actually. And I have to tell you, it's a LOT harder than it looks." ¶"OK, so I'm impressed, brainiac," Shelby said. "Hey, you could *use* that word . . . number fourteen across, starts with a *b*, eight-letter word to describe Palmer the Puzzle Writer . . ."

Edited Copy

Reformatted for easier reading

Palmer and Shelby were discussing ways each of them liked to pass the time while waiting. "Well," Palmer said, "Let's say you're at the dentist, right? You could like work a crossword puzzle."

"Oh, dude! That is so lame!" Shelby answered, laughing out loud. "Why wouldn't you just bring along a video game?"

"Because," said Palmer, "with crossword puzzles, you are actually *learning* something." He could see Shelby was still laughing. "It, like, tests your memory and stuff."

"Oh, right."

"No, man, really! Like I saw this show on television and they said that people who do puzzles or take quizzes actually make their brains smarter!"

"Yeah, right. If that's true, then why don't you write the puzzles yourself?" Shelby asked him.

"Have you ever tried it?" Palmer asked. "Because I *have*, actually. And I have to tell you, it's a LOT harder than it looks."

"OK, so I'm impressed, brainiac," Shelby said. "Hey, you could *use* that word . . . number fourteen across, starts with a *b*, eight-letter word to describe Palmer the Puzzle Writer . . ."

Revising for Readable Rhythm

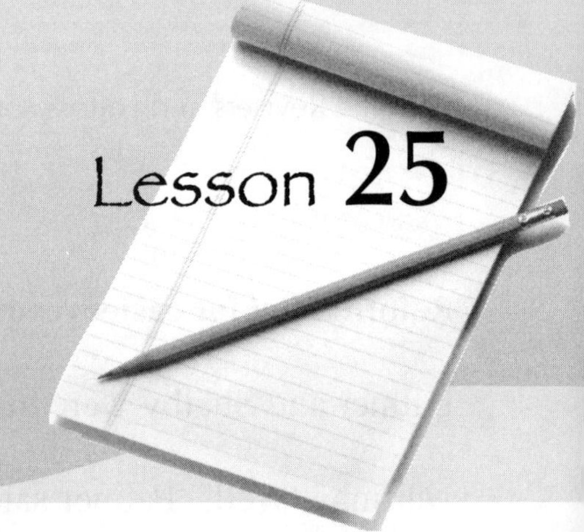

Lesson 25

Trait Connection: **Sentence Fluency**

Introduction

Nothing, absolutely nothing you do as a writer will be more helpful than reading everything you write aloud as you go. In this lesson, you'll have a chance to practice that strategy as you revise for fluency. By now, you've likely heard that the key to fluency is variety: variety in sentence length, variety in sentence beginnings. That's a good start. But sentences hold more secrets than that. Often, it helps to look closely at what great writers do. How do they begin their sentences? Do they follow any patterns? You'll have a chance to imitate the writing of some people who are masters at sentence crafting. Then you'll put all you know about sentences together to turn a nonfluent piece into something readable.

Teacher's Sidebar . . .

In this lesson, students combine several strategies: varying sentence length, varying sentence beginnings, imitating the writing of others, and, most important, reading aloud to hear the rhythm. We provide several "master" sentence writers your students can use as mentors. But you can extend the power of this lesson immeasurably by continuing this portion. Once a week or so, pull a well-crafted sentence from any literature source and ask students to discuss it and then write an original sentence, imitating its structure. You'll see their sentence writing abilities grow markedly.

Focus and Intent

This lesson is intended to help students:

- Understand the importance of reading text aloud to listen for fluency.
- Recognize several strategies for improving fluency in writing.
- Revise nonfluent text to increase its readability.

Teaching the Lesson

Step 1: Building Fluency

Reading aloud is part of *all* fluency-building strategies—so read each of the following samples aloud or ask students to do so as you go. Also remind students to read *their own* writing aloud as they work. Following are three strategies students will find helpful in crafting strong, fluent sentences.

Strategy 1
Vary Length and Structure
Revise the following sentences so that they begin differently and also vary in length. Feel free to combine sentences or word things differently.

> *A man in a raincoat stepped out of the door and put on his hat. The man looked up at the sky and then headed into the alley. He clutched his coat tighter against the wind and walked toward the street.*

Revision

____

____

Strategy 2
Sentence "Aerobics"
Rewrite the following sentence using the beginnings indicated.

> *Many writers become discouraged when critics fail to see the true value of their work.*

When ______________________________________

The failure _________________________________

The true value ______________________________

Discouragement _____________________________

Becoming discouraged ________________________

Critics ____________________________________

Their work _________________________________

Strategy 3
Learning from Mentors
Two masters of the sentence craft are Sandra Cisneros and Ernest Hemingway. They have very different styles. Cisneros is known for her poetic style—fluent, graceful, and marked by use of fragments: quick thoughts that capture images or feelings and make her prose sound poetic. Choose any place you know well, and describe it, using the following passage from Cisneros as a model:

> *Not a flat. Not an apartment in back. Not a man's house. Not a daddy's. A house all my own. With my porch and my pillow, my pretty purple petunias. My books and my stories. My two shoes waiting beside the bed. Nobody to shake a stick at. Nobody's garbage to pick up after. (*The House on Mango Street, *p. 108)*

____

____

Ernest Hemingway is known for the simple elegance of his language and sentences. Think of a person you know well, and describe him or her using this description of the old fisherman Santiago as a model:

> *The blotches ran well down the sides of his face and his hands had the deep-creased scars from handling heavy fish on the cords. But none of these scars were fresh. They were as old as erosions in a fishless desert. (*The Old Man and the Sea, *p. 10)*

____

____

Sources for mentor text:

1. *The House on Mango Street* by Sandra Cisneros. 1989. New York: Vintage Books.
2. *The Old Man and the Sea* by Ernest Hemingway. 2003. New York: Scribner.

Suggested responses appear at the end of "Next Steps," page 231.

Step 2: Making the Reading-Writing Connection

One of the best sentence writers around is Gary D. Schmidt. Read any of his work aloud, and you will be struck by the ease with which you can transform his written text into speech. This is the true test of fluency. Schmidt has a wonderful ear for patterns in language. In the following passage, Henry's family has just acquired a stray Labrador "temporarily" named Black Dog, and she's been left alone while the family goes to the hospital to see Henry's injured brother, Franklin. Black Dog breaks free from the carriage house where she's been tied *and* locked up, and manages to get into the main house—where she is *not* supposed to be. Here is a brief portion of her ensuing escapades. Listen for the pattern:

> *Black Dog had gone into the kitchen first, probably since she was familiar with it. She had nosed open the cupboards until she found the pantry, and she had pulled all of the soup cans and sacks of onions and jars of canned vegetables and applesauce and bottles of New Hampshire maple syrup out into the kitchen before she found what she wanted: a jar of peanut butter with a loose lid. She had licked it clean, eating what she wanted and then smearing the rest all over the quarried stone floors and the light maple cupboards.*
>
> (From *Trouble* by Gary D. Schmidt. 2008. Boston: Houghton Mifflin, p. 28)

Do you hear the pattern Schmidt uses to reinforce the trail of Black Dog's destruction? *Had gone . . . had nosed . . . had pulled . . . had licked.* Schmidt continues this pattern for several more paragraphs (since Black Dog is just warming up): Before long we learn that she "had gone into the library," "had jumped down onto the couch and sunk her toenails deep into the red leather," "had gone to the south parlor" leaving a peanut butter trail on the linen tapestry, and "had torn most of the stuffing" out of the cushions. What starts out as a description soon becomes a litany of Black Dog's transgressions. Such patterning, called *parallel structure*, is one of the most powerful tools a writer can use to drive home a point—or as in this case, a whole catalog of points.

Step 3: Involving Students as Evaluators

Ask students to review Samples A and B, asking which writer has created the more fluent piece. Have them work together, identifying particular strategies the writer of the stronger piece has used, and noting fluency problems in the weaker piece. Emphasize the importance of reading both pieces *aloud.*

Discussing Results

Most students should find Sample A stronger. Writer A shows variety, uses fragments selectively for emphasis, and also employs parallel structure. This piece is easy to read aloud. By contrast, Writer B begins most sentences in the same way, and the connections from sentence to sentence are not always clear, making oral reading more challenging. One possible revision of Sample B is provided.

Step 4: Modeling Revision

- Share Sample C (*Whole Class Revision*) with students. Ask one of your students to read the original aloud.
- Ask the reader—and other students—whether this writer has created a piece that is fluent and easy to read aloud. (Most should say *no.*)
- Give students time to discuss the piece with partners, talking through revision possibilities, and reading aloud (*softly*) to test various options. Ask them to imagine that this is an excerpt from a science textbook designed for fifth grade students.
- As a class, discuss revision possibilities, and work through the revision sentence by sentence, asking students to offer suggestions. You may wish to combine sentences, use fragments for emphasis or poetic effect, try parallel structure, simply weave in more variety—or use all of these strategies.
- Read the text aloud as you go. (You can call upon different student readers to do this.) Each time you revise a sentence, go back and read the full text *through the point of your revision.* This is a habit you want student writers to form.
- When you finish, ask another student to read the *whole revision* aloud, making any last-minute changes that could further improve the fluency.

Suggestion: Ask listeners (including yourself) not to read the text visually, but simply to listen to it. Your ear will pick up problems faster and more astutely if you don't use your eyes to help "interpret" the text.

- If you wish, compare your revision to ours, keeping in mind that your revision is likely to be quite different from ours.

Step 5: Revising with Partners

Share Sample D (*Revising with Partners*). Ask students to follow the basic steps you modeled with Sample C. *Working with partners,* they should:

- Read the passage aloud.
- Talk about fluency problems and possible revision solutions. Imagine that the copy will be read by a newscaster as the voice-under for a two-minute segment on *20/20* or a similar program.
- Revise sentence by sentence, using a variety of strategies and referring to any mentor text that may be useful. (Remind students to read aloud *as they write.*)
- Read the final revision aloud, with as much inflection as possible, testing the fluency and readability and tweaking the text as needed.

Step 6: Sharing and Discussing Results

When students have finished, have students *exchange their revisions* and read someone else's text aloud as a test of fluency. Ask readers to offer a critique on the general readability of the borrowed text. Truly fluent text should not require much rehearsal. (*Note:* Problems in reading handwriting do *not* count as fluency flaws!) After listening, ask the class as a whole to talk about which text sounded especially fluent. What strategies did various teams use? If you wish, compare your revisions with ours, keeping in mind that our changes are likely to be different.

Next Steps

- Ask students to exchange revisions of Sample D with other teams and to do a second round of revision, building on what the first team has already done. It is rare to reach *really strong* fluency with a single revision. The impact of two revisions, however, can be impressive.
- Invite students to review a sample of their own writing, reading it aloud carefully, sentence by sentence, and applying as many strategies as possible to improve the fluency.
- Look and listen for writers who craft strong sentences, and routinely use one of their sentences as a model to practice sentence construction. Recommended:

- *Trouble* by Gary D. Schmidt. 2008. Boston: Houghton Mifflin.
- **The House on Mango Street* by Sandra Cisneros. 1991. New York: Vintage.
- **Bad Boy by Walter* by Dean Myers. 2001. New York: HarperCollins.
- **Cuba 15* by Nancy Osa. 2003. New York: Delacorte Press.
- *Escape! The Story of the Great Houdini* by Sid Fleischman. 2006. New York: Greenwillow Books.
- **Fahrenheit 451* by Ray Bradbury. 1953 (renewed 1981). New York: Random House.
- **The Old Man and the Sea* by Ernest Hemingway. 1980. New York: Scribner.

■ *For an additional challenge:* Take any sample from a "sentence master," whether someone whose work is presented in this lesson, or any professional published author whose work you admire. Revise it once, twice, or more—just focusing on fluency and reading aloud as you go. See if you can improve on the original, and if you cannot, talk about why you think that is.

*Indicates a book written for a young adult *through* adult audience. These books may contain adult language and themes.

Suggested Responses to "Building Fluency," p. 227

Strategy 1
Vary Length and Structure

Revise the following sentences so that they begin differently and also vary in length. Feel free to combine sentences or word things differently.

> *A man in a raincoat stepped out of the door and put on his hat. The man looked up at the sky and then headed into the alley. He clutched his coat tighter against the wind and walked toward the street.*

Revision

A man in a raincoat stepped out of the door, put on his hat, looked up at the sky, and headed into the alley. Clutching his coat tighter against the wind, he walked toward the street.

Strategy 2
Sentence "Aerobics"

Rewrite the following sentence using the beginnings indicated.

> *Many writers become discouraged when critics fail to see the true value of their work.*

When critics fail to see the true value of their work, many writers become discouraged.

The failure of critics to sufficiently value their work discourages many a writer.

The true value of a writer's work is often ignored by critics—leading the writer to become discouraged.

Discouragement is common among writers whose work is not valued by critics.

Becoming discouraged is all too easy for an unappreciated writer.

Critics too unimaginative to spot a work's true value may undermine a writer's confidence.

Their work is so important to many writers that even slight criticism results in discouragement.

Question: Which sentence is most powerful? Why?

Strategy 3
Learning from Mentors

Cisneros imitation

Not a guest house. Not an office. Not a hideaway. Not a child's playhouse. A retreat all my own. With my rocker and my old rug, my sketches and photographs. My poems. My favorite books waiting to be opened. No telephone to ring. Nobody's voice to interrupt the silence.

Hemingway imitation

The creases burrowed deep into the borders of her cheeks, and her hands had a spotted, leathery look from too many hours in the sun. And the creases were no longer erasable. They were as indelible as the folds of a newspaper buried for years in a forgotten attic trunk.

Sample A

Varied structure? Easy to read aloud?

Real Drama on the High Seas*

When many people think of pirates, they imagine daring heroes, loathsome villains, alluring treasure, and romantic adventures in far-off ports. Real life piracy is not in the least romantic, however. Anything but. It is a treacherous business that threatens human lives and the economic welfare of shippers throughout the world. Nearly every day, a ship is attacked somewhere, by pirates who no longer wield swords, but are now armed with GPS units, rocket-grenades, and machine guns. Today's pirates are more ruthless than ever. They steal whatever they can, from food to jewelry; kidnap and hold crew or passengers for ransom; and even take over ships, repainting them and then selling or using them for further piracy.

Fortunately, shippers are fighting back. Effectively, too. Hidden transmitters aboard most ships trace the ship's route, and inform rescuers at once of any attack. Unmanned planes patrol the oceans, actively looking for pirates—as do remote-controlled interceptor boats. Many ships now carry Secure-Ship, a 9,000 volt electric fence which, while not lethal, delivers a jolt sufficient to interrupt even the most determined attempts at boarding. Acoustic barriers can deliver up to 125 decibels of deafening noise—intolerable to the human ear and distracting in the bargain. And if all this isn't sufficient to discourage the pirates, ships' crews may resort to a less high-tech method of defense: blasting pirates with ship-mounted firehoses.

While defensive measures are taking a real cut out of pirates' bounty, the number of attacks remains high in some portions of the world—including the waters off Sumatra and Indonesia. Piracy is not just the stuff of movies. It's real world drama.

*Information for this sample is based, in part, on "The High-Tech Battle Against Pirates," in *Science Illustrated.* March/April 2008. ed. Mark Jannot. Copenhagen: Bonnier Publications, pp. 68–71.

Sample B

Varied structure? Easy to read aloud?

Iceberg Migration

Icebergs are so massive that we usually think of them as stable. We also think of them as non-moving. Migrating, however, icebergs can break free from larger ice flows. Then, the icebergs travel, sometimes long distances. Icebergs that can migrate for hundreds of miles. They are often extremely large, ranging up to two or three hundred feet in length and being even longer than this in some cases. Icebergs melt so slowly that it is possible they may make it to fairly warm waters before they melt entirely. They have been spotted south of Ireland. Very large icebergs pose a significant threat to ships. The threat is made worse by the fact that ships' captains do not expect to encounter icebergs in warmer waters. The most famous encounter of an iceberg and a ship is the disaster involving the Titanic, which was rammed by the Titanic although not in truly warm waters. It was, however, south of Newfoundland. That is still a long way for an iceberg to travel. Icebergs, as it turns out, move a lot. Plus you can't predict them. Icebergs are dangerous because of this.

Revision of Sample B

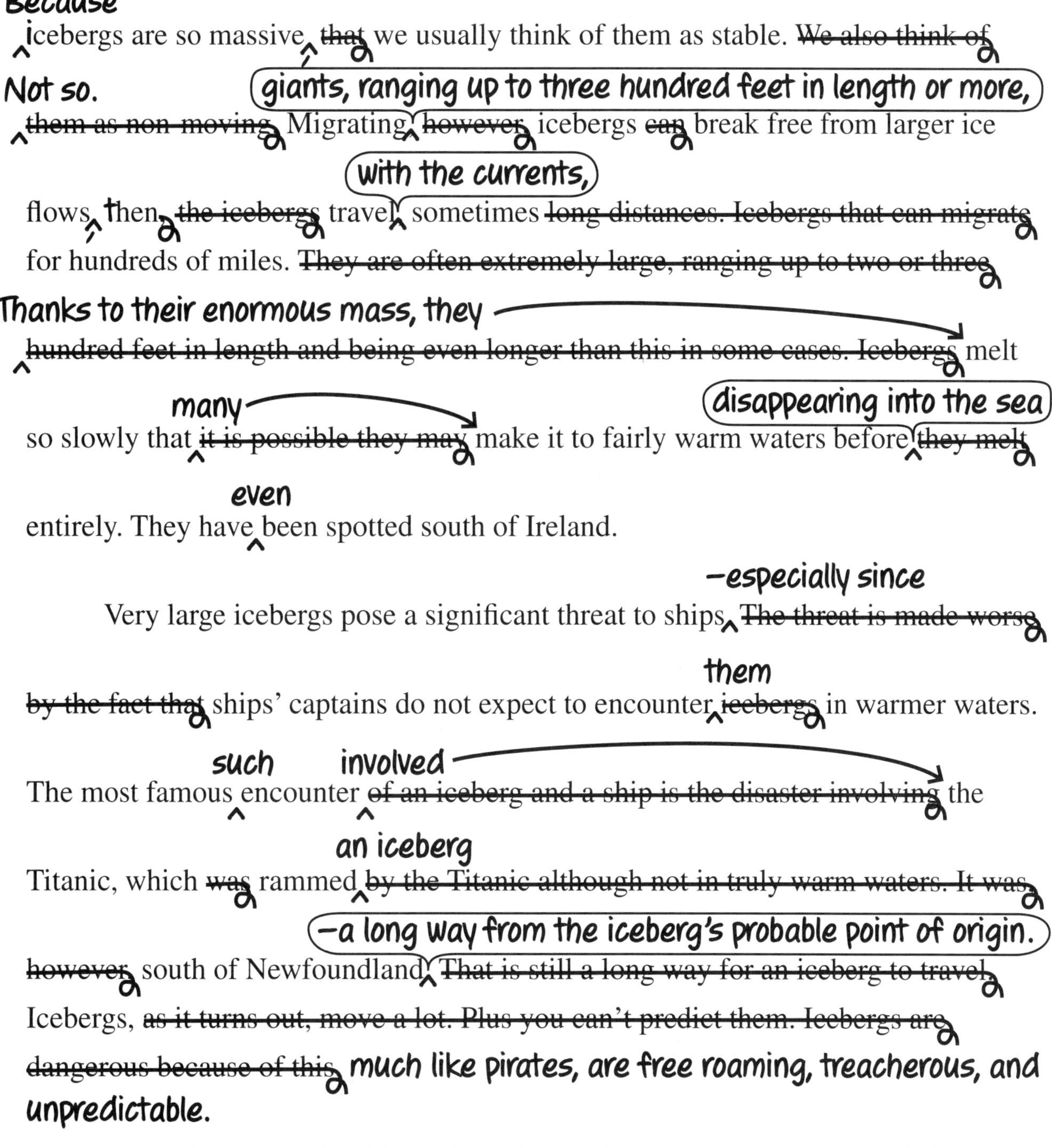

Iceberg Migration

Because icebergs are so massive, ~~that~~ we usually think of them as stable. ~~We also think of them as non-moving.~~ Not so. Migrating, giants, ranging up to three hundred feet in length or more, ~~however,~~ icebergs ~~can~~ break free from larger ice flows; then, ~~the icebergs~~ travel, with the currents, sometimes ~~long distances. Icebergs that can migrate~~ for hundreds of miles. ~~They are often extremely large, ranging up to two or three hundred feet in length and being even longer than this in some cases. Icebergs~~ Thanks to their enormous mass, they melt so slowly that ~~it is possible they may~~ many make it to fairly warm waters before disappearing into the sea ~~they melt~~ entirely. They have even been spotted south of Ireland.

Very large icebergs pose a significant threat to ships—especially since ~~The threat is made worse by the fact that~~ ships' captains do not expect to encounter them ~~icebergs~~ in warmer waters. The most famous such encounter involved ~~of an iceberg and a ship is the disaster involving~~ the Titanic, which ~~was~~ rammed an iceberg ~~by the Titanic although not in truly warm waters. It was, however,~~ south of Newfoundland—a long way from the iceberg's probable point of origin. ~~That is still a long way for an iceberg to travel.~~ Icebergs, ~~as it turns out, move a lot. Plus you can't predict them. Icebergs are dangerous because of this~~ much like pirates, are free roaming, treacherous, and unpredictable.

Note that in this revision, we also broke the text into two paragraphs.

Sample C: Whole Class Revision

Varied structure? Easy to read aloud?

Dinosaurs in Living Color

Dinosaurs usually appear in children's books as brown, green or gray. Dinosaurs seen onscreen typically look about the same. In real life, though, dinosaurs may or may not have had these precise colors. We may never know for sure. Fossils do not preserve pigmentation, so the precise color a dinosaur's skin was is an unknown. Fossils *do* preserve form, giving us the knowledge that dinosaurs had scales much like modern day reptiles do as well. The fossils, unfortunately, cannot reveal much about skin color, but we can speculate. Dinosaurs that were prey for other dinosaurs may have had spots or stripes, for example. These dinosaurs likely lived on vegetation, which colors would allow them to blend into surrounding foliage to escape predators. Dinosaurs that lived more in the open as hunters may have been colored like today's predators. For example, they may have been some sort of neutral color, much like a lion has to hide in the grass when stalking prey. Today, lizards are often brown or green. But this should not encourage generalization. The dinosaurs of yesterday may have been a different color altogether.

Sample D: Revising with Partners

Varied structure? Easy to read aloud?

Make Way for the PAL-V

Many people have dreamed of a car that could fly. But many people did not believe it was possible until recently. Now more recently, people who have been waiting may have an answer. Their wait is over because a firm in Holland is announcing plans to bring a new three-wheel vehicle to the market. The firm says that the vehicle will have three wheels and run like a car. The vehicle will also be capable of flying, however. This vehicle is very narrow, and can corner without tipping, like a motorcycle. Because the vehicle has folding wings that fold down when it is on land. The wings however flip up and extend at the moment when it is time to fly. The vehicle is called the PAL-V, which means "Personal Air and Land Vehicle." This vehicle can go up to 120 miles an hour on land. It goes about the same speed when in the air. The vehicle has a range of 375 miles on land. It can also go about 340 miles in the air. It takes off and lands in a way that is vertical which means it is like a helicopter in the way it moves. This means it does not need a lot of runway space for takeoff and landing. It flies under 4,000 feet, so no flight plan is required. The people who plan to manufacture the PAL-V see it as a popular commuter vehicle. They imagine commuters looking down on the traffic and feeling very good about their choice!

Information for this sample is taken from two websites:
http://www.pal-v.com/
http://www.technologynewsdaily.com/taxonomy/term/28

Suggested Revisions of C and D

Sample C: Whole Class Revision

Dinosaurs: Creatures of Another Color ~~Dinosaurs in Living Color~~

Dinosaurs ~~usually appear in~~ that roam the pages of children's books ~~as~~ are usually brown, green or gray—just as they are onscreen. ~~Dinosaurs seen onscreen typically look about the same.~~ In real life, though, dinosaurs may have been spotted, striped or buff colored. ~~or may not have had these precise colors.~~ We may never know for sure. Fossils, which provide our primary clues about these ancient creatures, do not preserve pigmentation, so the precise color of a dinosaur's skin ~~was is an unknown.~~ remains a mystery. Fossils *do* preserve form, however, telling us ~~giving us the knowledge~~ that dinosaurs had scales much like those of modern day reptiles. ~~do as well. The fossils, unfortunately, cannot reveal much~~ As for ~~about~~ skin color, ~~but~~ we can speculate. Dinosaurs that ~~were prey for other dinosaurs may have had spots or stripes, for example. These dinosaurs likely~~ lived on vegetation ~~which colors would allow~~ needed mottled colors that would help them ~~to~~ blend into surrounding foliage to escape predators. The predatory dinosaurs that lived ~~more~~ in the open as hunters may have needed neutral colors ~~been colored like today's predators. For example, they may have been some sort of neutral color, much like a lion has to hide~~ that would help them disappear in the grass when stalking prey—much like today's lions. ~~Today, lizards are often brown or green. But this should not encourage generalization.~~ It's tempting to look at a modern day lizard and think, "Dinosaur—only smaller." Too simple. The dinosaurs of yesterday ~~may have been a different~~ were creatures of another color altogether.

Sample D: Revising with Partners

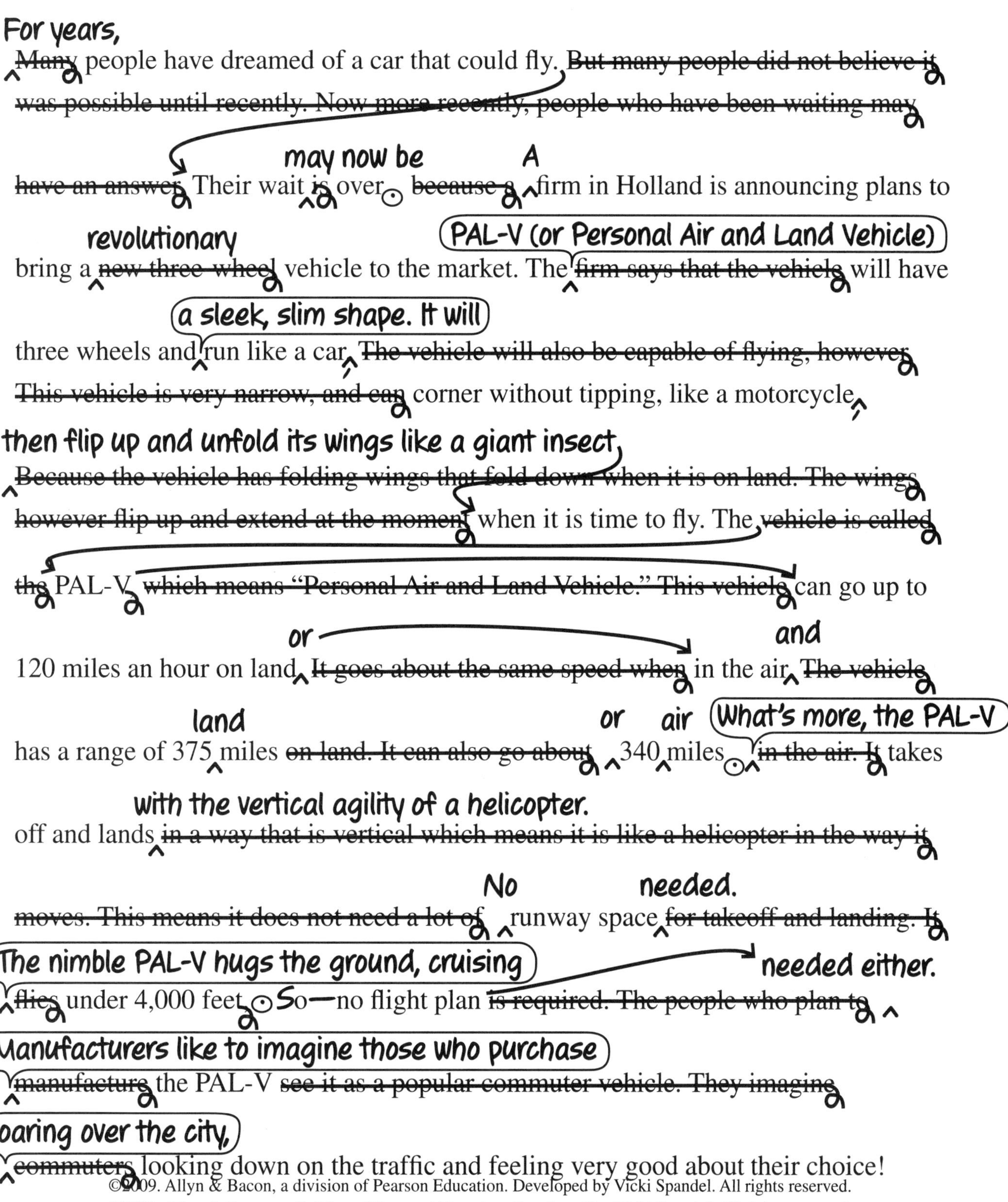

Make Way for the PAL-V

For years,
Many people have dreamed of a car that could fly. But many people did not believe it
was possible until recently. Now more recently, people who have been waiting may

may now be A
have an answer. Their wait is over because a firm in Holland is announcing plans to

revolutionary PAL-V (or Personal Air and Land Vehicle)
bring a new three-wheel vehicle to the market. The firm says that the vehicle will have

a sleek, slim shape. It will
three wheels and run like a car. The vehicle will also be capable of flying, however.
This vehicle is very narrow, and can corner without tipping, like a motorcycle,

then flip up and unfold its wings like a giant insect,
Because the vehicle has folding wings that fold down when it is on land. The wings
however flip up and extend at the moment when it is time to fly. The vehicle is called

the PAL-V, which means "Personal Air and Land Vehicle." This vehicle can go up to

or and
120 miles an hour on land. It goes about the same speed when in the air. The vehicle

land or air What's more, the PAL-V
has a range of 375 miles on land. It can also go about 340 miles in the air. It takes

with the vertical agility of a helicopter.
off and lands in a way that is vertical which means it is like a helicopter in the way it

No needed.
moves. This means it does not need a lot of runway space for takeoff and landing. It

The nimble PAL-V hugs the ground, cruising needed either.
flies under 4,000 feet. So—no flight plan is required. The people who plan to

Manufacturers like to imagine those who purchase
manufacture the PAL-V see it as a popular commuter vehicle. They imagine

soaring over the city,
commuters looking down on the traffic and feeling very good about their choice!

©2009. Allyn & Bacon, a division of Pearson Education. Developed by Vicki Spandel. All rights reserved.

Sharpening Your Editor's Eye

Lesson **26**

Trait Connection: **Conventions**

Introduction (Share with students in your own words—or as a handout.)

Have you ever proofed a document so carefully that you were sure you caught *every tiny problem*—only to have an error pop right out at you just as you were turning the final copy in? If so, you know how hard it can be to spot the small things—missed letters or words, for example. As writers, we already know what we *mean* to say. And often, that's what we "read" on the page—whether the meaning came through clearly or not. A good editor's eye develops with practice—lots of it. It also comes with taking time to read copy through, *slowly*—more than once. By the way, don't rely too heavily on your computer. Computers are helpful, to be sure, but far from infallible. Not only do they overlook some things that later seem obvious, but they occasionally identify things as errors that in reality are correct. Electronic editorial programs are still being perfected. This doesn't mean we shouldn't use them; we need all the help we can get! It does mean, however, that when it comes to editing your own work, *you* need to be the final authority. In this lesson, you'll have a chance to test your editor's eye, looking for little things that can easily slip by undetected. Let's warm up. How many errors can you spot in these seven sentences?

Warm-Up

1. He estamated the cost at thousand dollars and was only of by a six percent
2. Phyllis new her cruise to Alask was. going tobe the trip of a lifetime.
3. Ive asked him at least for times to provide use with now estimate's.
4. Greenpaece calculate that global warming is ever more of an problem then original estimates predicated.
5. In informational, writing it is important to to site sources acurately.
6. Its a customary when World series games ran long too continue right though the night, even of that means going for many innings.
7. If ever American turns of lights duing Earth Hour, we can prevent over sixteen thousand ton of CO_2 for entering th atmosphere.

If you found *at least* four errors per sentence, you are developing a good editor's eye. If you found *more*, you're a natural editor. If you did not find all the errors, here are four tips for editing carefully when it counts:

1. **Read aloud**. It will slow you down a little, and also help you hear things like repeated or missing words or missing punctuation.
2. **Use a ruler** to mark the line you're currently reading. This keeps your quick reader's eye from skipping ahead.
3. When you write a draft, **double space** to make revising and editing easy. Do this even if you compose on the computer because it will give you "breathing room." It's easy for small errors to go undetected in tightly compressed text. They stand out more when there's room to see things.
4. **Leave your rough draft alone for two to three days** (if time permits). Later, read your draft both silently and aloud to look and listen for errors, pencil in hand, handbook at your side. You'll be surprised how many errors you'll catch when your editor's eye and mind have had time away from your text.

Teaching the Lesson (General Guidelines for Teachers)

1. Share the examples above, or make up your own examples to offer students practice in spotting small errors.
2. Let them know that this lesson does not focus on any particular rules, but covers a wide range of *small* errors likely to show up in unedited or hastily edited text: missing or repeated words, misspellings, missing punctuation, faulty capitals, words run together, and so on.
3. Make sure students have access to a good handbook (*Write Source: New Generation* is recommended) to which they can refer during the lesson.
4. Share the editing lesson on the following page. Ask students to read the text aloud, looking and listening for small errors, such as missing words or letters, unneeded words, letters, or punctuation—or anything else likely to be overlooked with a hasty reading. *It may be helpful for some students to use a ruler to set off lines of text as they read.* They should find 41 errors altogether. (*Note:* Most students will not find all 41 errors in a single reading. That is the point of the lesson. Ask them to read through once, making as many corrections as possible. Then let them know how many errors there are altogether.)
5. Ask students to edit individually first, then check with a partner.
6. When everyone is done, ask them to coach you as you edit the same copy.
7. *Note:* If students have difficulty with so many corrections at one time, divide the lesson into two or four parts, either doing half at a time, or doing one paragraph at a time.
8. When you finish, compare your edited copy with our suggested text on page 245.

Editing Goal: Catch 41 small errors.
Follow-Up: Watch for small errors in your own work.

Answers to Warm-Up Sentences

1. He estamated the cost at thousand dollars and was only of by a six percent
2. Phyllis new her cruise to Alask was going tobe the trip of a lifetime.
3. I've asked him at least for times to provide use with now estimates.
4. Greenpeace calculate that global warming is ever more of an problem then original estimates predicated.
5. In informational writing it is important to to site sources acurately.
6. It's a customary when World series games ran long too continue right though the night, even of that means going for many innings.
7. If ever American turns of lights duing Earth Hour, we can prevent over sixteen thousand ton of CO_2 for entering th atmosphere.

Editing Practice

Look for small errors.

People are find it increasingly creative ways too "go green in today's world. For example, their is now hotels with the "intelligence" to detect when patrons left, an turn off th heat or air conditioning, thus saving thousands of dollars per year on energy costs—and also conserving fule. Not only are soler panels and windmill popping up everywhere, but some nightclubs actually finding ways to absorb energy from patron's dancing feet—and us that energy to power lightning ore sound.

Increasing numbers of people are "adopting" endanger animals, suchas sea turtles. The adoption fees pays the cost of rehabilitating injured turtles, as well a tracking turtles accross their ocean to monitor there habit and learn more abot what threatens or sustains the.

At a website called 1UglyShirt.com, people can purchase recycle, vintage clothing. Supporters of the site suggest that be recycling cloths, we can cute down on the pollution, shiping costs, or (in some cases poor working conditions asociated with the manufacture of knew clothes

From organic fod preparation, to water eficiency, recycling, or fragrance-free policies, America continued to seek eco-friendly policies that not only working, but also captures the imagination.

Edited Copy

42 small errors corrected

People are find it increasingly creative ways too “go green in today's world. For example, their is now hotels with the “intelligence” to detect when patrons left an turn off th heat or air conditioning, thus saving thousands of dollars per year on energy costs—and also conserving fule. Not only are soler panels and windmill popping up everywhere, but some nightclubs actually finding ways to absorb energy from patron's dancing feet—and us that energy to power lighthing ore sound.

Increasing numbers of people are “adopting” endanger animals, suchas sea turtles. The adoption fees pays the cost of rehabilitating injured turtles, as well as tracking turtles accross their ocean to monitor there habit and learn more abot what threatens or sustains the.

At a website called 1UglyShirt.com, people can purchase recycle, vintage clothing. Supporters of the site suggest that be recycling cloths, we can cute down on the pollution, shiping costs, or (in some cases poor working conditions asociated with the manufacture of knew clothes

From organic fod preparation, to water eficiency, recycling, or fragrance-free policies, America continued to seek eco-friendly policies that not only working but also captures the imagination.

Revising the Opening Scene

Trait Connection: **Sentence Fluency**

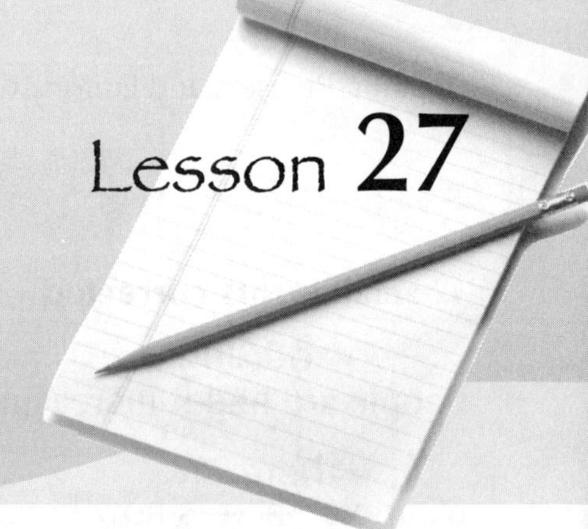

Introduction

Good dialogue is a happy surprise in writing. It reveals something about the characters who are speaking, creates a mood, and offers important information about what's happening or about to happen. Maybe that's why so many films open with a scene that involves dialogue. Bad dialogue, on the other hand, is a chore to process. As readers, we scramble to rewrite it in our heads—and if we can't, the characters lose credibility—and so does the writer. Writing good dialogue is an art. It requires listening to how real people talk. In addition, it requires knowing your characters as if they were real people. Since the dialogue you'll revise in this lesson was written by someone else, that won't be as *quite as easy* as if you'd created the characters yourself. With imagination, though, you can still give this dialogue authenticity. Pay special attention to the text linking the lines of dialogue. Think of that part as "stage direction." Imagine that each sample you revise will be a script for the opening scene of a film.

Teacher's Sidebar . . .

The most important goal of this lesson is to create dialogue that rings true. This requires reading aloud—and perhaps even performing the dialogue with a partner. Students should expect to go through each dialogue set more than once. As one character's speech changes, it tends to alter the response from the other character. And remind them not to forget the linking text that connects lines of dialogue. It is the writer's opportunity to give the reader important clues about how to read the dialogue with the right inflection. In this lesson, students are also asked to apply some editing skills, paragraphing dialogue appropriately. Punctuation is correct.

Focus and Intent

This lesson is intended to help students:

- Recognize the many roles good dialogue plays in advancing a narrative.
- Distinguish between authentic and artificial dialogue.
- Revise a piece so that the dialogue is authentic, the linking text is effective, and the paragraphing is correct.

Teaching the Lesson

Step 1: Going for Authenticity

Following are some samples of first-draft dialogue that will serve as the opening two lines of a film. In each case, there are two speakers. Ask students to work in pairs, taking turns reading the parts aloud, and revising each sample for authenticity—or do them as a whole class. For each set, try to imagine the situation: What's the setting? What's the circumstance? What sort of film is this? Invent answers to suit yourself. Try to picture the characters. What are they like? Who would play these parts? What is each character *really* trying to project?

Set 1

Ramon: I want you to marry me. We'll be extremely happy.
Isabel: I'm afraid I can't. Marrying you would not be a sound decision.

Revision ____

____

Set 2

Louis: Could you possibly put your dog on a leash?
Mildred: I don't think so. He might not like that. Please try to put up with him.

Revision ____

____

Set 3

Deirdre: Isn't it thrilling to be here and to take part in this event?
Daisy: I can see that you are thrilled. I am less than thrilled, however.

Revision ____

____

Step 2: Making the Reading-Writing Connection

In *No More Dead Dogs*, author Gordon Korman creates characters who speak with a great deal of voice—and attitude. It is generally very easy to tell just how to read the dialogue, as in the following scene. Wallace Wallace, the book's intrepid hero, is in detention for writing an honest book report demeaning a book he hates: *Old Shep, My Pal*. Though Wallace finds it trite and phony, the book is, unfortunately, a favorite of Mr. Fogelman, the English teacher and drama coach. Now, as if detention alone were not enough, Wallace is being tormented by another student, the alarmingly self-absorbed Cavanaugh, who has "all the charm of a cobra" and cannot stop combing his "ridiculously straight, ridiculously long, ridiculously blond hair":

> *"Stop combing," I seethed. "You're driving me crazy."*
>
> *"It's tough to be me." He smiled, pocketing his comb. "Every day is a good hair day." His grin never wavered. "So, Doofus Doofus, I have to tell you about this fantastic book I've been reading."*
>
> *"I didn't know you could read," I muttered.*
>
> *"It's called Old Shep, My Pal," he continued airily. "By Zack Paris. What a genius! You'd have to be a complete idiot not to love this masterpiece."*
>
> *I glared at him. "All right, enough. You know why I'm on detention. Who told you?"*

(From *No More Dead Dogs* by Gordon Korman. 2000. New York: Hyperion, pp. 27–28)

Notice the paragraphing in this sample. How do you know it's correct? Look through this piece for the clues that tell you how each character feels, and what the character is like. How many do you find? What's a good word to describe Cavanaugh? Does this dialogue sound real to you? If you were writing it, would you change anything? Here's a test of authenticity. See if you can read Korman's dialogue in this brief excerpt with *just the right inflection* to show how each character is feeling—and what he is thinking. If you find that easy, you know the dialogue rings true. By the way, how does a person speak "airily"? Try it. Do you like Korman's use of this word? Imagine that this is going to be filmed. Who would you cast as Cavanaugh? As Wallace?

Step 3: Involving Students as Evaluators

Ask students to review Samples A and B, asking which writer has created more authentic and revealing dialogue. Have students work in teams, identifying clues that tell a reader what the characters are like, what's happening, and how to read the dialogue with the right inflection. Emphasize the importance of reading both pieces *aloud*. Also ask students to check for correct paragraphing; a new paragraph should begin *each time a different character speaks.*

Discussing Results

Most students should find Sample B stronger. Writer B's characters sound like real people. The paragraphing is also correct. Writer A's characters, by contrast, do not sound authentic. No one speaks this way in real life. In addition, Sample A is not paragraphed correctly. One possible revision of Sample A is provided.

Step 4: Modeling Revision

- Share Sample C (*Whole Class Revision*) with students. Ask *two* of your students to read the original aloud, each one taking a part.
- Ask the readers—and other students—whether the dialogue sounds authentic, whether it's easy to read with the right inflection, and whether it would make a captivating opening scene for a film. (Most should say *no.*)
- Give students time to discuss the piece with partners, talking about the situation and the characters. What is each one like, and how would the character really speak?
- As a class, work through the revision line by line, with students offering suggestions. Feel free to make any changes at all. Be inventive. The goal is authenticity; you do not need to stay true to the plot, sketchy as it is. Pay attention to linking text (text linking one line of dialogue to another) also.
- Read the new dialogue aloud as you go. (You can call upon different student readers to do this.)
- When you finish, ask another pair of students to read the *whole revision* aloud, making any last-minute changes that could further heighten authenticity, add to the mood, or advance the plot. Think about changing the characters' names. Cast the parts as you would if actually making a film.
- If you wish, compare your revision to ours, keeping in mind that your revision is likely to be quite different from ours.

Step 5: Revising with Partners

Share Sample D (*Revising with Partners*). Ask students to follow the basic steps you modeled with Sample C. *Working with partners,* they should:

- Read the passage aloud.
- Talk about the situation and the characters.
- Revise line by line, using a variety of strategies, reading aloud as they go, and always imagining how the dialogue will play on film.
- Read the final revision aloud, with as much inflection as possible, testing the authenticity, and revising as needed.

Step 6: Sharing and Discussing Results

When students have finished, ask pairs of students to perform their revised dialogue. Ask listeners to comment on the authenticity of the dialogue and to cast the parts. After listening, ask the class as a whole to vote for those they think are "film ready" without further revision. If you wish, compare your revisions with ours, keeping in mind that our changes are likely to be different.

Next Steps

- Ask students to extend the dialogue for Sample D, building on what they have already done. Ask them to add two to four additional lines per character. Then, ask them to meet in small groups to share their revisions. Did the pieces take different directions in terms of character development and plot?
- Dialogue is refreshing because it brings the human voice into writing. In writing where dialogue seems out of place, what are the options for bringing in a human voice?
- Look and listen for good dialogue in the literature you share aloud. Recommended:
    - *No More Dead Dogs* by Gordon Korman. 2000. New York: Hyperion.
    - **Cuba 15* by Nancy Osa. 2003. New York: Delacorte Press.
    - *Everest* by Gordon Korman. 2002. New York: Scholastic.
    - *Stargirl* by Jerry Spinelli. 2004. New York: Laurel Leaf.
    - *Trouble* by Gary D. Schmidt. 2008. Boston: Houghton Mifflin.
- *For an additional challenge:* Ask students to obtain a sample script for a film or play and to perform one scene for the class. (They will need time to rehearse this.) Give them license to modify the dialogue if they wish, but ask them to provide a rationale for any changes they make.

*Indicates a book written for a young adult to adult audience. May contain mature language or themes.

Suggested Responses to "Going for Authenticity," p. 247

Set 1

Ramon: I want you to marry me. We'll be extremely happy.
Isabel: I'm afraid I can't. Marrying you would not be a sound decision.

Revision

Ramon: Marry me. Make a decision for once in your life, Isabel. What's stopping you?

Isabel: Are you insane? OK—here are the stoppers: We're both unemployed, I throw up on ships, and you're allergic to cats. How many reasons do you need?

Set 2

Louis: Could you possibly put your dog on a leash?
Mildred: I don't think so. He might not like that. Please try to put up with him.

Revision

Louis: Did you ever think of putting that monster attack dog on a leash?

Mildred: That isn't going to happen, Indiana, so get used to it. Cujo doesn't like leashes—or rude people.

Set 3

Deirdre: Isn't it thrilling to be here and to take part in this event?
Daisy: I can see that you are thrilled. I am less than thrilled, however.

Revision

Deirdre: Aren't weddings the best? I can't believe we're here! It's like we're dreaming it!

Daisy: Deirdre, you love everything. It's your most endearing and annoying trait. Personally, I wish I were home.

Sample A

Authentic dialogue?
Strong linking text?
Correct paragraphing?

Unfair

Debbie thought to herself that she didn't feel like talking with Heather, but since Heather had already spotted her, there was no getting out of it now.

"Hello!" Heather said, flicking her hair over her shoulder. "Hello," Debbie answered. "What's new with you today?"

"Nothing in particular," Heather replied. She wondered if she should mention that she was going out that night with Brad, Debbie's former boyfriend. He had only been her "former" boyfriend since 10 o'clock that morning, when he had asked Heather to go to the movies with him. "Shall we walk to math together?" "I would love to, but I think I need to pick up something in my locker," Debbie replied. Heather couldn't help wondering if she somehow knew about Brad and the movies. "OK, then—I will see you in math class shortly," she said.

Debbie watched Heather walk off toward the cafeteria. Brad came through the door, and offered to carry Heather's backpack. Debbie watched them for a few moments. Then she turned and headed in the other direction. "That is very upsetting," she muttered to herself.

Sample B

Authentic dialogue?
Strong linking text?
Correct paragraphing?

The Dare

Tara and Kevin were two of four students accepted for an intership aboard the Seal, an eco-vessel charged with tracking marine life in the Pacific. They were photographing small reef sharks—which Tara loved. "Come in the water," she challenged Kevin. "You're a better swimmer than I am. What are you afraid of?"

"Fear has nothing to do with it, Captain Nemo," Kevin answered. "They need me on deck." He knew that was lame, and tried not to look at the irresistibly beautiful grin splashed all over Tara's face. She was definitely not buying it.

"What do you have to do that's so important? Make *lunch*?" she mocked him, slipping on her swim fins and checking the oxygen tank. "Listen—the surf's down and the water's clear. The only thing holding you back today is that tattoo on your forehead screaming 'I'm a chicken.'" She slipped in her mouth piece, grabbed her camera, and prepared to somersault off the boat.

"I like you better when you can't talk," Kevin remarked, smiling so she'd know he was kidding—sort of. He reached for his SCUBA gear. "Listen, when I die down there, you'll be sorry when your scrawny, pathetic arms aren't strong enough to haul me back to safety." He felt a chill then, and hoped those words weren't prophetic.

Revision of Sample A

Unfair

Debbie thought to herself that she ~~didn't feel like talking~~ would rather grow moss on her face than talk with Heather, but since Heather had already spotted her, there was no getting out of it now.

~~"Hello!"~~ "Hey!" Heather said, flicking her long, perfect hair over her shoulder.

~~"Hello"~~ "Hey, yourself," Debbie answered. "What's ~~new with you today?"~~ up?"

~~"Nothing in particular,"~~ "The usual," Heather replied. She wondered if she should mention that she was going out that night with Brad, Debbie's former boyfriend. He had only been her "former" boyfriend since 10 o'clock that morning, when he had asked Heather to go to the movies with him. ~~"Shall we walk~~ "C'mon—let's go to math ~~together?"~~ class."

~~"I would love to, but I think I need to pick up something in~~ "Um, I can't—listen, I need something from my locker," Debbie replied, trying hard to keep her voice steady.

¶Heather stared into Debbie's unsmiling eyes. She couldn't help wondering if ~~she~~ Debbie somehow knew about Brad and the movies. ~~"OK, then—I will see you in math class shortly"~~ "Suit yourself. See ya," she said. She couldn't spend all her time worrying over someone's stupid hurt feelings—could she? She whirled around without another word.

Debbie watched Heather ~~walk off~~ sashay toward the cafeteria. Brad came through the door just as Debbie was about to walk away, and offered to carry Heather's backpack. Debbie ~~watched them for a few moments.~~ stared in disbelief as they laughed together. Then she turned and headed in the other direction. ~~"That is very upsetting,"~~ "I totally hate her," she muttered to herself.

Sample C: Whole Class Revision

Authentic dialogue?
Strong linking text?
Correct paragraphing?
A good film opening?

Not Guilty

Chad was out of breath, but the officer wasn't even breathing hard, even though he had to be older. He looked at Chad. "What were you doing in the music store?" he asked. "Nothing," Chad replied.

The officer kept staring. "I need to ask you once more," he said. "Tell me what you were doing in the music store." "I was not in the music store, officer," Chad answered. He looked back at the officer's face, hoping he would believe him.

Actually, he *had* been in the store, but hc had not taken anything. His friend had, though. It was not the first time Riley had stolen something, and it probably would not be the last. "Is it all right if I go now?"

The officer looked away for a minute, then back at Chad. "I am going to release you this time, but I will not forget your face," he said, speaking slowly. Chad was very close right then to telling the truth about Riley. "There's a certain kid . . . " he started to say. "Yes?" the officer said, looking impatient. "Never mind," Chad said. The officer walked away then, mumbling something under his breath. "You are fortunate to have my friendship, Riley," Chad said to himself. He was not quite so sure he was lucky to have Riley, however.

Sample D: Revising with Partners

Authentic dialogue?
Strong linking text?
Correct paragraphing?
A good film opening?

Reluctant Romeo

Kyle had never kissed anyone in his whole life—and now he was going to have to kiss Jennifer, on stage, in front of everyone. The most beautiful girl in school. It was hideously embarrassing. Should he put his arms around her? Should he keep his lips together—or let them part? How hard should he press? How was his breath?

"Kyle," Mrs. Krenshaw interrupted his daydreams. "We need to have your full attention, please." Other students were giggling, staring at him. He wished they would go away. "Are you quite ready to give us your best performance?" Mrs. K continued.

"I do not think so," Kyle thought to himself, but out loud, he said, "I am quite ready, Mrs. K." She nodded and turned to Jennifer. "And are you ready as well, Jennifer?" she asked, smiling.

"I am not completely sure," Jennifer replied, looking at Kyle somewhat uncertainly. "Perhaps we could just hug," she added.

"That might not quite work for this scene," Mrs. K replied, frowning. "This is *Romeo and Juliet*, after all."

Kyle slipped up behind Jennifer. "I will kiss you very quickly," he whispered—but his voice startled her, and she screamed. Kyle's best friend Wilson laughed so hard he had to sit on the floor. "You need to be in a different kind of play," Wilson called out to Kyle, as Mrs. K's frown deepened.

Suggested Revisions of C and D

Sample C: Whole Class Revision

Not Guilty

Chad was out of breath, but the officer wasn't even breathing hard, even though he had to be pushing fifty. ~~older.~~ He looked at Chad. "You wanna tell me just what the heck you were doin' ~~"What were you doing~~ in the music store?" he asked.

"Nothing," Chad replied, shrugging, and doing his best to look innocent. "I wasn't even in there. Honest." He thought maybe he should shut up now.

The officer sighed like this was the kind of lie he heard about 15,000 times a day. His eyes drilled a hole into Chad's forehead. "OK, kid," he said, "I'll ask you this just one more time. Stretch your feeble memory, and tell ~~kept staring. "I need to ask you once more," he said. "Tell~~ me exactly what you were doing in the music store."

"I was not in the music store, officer," Chad answered, trying to sound as calm as someone caught in a lie can sound. He looked back at the officer's face, ~~hoping he would believe him~~ and noticed a small trickle of saliva running down his chin. He thought if he stared at that, it might keep him from feeling so nervous.

Actually, he *had* been in the store, but he had not taken anything. His friend had, though. It was not the first time Riley had stolen something, and it probably would not be the last. The really bad part was that Chad and Riley looked so much alike they could pass for twins.

"Is it all right if I go now?" Chad asked politely, wondering to himself just where old Riley had gone.

The officer looked away for a minute, then back at Chad. "I am going to let you go ~~release you~~ this time, but I will not forget your face," he said, speaking slowly.

Chad had a sudden impulse to confess. ~~was very close right then to telling the truth about Riley.~~ "There's ~~a~~ this kid I know ~~certain kid~~ . . . " he started to say.

"Yes?" the officer said, looking ~~impatient~~ like someone had just pulled him off brain surgery and he had to rush back.

"Never mind," Chad said. Confessing was just too complicated.

The officer walked away then, mumbling something about dumb kids under his breath.

"You are one lucky dude to have me for a friend, ~~fortunate to have my friendship,~~ Riley," Chad said to himself. He ~~was~~ didn't feel quite so ~~not quite so sure he was~~ lucky to have Riley, however.

Sample D: Revising with Partners

Reluctant Romeo

Kyle had never kissed anyone in his whole life—and now he was going to have to kiss Jennifer, on stage, in front of everyone. The most beautiful girl in school. It was hideously embarrassing. Should he put his arms around her? Should he keep his lips together—or let them part? How hard should he press? How was his breath?

"Kyle," Mrs. Krenshaw shattered ~~interrupted~~ his daydreams. "Could you possibly trouble yourself to give us ~~"We need to have~~ your full attention, please?" Other students were giggling, staring at him. He wished they would melt into the stage. ~~go away.~~ "Can you do a convincing Romeo—you know, at least look interested?" ~~"Are you quite ready to give us your best performance?"~~ Mrs. K continued.

"Can toads fly?" ~~"I do not think so,"~~ Kyle thought to himself, but out loud, he said, "Let the fun begin, ~~"I am quite ready,~~ Mrs. K." She nodded and turned to Jennifer. "And is my beautiful Juliet ready?" ~~"And are you ready as well, Jennifer?"~~ she asked, smiling.

"Actually, I was wondering if it would be, like, totally weird to rewrite Shakespeare—just for this one scene," ~~"I am not completely sure,"~~ Jennifer replied, looking at Kyle as if he were some sort of intrusive insect. "I was thinking ~~somewhat uncertainly. "Perhaps~~ we could just hug," she added. "Or just kind of, you know, smile at each other or something."

"Don't be ridiculous," ~~"That might not quite work for this scene,"~~ Mrs. K sighed, ~~replied,~~ frowning. "No one rewrites Romeo and Juliet. You'll live ~~"This is *Romeo and Juliet*, after all."~~

through it. Others have. Spit out your gum, Kyle. Romeo didn't chew gum, I'm quite sure."

Kyle slipped up behind Jennifer. "I'll make it really quick," ~~"I will kiss you very quickly,"~~ he whispered—but his voice startled her, and she screamed so loud Kyle actually jumped. Kyle's best friend Wilson laughed so hard he had to sit on the floor. "You oughta be in something like Frankenstein," ~~need to be in a different kind of play,"~~ Wilson called out to Kyle, as Mrs. K's eyes rolled and her frown deepened.

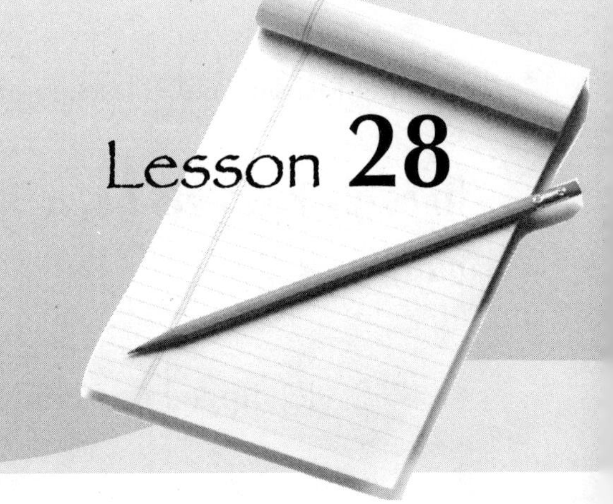

Lesson 28

Presentation

Trait Connection: **Conventions**

Introduction (Share with students in your own words—or as a handout.)

Picture yourself at a newsstand. Newspapers and magazines are everywhere. Which one will you buy? Which will you even pick up to look at? Chances are, presentation will have some influence on that decision. You may be drawn to a document because of the photographs, the font or fonts used in the title or subheads, the overall design and use of white space—or any of a dozen (perhaps hundreds) of little decisions, all intended to create eye appeal and readability—all intended to get the attention of readers like *you.* Design is an important element of every published document, from novels to textbooks, menus to greeting cards, campaign posters to advertisements. Good design makes writing enticing, and also guides the reader's eye to the most important information.

For narratives, informational research pieces, persuasive essays, and so forth, presentation deals mostly with such issues as font style and size, margin size, headings and subheadings, graphics, and footnotes or endnotes. These decisions may not seem as exciting as photo layout, but they're still important. Here is a list of everyday design decisions that could influence the appearance and readability of documents you produce for school:

1. What font (or fonts) will you use?
2. What *size* font will you use?
3. How big will your margins be?
4. Will your document be double spaced, single spaced, or something else?
5. Will you use *italics*, **boldfaced** print, or underlining for emphasis?
6. Will you number pages? Upper right, lower right, or alternating right and left?
7. Will you have headings (titles and subtitles)? If so, will they appear in the same font—or a different font from the rest of your text?
8. Will you center them on the page—or place them differently?
9. Will you need to cite sources? If so, will you use footnotes (each page) or endnotes (at the end of your document)? What format will you follow?

10. Will you use bulleted or numbered lists?
11. Will you have graphics? Photos? Charts? Cartoons?
12. Will anything appear in color? If so, how *many* colors?

You should be able to answer all of these questions. But know that even if you can, you have just *begun* to think about a few of the issues that design editors deal with each day. Pay attention to the printed documents in your life, and even though you may not have the technology to imitate everything you see, you'll gather a wealth of ideas you can use to give your own documents eye appeal—and ensure that readers can quickly, easily find the information they're looking for.

In the lesson that follows, you'll have a chance to do a critique of the design and layout of a one-page ad for a writing contest. With a partner, you'll consider as many issues as occur to you, imagining that you could re-do the design *completely*. There are no rights or wrongs here. This is about making information accessible—and appealing.

Teaching the Lesson (General Guidelines for Teachers)

1. Share the list of 12 presentation questions, encouraging students to think through how they would design one of their own documents if they had the technology and resources to make *any decisions they wished*. You may want to take some time for this discussion. (Students' answers will depend, in part, on whether they have computer access, and what programs are available to them. Take some time to discuss this, too.)
2. To expand this part of the lesson, consider looking at the covers, front matter, and internal design of several different books. Also compare front pages of major newspapers, such as the *Wall Street Journal*, the *New York Times*, and *USA Today*. Talk about what your students find appealing—or any changes they would like to see. If you have other documents available (books, brochures, menus, greeting cards, magazines, advertisements), you may wish to include those also.
3. Take time to discuss how presentation fits within your own curriculum. What issues are *most* important (or less important) for the kinds of documents your students produce in your classroom? What are your *personal* expectations? What issues are important for specific kinds of documents? (Think résumés, graduation announcements, job application letters, letters to the editor, etc.) Do you have a style sheet summarizing these preferences? If not, consider creating one.
4. Remind students that this lesson focuses not on rules but on what is most (1) appealing to the eye, and (2) helpful to a reader seeking specific information. With respect to point 2, for example, a list can be buried within the text, or

made to stand out with numbers or bullets. Key points can be emphasized with subheads (or at least paragraphs) or blended together in one large body of text.

5. Share the editing lesson on the following page. Ask students to read the text aloud, thinking about how the information could be more effectively organized. Ask them to think of as many ideas for making this piece visually striking as they can—and with their partners, to make a list.
6. When everyone is done, invite students to join in a class discussion of possibilities, and if you wish, make a class list of design recommendations.
7. If your students have computer access, consider putting the writing contest copy on the computer and asking students to actually work up a design.
8. When you finish, compare your list with our reformatted revision. Talk about what the reformatted design accomplishes that is missing from the rough. Also talk about any of your own design ideas that we did not implement. (Note that the original is written in Officina Sans Bold 11 point text. Revised text is Helvetica 12-point, with heads done in Marker Felt Thin 26-point (main head) and 18-point (subheads).)

Editing Goal: Think about issues of design.
Follow-Up: Do whatever is practical and possible to make your own documents visually appealing and readable.

Editing Practice

Consider visual presentation.
Suggest possible design revisions.

Announcing a writing contest

Our community is sponsoring the first annual William C. Fields
Writing Contest. Entries should be no more than 2000 words long. Entries should be double spaced, not single spaced. It is suggested that people wishing to enter choose their own topics. The writing may take the form of a story or essay. No poems, please. All writing must be prose. Entries will be judged by several readers. The readers will work independently. The top ten (10) essays will all receive rewards/ prizes of various types. Prizes include money (ranging from $100 to $1,000) and the Grand Prize winner will receive an all-expense paid trip to New York, including a three-night stay, tour of the city, tickets to a Broadway production, and tour of a New York publishing house.

Entries will be judged on original ideas, voice, readability, correct and creative use of conventions, and presentation (eye appeal). Original art is allowed, but please, no photographs. Entries should be sent to William C. Fields Writing Contest, 1200 Baltimore Street, Field City, Oregon 97709. Entries will not be returned. Please allow six weeks for judging. Entries should be submitted (2 copies) no later than June 1 of this year. No entries will be returned. We wish all competitors the best of luck.

Design Suggestions:

Re-Designed Copy

Calling all writers . . . to the first annual

William C. Fields Writing Contest

Do you love to write? You could be headed to New York! Just send us a piece of your own writing *by June 1 of this year*, and a panel of independent judges will review it for originality, voice, conventional correctness—*and* eye appeal. It's that simple. Please note the following . . .

Requirements

- Original topics—your choice!
- Stories or essays (No poems, please)
- Original art *allowed* (No photographs)
- 2000-word limit
- Double-spaced text
- Two copies (Not returnable)
- Mail all entries to
  William C. Fields Writing Contest
  1200 Baltimore Street
  Field City, Oregon 97709

Prizes

- Cash winnings from $100 to $1,000
- Prizes for *each* of the top ten entries
- Grand Prize: Trip to New York City!

If you are the Grand Prize winner, you will spend three nights in beautiful New York City—all expenses paid! Take in the sights, enjoy a fabulous Broadway production, and tour a famous New York publishing house—all courtesy of William C. Fields! *Don't wait—we must receive your entry no later than June 1 of this year*. Please allow six weeks for judging.

Share your voice!

Revising for the Reader in a Rush

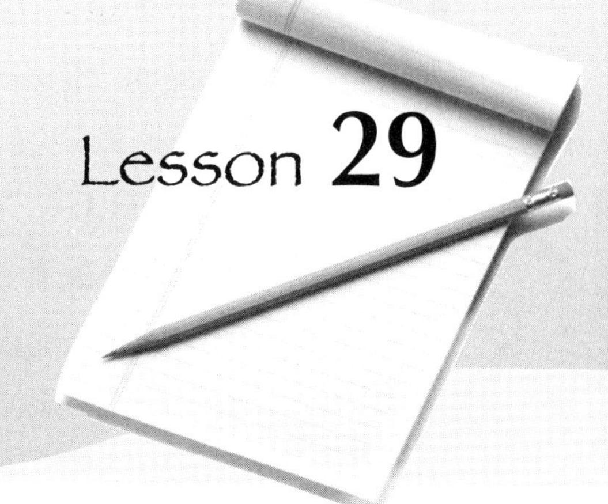

Lesson **29**

Trait Connection: **Sentence Fluency**

Introduction

Maybe you've thought that the more fluent you became as a writer, the longer your sentences would get. There's *some* truth to that. It's difficult not to admire the grace with which Norman Mailer, Gary Paulsen, Toni Morrison, William Faulkner, Gary D. Schmidt—or Dylan Thomas in *A Child's Christmas in Wales*—create sentences that hold up like marvelous suspension bridges despite their disarming length: "Years and years and years ago, when I was a boy, when there were wolves in Wales, and birds the colour of red-flannel petticoats whisked past the harp-shaped hills, when we sang and wallowed all night and day in caves that smelt like Sunday afternoons in damp front farmhouse parlours and we chased, with the jawbones of deacons, the English and the bears, before the wheel, before the duchess-faced horse, when we rode the daft and happy hills bareback, it snowed and it snowed." That's not just a sentence; it's an 84-word masterpiece. Just for fun, let's diagram it . . . (I *am* kidding.) It's fun to lose ourselves in poetic language of this sort that's meant to be read as you're curled up by the fire. But for the reader in a rush, nothing beats the straightforward, direct sentence that drives the message home. In this lesson, you'll get at the heart of the message, and write sentences to support that message.

Teacher's Sidebar . . .

The beauty of fluent English is that it is so variable. Endless patterns are possible. Though this lesson focuses on the short, direct sentence, remind students that *all styles* have a place. The key, as always, is purpose. For a descriptive or poetic piece, a long, lyrical sentence—like that of Dylan Thomas—may be perfect. But for business writing, directions, or news—where the reader has to "get it" as quickly as possible—nothing eclipses the power of straightforward prose.

Quotation is taken from Dylan Thomas, *A Child's Christmas in Wales*, 1993. London: Orion House, unpaginated.

Focus and Intent

This lesson is intended to help students:

- Recognize the part that short, direct sentences play in clear writing.
- Identify separate messages within a single long sentence.
- Revise a series of long sentences into crisp prose with short, direct sentences.

Teaching the Lesson

Step 1: Breaking Down the Message

Following are some longer sentences, each containing several messages. Imagine that each of these is a memo going to new employees at a company. They have only a short time to read the memo, and they must interpret the message quickly and accurately. First, figure out what key messages the writer is trying to convey. Then, break each message into two or three short, direct sentences that capture those messages, and are also easy to understand. *Clarity* is the goal. Feel free to condense and to change any wording. Suggested revisions appear on page 270.

Memo 1

In the interest of better serving our customers, we will begin a new practice as of tomorrow that will involve surveying our customers as they come in to see how we may better meet their needs in the future.

Revision

____

____

Memo 2

Because a number of employees have expressed concern over a breakdown in communications between employees and management, managers have together reached a decision that involves bringing in a specialist from Making Words Count who will work with us in improving our internal communications.

Revision

____

____

Memo 3

After a careful review, it has come to our attention that creating a more eco-friendly environment within our company will prove beneficial not only to customers but to employees as well, and a list of ideas designed to accomplish this goal will be posted on each floor next to the elevator, where we hope they will be noticed by all employees.

Revision

____

____

Step 2: Making the Reading-Writing Connection

The short sentence is useful in many contexts other than the sort of business writing you did in the warm-up. Consider this opening to Stephen R. Swinburne's informational text, *Once a Wolf*:

> *Hatred of wolves goes far back in history. As soon as people began raising livestock, wolves became the enemy and the symbol of savagery.* (Swinburne, p. 5)

This very direct opening sets a clear direction for the discussion to follow. Swinburne wants to get our attention and make sure we know how much wolves have been despised through history. Now we know. Short sentences can be used dramatically to create a sense of urgency. In *Teammoon*, author Catherine Thimmesh explains that for astronauts involved in the Apollo 11 moon landing, cosmic "shorthand" was a lifesaver. Astronauts who are in danger do not have time for wordy explanations, and the expression "twelve-oh-two" had a special meaning:

> *Translation: We have a problem! What is it? Do we land? Do we abort? Are we in danger? Are we blowing up? Tell us what to do. Hurry!* (Thimmesh, p. 18)

Author Sandra Cisneros often favors short sentences—sometimes intermixed with deliberate fragments, for emphasis. In a chapter called "Boys and Girls" (from *The House on Mango Street*), she speaks in a heartfelt way that seems to say, "I *need* you to understand this." She explains that "Nenny is too young to be my friend. She's just my sister and that is not my fault" (p. 8). Then she closes the chapter with this comment:

> *Some day I will have a best friend all my own. One I can tell my secrets to. One who will understand my jokes without my having to explain them. Until then I am a red balloon, a balloon tied to an anchor.* (p. 9)

Try re-connecting any of these passages to form one longer sentence and see what is lost. While sentence combining is in itself a powerful way of creating fluency, sometimes the punch of the short sentence is just what's needed.

Quotations from:

- *Once a Wolf: How Wildlife Biologists Fought to Bring Back the Gray Wolf* by Stephen R. Swinburne. 1999. Boston: Houghton Mifflin.
- *Teammoon: How 400,000 People Landed Apollo 11 on the Moon* by Catherine Thimmesh. 2006. Boston: Houghton Mifflin.
- *The House on Mango Street* by Sandra Cisneros. 2004. New York: Vintage Books.

Step 3: Involving Students as Evaluators

Ask students to review Samples A and B, asking which writer has used direct, short sentences to make meaning clear. Ask students to work in teams, breaking down the messages in the passage with longer sentences, and brainstorming possible revisions. Emphasize the importance of reading both pieces *aloud.*

Discussing Results

Most students should find Sample A stronger. Writer A uses short, direct sentences to make the message clear and easy to read—even for someone in a hurry. Writer B, by contrast, creates convoluted sentences that make the message difficult to decipher. One possible revision of Sample B is provided.

Step 4: Modeling Revision

- Share Sample C (*Whole Class Revision*) with students. Read the passage aloud, or ask a student to do so.
- Ask students whether the message is easy to decipher on a quick first reading. (Most should say *no.*)
- Give students time to discuss the piece with partners, talking about individual messages buried within each sentence, and brainstorming ways to rewrite sentences. Ask them to imagine that this is copy that an anchor person will read aloud on the evening news.
- As a class, work through the revision sentence by sentence, asking students to offer suggestions. Feel free to make any changes at all. Condense, rewrite, begin sentences in new ways, change wording. The goal is clarity. As you go for clarity, feel free to also add the voice that comes with crafting strong short sentences.
- Read aloud as you go. (You can call upon different student readers to do this.) You want the sentences to be strong, but not choppy. So be careful to *vary your sentence beginnings.*
- When you finish, ask a student to read the *whole revision* aloud, making any last-minute changes that could further heighten clarity or voice.
- If you wish, compare your revision to ours, keeping in mind that your revision need not match ours.

Step 5: Revising with Partners

Share Sample D (*Revising with Partners*). Ask students to follow the basic steps you modeled with Sample C. *Working with partners,* they should:

- Read the passage aloud.
- Talk about the messages buried within each long, complex sentence.
- Revise sentence by sentence, making the sentences forceful and direct—but taking care to maintain variety so that the result is not choppy.

- Read the final revision aloud, with as much inflection as possible, testing the fluency and clarity, and revising as needed.

Step 6: Sharing and Discussing Results

When students have finished, ask students to exchange passages. Have readers go through the revisions quickly, as if reading under pressure. Are the revisions easy to understand? Then, ask readers to share any revisions that seem especially clear and strong. Discuss the specific strategies revisers used. If you wish, compare your revisions with ours, keeping in mind that your revisions need not match ours in any way.

Next Steps

- Look for samples of short, direct sentences in real-world writing. Make a collection, and discuss the contexts in which this style works well. You are likely to find it in directions, advertising, recipes, some technical writing, journalistic writing, and textbooks. You may also wish to look for samples of longer, more convoluted sentences—and to discuss the writers' reasons for using this style.
- Invite students to review their own writing—particularly informational and persuasive samples—looking for one or two passages that might benefit from a more direct approach. Remind students that it is not necessary to write a whole piece in the simple, direct style. It should be reserved for short documents, or selections in which it is important to get a message across clearly and quickly. Short sentences have even more power when contrasted with longer sentences. For an example of this, read the chapter "Hair" aloud from Sandra Cisneros's book, *The House on Mango Street*. Listen for the striking contrast.
- Look and listen for short, powerful sentences in the literature you share aloud. Recommended:
    - *Once a Wolf: How Wildlife Biologists Fought to Bring Back the Gray Wolf* by Stephen R. Swinburne. 1999. Boston: Houghton Mifflin.
    - *Teammoon: How 400,000 People Landed Apollo 11 on the Moon* by Catherine Thimmesh. 2006. Boston: Houghton Mifflin.
    - *The House on Mango Street* by Sandra Cisneros. 2004. New York: Vintage Books.
    - *The Lightning Thief* by Rick Riordan. 2005. New York: Hyperion Books.
    - *Son of the Mob* by Gordon Korman. 2004. New York: Hyperion Books.
- *For an additional challenge:* Long sentences can lose readers—even skillful, determined ones. Sometimes, that's unintended; other times, of course, it's the goal. Invite students ready for a challenge to tackle something truly com-

plex—such as a higher level textbook or a legal contract. See if they can turn a short passage (two to three long sentences) into something digestible even for a reader in a rush.

Suggested Responses to "Breaking Down the Message," p. 266

Memo 1

In the interest of better serving our customers, we will begin a new practice as of tomorrow that will involve surveying our customers as they come in to see how we may better meet their needs in the future.

Revision

We want to make every customer's experience the best it can be. Beginning tomorrow, we'll ask them to share their ideas about how we can do our job better.

Memo 2

Because a number of employees have expressed concern over a breakdown in communications between employees and management, managers have together reached a decision that involves bringing in a specialist from Making Words Count who will work with us in improving our internal communications.

Revision

Everyone's noticing it. Employees and managers in our company need to communicate better. Beginning Monday, a specialist from Making Words Count will help us develop the strategies we need to speak and listen effectively.

Memo 3

After a careful review, it has come to our attention that creating a more eco-friendly environment within our company will prove beneficial not only to customers but to employees as well, and a list of ideas designed to accomplish this goal will be posted on each floor next to the elevator, where we hope they will be noticed by all employees.

Revision

An eco-friendly company environment benefits customers and employees alike. Ideas for making this happen are now posted on each floor, right by the elevator. We hope you'll take time to read them.

Sample A

Imagine the following copy as text to be read aloud on the evening news. It should require no more than a 30-second spot.

Short, direct sentences? Easy to read? Good for the reader in a rush?

Golden Frogs Found

The Golden Frog—also sometimes referred to as the Golden Toad—has been found alive and well. For many years, scientists believed that the Golden Frog was extinct. And no wonder. The creature is less than an inch long. What's more, its gold and green color keeps it camouflaged in the trees and shrubs of the rainforest. Recently, several were spotted in the largely unpopulated rainforests of Colombia. It is hoped even more will be found as time goes on. If the existing population is too small, scientists say, the frog could still be in danger of extinction. Luckily, the tiny frog has few natural enemies. It seems that in nature, the colors of yellow and orange are sometimes warnings to predators. That is the case with the Golden Frog. Its yellow-orange skin can be toxic to any creature that tries to swallow it. That holds true for humans, too—who do sometimes eat frogs. That wouldn't be a good choice for the Golden Frog—or the human diner!

Sample B

Imagine the following copy as text to be read aloud on the evening news. It should require no more than a 30-second spot.

Short, direct sentences? Easy to read? Good for the reader in a rush?

A Local Earthquake

Our local area experienced an earthquake earlier this morning which registered 3.8 on the Richter Scale, strong enough to be felt, but generally not strong enough to cause any serious damage, although it did produce small cracks in one of the local bridges. Inspectors investigating the site stated upon inspection of the bridge that the construction did not meet code, speculating that this was the reason for the structural damage. The bridge is part of Highway 18, which spans the Rolling River just southeast of town, a bridge that is heavily traveled, which could account for a portion of the structural damage, together with the weak construction, a problem then aggravated by the earthquake. Geologists consulted following the quake provided assurance that quakes of any significant magnitude are fairly infrequent in our area, offering no particular explanation for this most recent event, but emphasizing that there is no need to panic. The bridge will undergo further inspection and is scheduled for repair sometime within the coming month.

Revision of Sample B

A Local Earthquake

Our local area experienced an earthquake ~~earlier~~ around 10 a.m. this morning which registered 3.8 on the Richter Scale~~,~~. That's strong enough to be felt, but generally not strong enough to cause ~~any~~ serious damage~~,~~. This quake, however, may have contributed to ~~although it did produce~~ small cracks in ~~one of the local bridges~~ the Highway 18 bridge spanning the Rolling River southeast of town. It seems the earthquake is not solely to blame, however. Inspectors investigating the site ~~stated upon inspection of~~ pointed out that the bridge ~~that the~~ construction did not meet code~~,~~. They speculated that faulty construction played a part in ~~speculating that this was the reason for~~ the structural damage. ~~The bridge is part of Highway 18, which spans the Rolling River just southeast of town, a bridge that is~~ Further, the bridge is heavily traveled, which could ~~account for a portion of the structural damage, together with the weak construction, a problem then aggravated by the earthquake~~ have weakened it over time, inspectors say. Geologists ~~consulted following the quake provided assurance~~ assure us that quakes of ~~any~~ significant magnitude are ~~fairly~~ infrequent in our area, ~~offering no particular explanation for this most recent event, but emphasizing~~ and say that there is no need to panic. The Highway 18 bridge ~~will undergo further inspection and~~ is scheduled for repair ~~sometime~~ within the coming month.

Sample C: Whole Class Revision

Imagine that the following text will appear online in a "News at a Glance" summary designed for busy people. Expect them to spend no more than 20 seconds on a piece (reading silently).

Short, direct sentences? Easy to read? Good for the reader in a rush?

Good Willed Chimps

Until recently, it was assumed that altruism, or the capacity to perform particular acts unselfishly for the betterment of another individual, was exclusively a human trait, even though pet owners (particularly dog owners) have argued for years that other animals are capable of unselfish acts, which apparently is true. Recent experiments with chimpanzees have shown that these animals, much like human toddlers, will offer assistance to one of their own kind if that individual is experiencing difficulty with a particular kind of task, such as an inability to reach a piece of food. When presented with an opportunity to provide such assistance, the chimps, like the human children, will often—though not always—come to the aid of another individual, supporting the theory long-held by many that altruism is not, after all, an exclusively human trait, but may be one that arose far earlier in our evolution than previously believed.

Sample D: Revising with Partners

Imagine that the following text will appear online in a "News at a Glance" summary designed for busy people. Expect them to spend no more than 20 seconds on a piece (reading silently).

Short, direct sentences? Easy to read? Good for the reader in a rush?

Universal Donor

Type O has long been known as the "universal donor" blood type because of the fact that type O has zero antigens (think O for zero), a kind of sugar on the blood cell's surface that characterizes other blood types, including A, B, and AB. In transfusions involving differing antigens, such as A to B, for example, the recipient may produce antibodies to the sugar groups that do not match the recipient's own blood type, setting off a dangerous immune reaction, and making O the only safe universal donor since it lacks the antigens to trigger such a reaction. Now, however, scientists have discovered that certain types of bacteria and fungi produce enzymes with the capability to break up sugar molecules, so that when these enzymes are added to other blood types, they produce an antigen-free blood that is similar to type O. The result is that other blood types may be used as universal donors—just as effectively as type O, and with additional research, this procedure may soon be used widely at blood banks everywhere.

Suggested Revisions of C and D

Sample C: Whole Class Revision

Good Willed Chimps

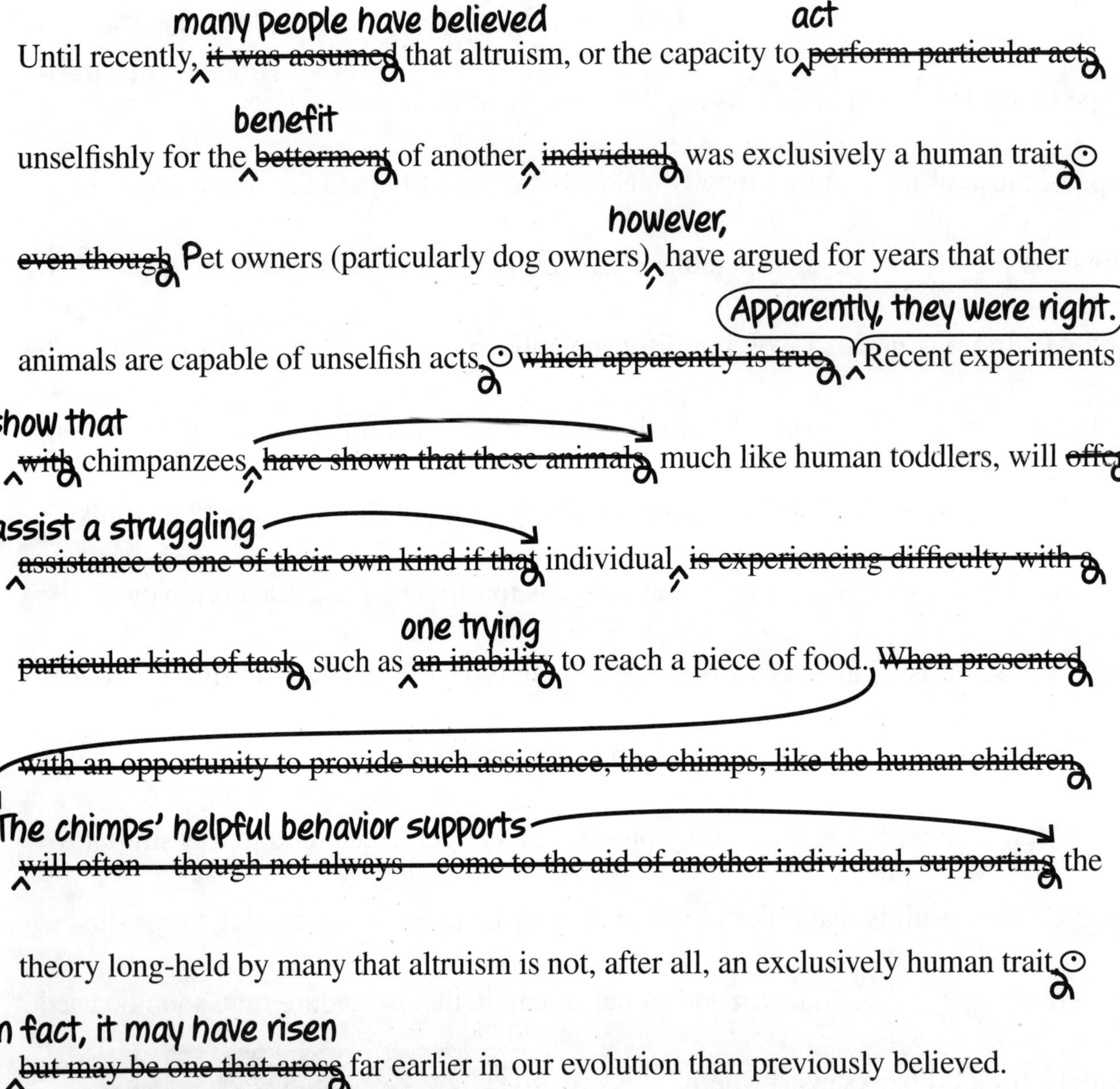

Until recently, ~~it was assumed~~ many people have believed that altruism, or the capacity to ~~perform particular acts~~ act unselfishly for the ~~betterment~~ benefit of another, ~~individual~~ was exclusively a human trait. ~~even though~~ Pet owners (particularly dog owners), however, have argued for years that other animals are capable of unselfish acts. ~~which apparently is true~~ Apparently, they were right. Recent experiments ~~with~~ show that chimpanzees, ~~have shown that these animals~~ much like human toddlers, will ~~offer assistance to one of their own kind if that~~ assist a struggling individual, ~~is experiencing difficulty with a particular kind of task~~ such as ~~an inability~~ one trying to reach a piece of food. ~~When presented with an opportunity to provide such assistance, the chimps, like the human children will often—though not always—come to the aid of another individual, supporting~~ The chimps' helpful behavior supports the theory long-held by many that altruism is not, after all, an exclusively human trait. ~~but may be one that arose~~ In fact, it may have risen far earlier in our evolution than previously believed.

Sample D: Revising with Partners

Universal Donor

Type O [blood] has long been known as the "universal donor" ~~blood type~~ because of the fact that [it] ~~type O~~ has zero antigens (think O for zero)~~.~~ [. Antigens are] a kind of sugar on the blood cell's surface [and they are different for each blood type:] ~~that characterizes other blood types, including~~ A, B, and AB. In transfusions ~~involving differing antigens, such as A to B, for example~~ the recipient may produce antibodies to [any] ~~the~~ sugar groups that do not match the recipient's own blood type[.] [This, in turn, can set] ~~setting~~ off a dangerous immune reaction[.] ~~and making O the only safe universal donor~~ [S]ince it lacks the antigens to trigger such a reaction[, type O has been, until recently, the only safe universal donor.] Now, however, scientists have discovered that certain types of bacteria and fungi produce enzymes with the capability to break up sugar molecules[.] ~~so that~~ [W]hen these enzymes are added to other blood types, they produce an antigen-free blood that is similar to type O. ~~The~~ [As a] result[,] ~~is that~~ other blood types may be used as universal donors—just as effectively as type O[.] ~~and with~~ [Following] additional research, this procedure may soon be used widely at blood banks everywhere.

Editing Wrap-Up
(All Editing Lessons for Grade 8)

Lesson **30**

Trait Connection: **Conventions**

Introduction (Share with students as a handout or in your own words.)

In this lesson, you will have a chance to practice editing for errors and problems covered in all previous editing lessons. An editing checklist is provided to remind you what to look for.

Teaching the Lesson (General Guidelines for Teachers)

1. Share copies of the editing checklist (page 280) with students if you have not done so previously. Review anything about which your students have questions. You may wish to laminate the checklist or insert it into a plastic protective cover so students can mark it with a dry erase marker.
2. Make sure that students have access to a student handbook (such as *Write Source: New Generation*) that reflects conventional rules applied in your classroom.
3. Remind students that this is *not a test.* It is a personal assessment, a chance for them to see how many conventional rules and suggestions they can recall and apply. (**Suggestion:** If you wish to *test* students' knowledge of conventions, use this lesson as a warm-up, and then have them (as soon as possible following the lesson) edit a piece of their own work. Base your assessment on the editorial quality of the final draft combined with the degree of change from rough to final.)
4. Share the editing lesson on the next page.
5. Students should read the passage aloud *(softly),* looking *and listening* for errors or problems. In addition, ask them to think about presentation, and to be prepared to offer at least *three suggestions* for improvement. In addition, students should mark new paragraphs using this symbol: ¶
6. Ask students to edit individually first, then check with a partner.
7. When everyone is done, ask them to coach you as you edit the same copy, making any changes you and they identify. Use carets, inverted carets, and delete symbols to make your corrections. Circle new periods.

8. When you finish, read your edited copy aloud to make sure you and your student editors have caught *everything*, and pause to discuss your editorial changes. Also discuss suggestions for improving the presentation, considering both (1) eye appeal, and (2) accessibility of information. Compare your version to our suggested copy on page 283. If you have computer access, consider creating a new layout for the page.
9. If students have any difficulty, review as necessary and repeat this lesson, asking students to work with different partners.

Editing Goal: Correct 48 errors. Mark 3 new paragraphs.
Make design suggestions.
Follow-Up: Look for editorial changes needed in your own work.

Editing Checklist for Grade 8

___ **Carets** (^) used to insert words or corrections
___ **Delete symbol** (ꝺ) used to take things out
___ **Paragraph symbol** (¶) used to mark new paragraphs

___ **Commas** used to set off items in a series: *For dinner we had fried zucchini, lettuce wraps, and sushi.*
___ **Commas** used to set off a sentence introduction: *Once the rain had stopped, fans returned to the stands.*
___ **Commas** used to set off a sentence interruption: *Gabrielle and Siobhan, unlike other members of the team, kept practicing after sundown.*
___ **Commas** used to set off an appositive (words that rename or describe a noun): *Mr. Fixx, a most unusual teacher, did not believe in homework.*
___ **Unneeded commas** deleted: *This year, Ann plans to see Europe.* (second comma not needed)

___ Making sure **subjects and verbs** agree:

- *The* ***band****, despite the urging of their fans,* **is** *not going to do an encore.*
- *Either* ***asparagus or carrots go*** *well with chicken.* (**carrots** is closer to the verb **go**)
- *Either* ***carrots or asparagus goes*** *well with chicken.* (**asparagus** is closer to the verb **goes**)
- *Our biggest* ***worry is*** *forest fires.* (**worry,** the subject, is singular)
- ***Forest fires are our biggest worry.*** (**fires,** the subject, is plural)
- ***Economics is*** *hard for some people.* (special case—singular)
- *Your* ***trousers are*** *pressed.* (special case—plural)

___ **Indefinite pronouns** take the right form (one word or two):

- ***Everyone*** *loves a great surprise.* (one word, meaning *all of us*)
- ***Every one*** *of the cupcakes got eaten.* (two words, *every single cupcake*)

___ **All right, all ready, a lot,** and **already** used correctly:

- *Spring is* ***all right*** (not *alright*)*, but summer is even better.* (two words)
- *Three-year-old Jack was* ***all ready*** (not *already*) *for his birthday.* (meaning *all set, prepared*)
- *He had* ***already*** (not *all ready*) *opened two gifts.* (meaning *by this time*)
- *We all had* ***a lot*** (not *alot*) *of fun at the celebration.* (two words)

___ **Sound-alike words** used correctly:

- ***There*** *was a lot of commotion when* ***their*** *plane landed.*
- *It takes* ***two*** *people* ***to*** *have an argument.*
- *My request had little* ***effect****.* (*impact, result,* a noun)
- *How will attendance* ***affect*** *our grades?* (*influence,* a verb)
- *Her report included an* ***allusion*** *to the story "Cinderella."* (*reference*)

- *You must be under the **illusion** that my opinion counts.* (*misguided belief*)

___ **Capitals used** to mark specific, proper names:
- *He attends **H**arvard **U**niversity.*
- *The entire **E**nglish **D**epartment is going on the cruise.*
- *The **P**resident is holding a press conference.*
- *Harold said that **P**sych 101 was his favorite class.*
- *Several **A**sian students have transferred to our school.*
- *I love living in the **W**est.*
- *Did **M**om buy **K**leenex?*

___ **Capitals avoided** on generic words referring to categories, not names:
- *He attends a local university.*
- *The entire department is going on the cruise.*
- *Many presidents have held press conferences.*
- *Harold said that psychology is his favorite subject.*
- *Several students have transferred to our school.*
- *I love living in the western part of the U.S.*
- *Did your mom buy tissue?*

___ **Quotation marks** used to set off speech:
- "What a great day!" exclaimed Dale.
- "I would agree," Robin rejoined, "except that I am not a fan of hail."
- "Don't you enjoy some variety?" asked Dale.
- Had Dale really called this stormy day "great"?

___ **New paragraphs** used to indicate a turn in the conversation or a new speaker.

___ Careful editing to catch **little things**: missing or repeated words and letters, missing punctuation, words run together, misspellings, etc.

___ Review of **presentation** to be sure it is pleasing to the eye, and directs readers' attention to key information

___ *Everything* read both silently AND aloud, pencil in hand, handbook nearby

Author's Note

Please remember that this editing checklist is designed for use with these Grade 8 lessons, and is *not meant to be comprehensive.* For a review of numerous other conventional issues, I invite you to explore editing lessons (and corresponding Editing Checklists) for other grade levels in the *Creating Revisers and Editors* series.

Editing Practice

Correct any errors you find. Make 3 or more recommendations for effective presentation.

An agency know a Earthwatch (www.earthwatch.org) provides opportunities for people who like to travel to also give something back to the Environment. The concept is simple. Travelers team with scientists to observe and record what they sea in parts of the world where Human Presence are threatening plant or animal life. Participants may track Whales in hawaii herbivores in south Africa, orangutans in Borneo gulls in the maine, or monkeys in Costa rica. Most of th time travel costs are borne by the volunteers themselves, though some Grants are all ready being made avalable. The project has become particularly popular wit teachers, who are sometimes outfitted with satellite technology that allow them too send messages an video communications back to students in they're classrooms. In adition, some tours except teenagers, who become part of so-called "Teen Teams." A warning, though. This kind of travel which takes volunteers into some pretty remote an undeveloped areas are not for those who require luxury or who are squeamish. Volunteers may find themselves face too face with Crocodiles, or counting "guano hits" one they're hats, as sea gulls sore overhead. They take turns cooking spend long hours working, and seldom have comfy mattresses for resting there weary bodies at night. Their is not always running water readily available In short, they forego alot of modren convenences. Its not for every body! Still, for those who put purpose ahead of just lying in the sun, an earthwatch "vacation" could be just the thing. As one participant put it "It make the whole world feel like your laboratory.

Design Suggestions:

Edited Copy

45 changes plus 3 new paragraphs marked

An agency know a Earthwatch (www.earthwatch.org) provides opportunities for people who like to travel to also give something back to the Environment. The concept is simple. Travelers team with scientists to observe and record what they sea in parts of the world where Human Presence are threatening plant or animal life. Participants may track Whales in hawaii herbivores in south Africa, orangutans in Borneo gulls in the maine, or monkeys in Costa rica. Most of th time travel costs are borne by the volunteers themselves, though some Grants are all ready being made avalable. The project has become particularly popular wit teachers, who are sometimes outfitted with satellite technology that allow them too send messages an video communications back to students in they're classrooms. In adition, some tours except teenagers, who become part of so-called "Teen Teams." A warning, though. This kind of travel which takes volunteers into some pretty remote an undeveloped areas are not for those who require luxury or who are squeamish. Volunteers may find themselves face too face with Crocodiles, or counting "guano hits" one they're hats, as sea gulls sore overhead. They take turns cooking spend long hours working, and seldom have comfy mattresses for resting there weary bodies at night. Their is not always running water readily available In short, they forego alot of modren convenences. Its not for every body! Still, for those who put purpose ahead of just lying in the sun, an earthwatch "vacation" could be just the thing. As one participant put it "It make the whole world feel like your laboratory.

Edited Copy (as it would appear in print)

Making the World Your Laboratory

An agency known as Earthwatch (www.earthwatch.org) provides opportunities for people who like to travel to also give something back to the environment. The concept is simple. Travelers team with scientists to observe and record what they see in parts of the world where human presence is threatening plant or animal life. Participants may track whales in Hawaii, herbivores in South Africa, orangutans in Borneo, gulls in Maine, or monkeys in Costa Rica. Most of the time, travel costs are borne by the volunteers themselves, though some grants are already being made available.

The project has become particularly popular with teachers, who are sometimes outfitted with satellite technology that allows them to send messages and video communications back to students in their classrooms. In addition, some tours accept teenagers, who become part of so-called "Teen Teams."

A warning, though. This kind of travel, which takes volunteers into some pretty remote and undeveloped areas, is not for those who require luxury or who are squeamish. Volunteers may find themselves face to face with crocodiles, or counting "guano hits" on their hats as sea gulls soar overhead. They take turns cooking, spend long hours working, and seldom have comfy mattresses for resting their weary bodies at night. There is not always running water readily available. In short, they forego a lot of modern conveniences. It's not for everybody!

Still, for those who put purpose ahead of just lying in the sun, an Earthwatch "vacation" could be just the thing. As one participant put it, "It makes the whole world feel like your laboratory."

Note on Presentation: We divided the copy into four paragraphs, with paragraphs single spaced, and double spacing between. We added a heading, set in 24-point Marker Felt Thin. The body of the text has been changed from Times 14-point to Helvetica 11-point. The graphic of the orangutan is woven into the text. A page border has been added.